Accidental Immigrants and
the Search for Home

CAROL E. KELLEY

Accidental Immigrants and
the Search for Home

WOMEN, CULTURAL IDENTITY,
AND COMMUNITY

TEMPLE UNIVERSITY PRESS • PHILADELPHIA

TEMPLE UNIVERSITY PRESS
Philadelphia, Pennsylvania 19122
www.temple.edu/tempress

Library of Congress Cataloging-in-Publication Data

Kelley, Carol E., 1959–
    Accidental immigrants and the search for home : women, cultural
identity, and community / Carol E. Kelley.
        p. cm.
    Includes bibliographical references and index.
    ISBN 978-1-4399-0945-4 (cloth : alk. paper) —
ISBN 978-1-4399-0946-1 (pbk. : alk. paper) —
ISBN 978-1-4399-0947-8 (e-book)   1. Immigrants—Cultural
assimilation—Case studies.   2. Immigrant women—Case studies.
3. Ethnicity—Case studies.   4. Group identity—Case studies.
5. Identity (Psychology)—Case studies.   6. Transnationalism—
Case studies.   I. Title.
    JV6342.K45 2013
    305.48'412—dc23
                                                    2012032081

Printed in the United States of America

2   4   6   8   9   7   5   3   1

For my sister, Chrissy

CONTENTS

ACKNOWLEDGMENTS

This book would not have been possible without the many people who provided support during the research and writing process. First and foremost I express my deepest thanks to the four anonymous women who participated in the research. They not only gave their time but also entrusted me with the intimate details of their lives. Listening to their stories was a privilege and offered me valuable lessons about the meaning of acceptance, commitment, resilience, and belonging. Their narratives are the heart of this work, and their generous contributions have inspired me every day.

I am fortunate to have friends and colleagues who not only allowed me to share my ideas and frustrations but also provided invaluable assistance along the way. My heartfelt thanks go to Richard Blot, Margarita Marnick, John Briggs, Mary Catherine Bateson, and Priscilla Claiborne for their close readings of the proposal and the manuscript. Ursula Lauper deserves special acknowledgment for the effort and enthusiasm she put into reading, rereading, and discussing the material with me. I extend a thank-you to Louis Herns Marcelin for urging me to begin this project and to Susan Schwartz Senstad for her valuable suggestions. Gail Martz, Susan Blair Hensley, and Barry Krzywicki all listened endlessly to my ideas and my hopes for the book. I also thank Gail for encouraging me to take risks and persevere when I hesitated.

My sister, Christine Kelley Lie, provided the inspiration for the book and gave me unfailing support every day before, during, and after the writing of it. I thank my brother-in-law, Arvid Lie, and my nephews, Thomas and Colin Lie, for their insights and for patiently accepting my frequent presence in their home. My gratitude goes to all of my family, who fostered my love of learning and who encouraged me and provided the opportunity for me to take the roads less traveled, even though they may not have understood my need to do so—especially Maureen S. Kelley, Mary Carol Smith, and Clarence T. Smith.

I am grateful to the anonymous peer reviewers provided by Temple University Press, who gave detailed and exacting comments and suggestions. The reviewers greatly improved my work, and their efforts are much appreciated. I thank all those at Temple who have been involved in the production of the book, including Joan S. Vidal, Kate Nichols, Gary Kramer, and Amanda Steele, as well as Rebecca Logan at Newgen. I am particularly grateful to Mick Gusinde-Duffy, who believed in the book and nurtured its progress with consistent good humor and patience.

My enduring gratitude goes to John S. Lofty for his extraordinary forbearance and generous help throughout the writing process. His skilled critiques and thought-provoking ideas raised the book to a higher level. Perhaps even more important, John's loving reassurance and continued faith in me have inspired and focused my work. Thanks to his steady companionship, I have begun to find my own sense of home.

Finally, I thank the friends who provided hospitality in the many places I called home while working on this project, including those in Norway, England, Florida, Colorado, New Hampshire, and Massachusetts.

*Accidental Immigrants and
the Search for Home*

INTRODUCTION

Approaching Home

Immigration is in the news every day. Many of the reports underscore generalized fears of "illegal" movement or the appropriation of domestic jobs and cultural change. Politically and socially controversial, immigration is often positioned in the media in terms of negative statistics rather than individual realities. This ideologically constructed standpoint creates an oppositional atmosphere. It can then be easy to forget that an immigrant can be any kind of person, from any background. Immigrants are our neighbors and our coworkers. Through marriage and children, immigrants often become part of our extended families. Like many non-migrants, they struggle to build a future, find contentment, and create a fulfilling life for themselves and their families. Regardless of how or why immigrants make their journey, they too are searching for a safe place that they can call home.

Worldwide there are around 200 million international migrants. About three-quarters of these migrants move to places that have higher living standards than those of their country of origin (UNDP 2009, 22–23). In 2005, there were 37 million immigrants living in the United States alone (Portes and Rumbaut 2006, 12). Many individuals are drawn to countries where work as strawberry pickers, meat packers, or domestics waits for them. They accept low-paying jobs and often get little respect, remaining virtually invisible to much of the public. We do not see the person who neatly cuts up our beef and wraps it in plastic. We do not see the backbreaking efforts of farm workers who labor in the heat and mud; we see only the colorful fruits and vegetables attractively displayed in the produce sections of our grocery stores. We do not see the cleaning crew working in our offices at night, but we smell freshly sanitized bathrooms and walk on newly vacuumed carpets.

Others leave their homes to escape repression, torture, or war. Though some are also escaping poverty, there are many refugees who are educated and who held prestigious positions in their home countries. The fortunate may find professional employment in their fields; more often, though, they count themselves lucky to find work in factories or restaurants.

Though at first glance the meaning of home may seem like a purely emotional concept, it has far-reaching political consequences. Aviezer Tucker has described human beings as "a migratory species," all of whom are searching for home (1994, 186). By assuming that a person's land of birth, or ethnicity, defines his or her "home," governments can use the word and the concept for their own purposes. Economic and political refugees are sent back "home," to a place that they have often risked their lives to leave and that—depending on their age at the time of migration—they may not even remember. The rationale that home is a singular location where a person must inevitably belong is used to exclude people from communities and prevent them from crossing borders. Although state-defined and personal perceptions of identity can differ, government authorities have an interest in maintaining the myth of historically linear and stable identities (Tucker 1994, 186; Ong 1999, 2).

The high numbers of immigrants worldwide demand that they be understood in ways other than those that serve institutional purposes. Viewing foreigners as the "other" not only separates and marginalizes them but also distances other people from the rich contributions immigrants make to their communities. Fair policy decisions therefore require an understanding of how the issues of identity, home, and migration are intertwined. Though individual immigration stories are, by their nature, personal, they are also intrinsically political (Furman 2005, 94; Benmayor and Skotnes 1994, 15–16) and can be a valuable means of informing policy.

INSIDER PERSPECTIVES

I became keenly aware of the personal challenges that immigrants face after my sister moved to Norway in 1985 to live in her future husband's hometown. Over the years, I have listened to the story of her immigrant experience and have seen how living as a foreigner has shaped her life and altered her sense of self and home. I once asked her if she realized when she left home that she would spend most of her adult life so far away from her roots. Her teasing response was "No, it was an accident." She knew she was moving, of course, but that decision was peripheral to the decision to marry, not an explicit decision to confuse her notion of home. She did not anticipate that she would struggle with unremitting feelings of dislocation for the next twenty years or more.

By witnessing my sister's life, I began to understand that the effect of immigration on individual lives is not short-lived. I discovered that feeling like a "foreigner" does not end when a person learns a new language, establishes residency, buys a house, or even changes citizenship. Instead, foreignness lingers and, as the years go by, creates fluid emotions about belonging, home, and identity. Those who stay in an adopted country go through a continual process of adjustment to and learning about both their new country and themselves.

These observations prompted me to look more closely at the immigrant experience. I wanted to explore whether the circumstances that led a person to immigrate might affect his or her ability to find comfort and a sense of belonging in a new home, how living in a different culture might transform perceptions of identity, and what meanings the journey of immigration might have to someone looking back over twenty or thirty years of life in a foreign country. And if a new sense of home and place is established, how do personal connections to a former home fit into this new life?

We hear about economic immigrants and political refugees because of their numbers and visibility. But there is another category of immigrants rarely covered by the media, perhaps because their stories are less dramatic: borrowing my sister's language, I refer to them as "accidental immigrants." These immigrants neither migrate to new countries to escape poverty or repression nor follow a pattern of movement by their fellow nationals or ethnic groups. Instead, accidental immigrants make intentional life decisions— such as those that involve marriage, education, or career advancement— that lead to the secondary and sometimes unanticipated outcome of long-term immigration. While at times they struggle with their choices, they have the advantage of being able to decide whether to stay in their adopted countries.[1]

The four women I feature in *Accidental Immigrants and the Search for Home* fall into this category. Though their circumstances can be differentiated from those of other migrants, they share the experience of having left home and the challenges and adjustments that come with living in a foreign country. The lives of the four accidental immigrants portrayed here provide insight into the lives of any immigrant from any setting: that they have had the opportunity to choose their home does not eliminate the compelling human need to belong and to feel at home.[2]

Anna Nielsen, born Ataahua Hakaraia, is Maori, from New Zealand. When she left home, she planned to return in a year; she never dreamed she would spend most of her life in Norway. Both Shirine Arya Cooper and Lisa Dwyre Nichols have experienced multiple immigrations but for different reasons: Lisa, born in Africa to working-class English parents, spent her childhood between Zambia and Canada and as a young woman immigrated to the United States to marry an American. Before marrying her husband, who is Jewish, Lisa converted from Christianity to Judaism, so conversion, too, is part of her cultural journey. Shirine, the daughter of an Iranian diplomat, spent her childhood moving between various countries before coming to the United States to study. She stayed in the United States for more than twenty years before finally moving to France. Originally from Connecticut, Barrett Meyer flew to Caracas and knew immediately that she would never want to leave. In Venezuela she has worked as a musician, a teacher, and a television executive.[3] All four women, who began their accidental immigrations in their twenties and are now in their forties or fifties, have lived their adult lives in adopted countries.

FINDING HOME THROUGH LIFE HISTORIES

While my sister provides me with an insider's perspective on immigration, our close relationship means also that her viewpoint influences mine. As a result, I tend to compare other immigrants' experiences to my sister's. Did they adapt to their new lives more or less easily than she did? Did they have the same experiences around children, work, and families abroad? As the point of reference from which I comprehend the stories that I have heard, my sister's life inevitably shapes my interpretations.

My own story also guides my research. Raised in the midwestern United States, I tend to find the themes of renewal and positive personal transformation in individual life narratives that are emblematic of my culture (see McAdams 2006). My focus also gravitates toward individual rather than group identity (see Appadurai 1996, 173). That I am an Anglo woman whose life has been relatively privileged undoubtedly affects my preconceptions and biases, even as I recognize them for what they are.

Having a close relative abroad profoundly altered my life in both positive and negative ways. In particular, my perspectives about belonging and home have become broader. Finding my own place to call home has been a lifelong endeavor; as I grow older, the need for grounding in a geographic location has become increasingly important. As a result, I am personally invested in researching the subject of home.

The portrayals I write, then, are a "joint production" (Maynes, Pierce, and Laslett 2008, 100) or "double biography," because my personality and biases necessarily flow through the narratives alongside those of the participants (Frank 1979, 89; Watson and Watson-Franke 1985, 12). The "truths" of the narratives are contingent on my interpretations, though I have made a conscious effort to refrain from imposing my own values as I retell and contextualize each story.[4]

To achieve an intimate understanding of the long-term effects of immigration, I explored the life stories of four immigrants from childhood through adulthood. I chose the participants for a variety of reasons: their similarity in age and in length of time as immigrants and their differences in terms of geographic location, ethnicity, personality, and perspective. As immigrants who have lived away from their first homes for many years, the participants were able to share the kind of insights that can come only from reflection—from a long-term view influenced by time and place. I was also drawn to them as my contemporaries, and therefore as women whose lives would be likely to resonate with my own.

The reasoning behind my decision to write about women was twofold: (1) the experiences of female immigrants would more closely resemble those of my sister, and (2) until recently women have been understudied in much immigration research (Brettell 2008, 128). Given that half the migrants (UNDP 2009, 25) and most of the refugees in the world are women (Croucher 2004, 163), it is vitally important that we understand how gender influences migration and, in turn, how migration influences the lives of women. Women, for example, tend to feel a greater need than men to belong in a new culture and tend to mourn the losses associated with immigration more than men do (Walsh and Horenczyk 2001). Men and women are also likely to differ in their responses to the meaning of home (Gurney 1997).[5] Stories told by women, including cross-cultural insights into family life, marriage, and gender, are necessary to any discussion of globalization (see Ong 1995, 367; 1999, 11–12).

Although the participants have had varying cultural influences during their lives, which include differing concepts of self, identity, and home, they have all lived in and internalized Western cultures such that they understand home and belonging from a viewpoint comparable to my own. Specifically, their understanding of the emotionally based notion of home encompasses Western ideas of time, space, boundaries, safety, and grounding (see Jackson 1995). While the term "Western" is not intended to suggest homogeneity, the participants' embedded understanding of the concepts of home and identity is similarly situated.

The purpose of the book is to gain insight into the interrelationship between immigration and individual perceptions of home. Life histories are particularly effective in the study of immigration, as they provide a retrospective, humanized view of the slow process of adjustment to life in a new place. While personal narratives cannot be generalized, they are a useful way to "get beneath the abstractions of migration theory in order to understand migration from an insider's perspective" and can inform broader observations about migration (Gmelch 1992, 311; see also Benmayor and Skotnes 1994, 14–15). The exploration of home is also particularly well suited to narrative and life history. As the author Michael Jackson has noted, home is not an essence that can be easily defined. "Being-at-home-in-the-world" is best described as a "lived relationship" (Jackson 1995, 123).

Life histories are based on memories, and memory changes as it is colored by time and experience. Memories are not absolute truths; they become, instead, a reflection of the feelings that remain. The fact that subjective truths may not correspond precisely with other versions of an event does not lessen the validity or meaning of the story told. The process of recalling may itself bring about new realizations and change how an event is understood or perceived (Watson and Watson-Franke 1985, 2–3). Stories, then, are told "about and around a life" (Behar 1993, 235); they are intensely personal and present the truths as they appear to the participant, even as later events and community narratives influence them (Bell 2002,

208). How a person relates his or her life story is also influenced by culture and by the value the culture places on different interpretations of any one event (McAdams 2006, 288–289).

NARRATIVE JOURNEYS

The many external factors that merge to create a person's response to immigration are addressed here only as they relate to the four participants. For example, economic and political forces (such as the independence of Zambia, the Iranian revolution, ethnic marginalization in New Zealand, and economic growth and collapse in Venezuela) certainly influenced how the participants viewed their immigration experiences. Only if they, as actors, felt historical or political pressures to be relevant to their stories, however, are these forces, or such factors as gender roles and cultural differences, discussed here. As Anna told me, she can make no wide-ranging statements about Norwegian culture; she can describe only her own personal experiences with the people she met. Her story and those of the other participants are therefore not offered as in-depth studies of any culture. They are the stories of each woman's life in the country or countries where she encountered these cultures.

In this book I retell the stories that *the participants wanted to tell me* about their immigrant experiences. The details and events that I have included are part of the narrative that each person expressed as important to her in terms of belonging and identity. The stories the women related to me emphasized their experiences of home, family, and personal change. Their stories were not about facts and events alone; they were also about the emotions and the meaning that they attributed to these experiences. What the participants chose to say and how they chose to say it in our interviews reflect how they make sense of their past and find coherence in their lives (McAdams 2006, 83–84). Although some of their self-reflections may not seem directly relevant to immigration and home, I have included those that appeared to affect how the participants themselves understand their immigrant experiences.[6]

Recent research across a variety of disciplines addresses theories of immigration and home (Mallett 2004). Although this book is based mainly in anthropology, I draw on other disciplines, most notably psychology, to understand issues around belonging, home, and identity. Borrowing from the methodologies of narrative inquiry, I not only tell the stories but also contemplate the insights and meanings that the stories hold (Bell 2002, 208). References to scholarly literature help frame the investigation, but my focus remains on the narratives and the understanding of immigration and home that can be drawn from them. As themes are revealed in the narratives, I explore relevant theoretical concepts, but I seek to avoid allowing any individual theory to overshadow the perspectives of the storytellers themselves

(Maynes, Pierce, and Laslett 2008, 10–11, 118). A full examination of any one particular theory is beyond the scope of this book.

By joining the rich details of the participants' lives with limited commentary and discussion, I hope to create a conversation between interpretation and story.[7] Relating the life stories of these four women is meant to raise questions about how individuals fit within theoretical models.[8] My hope is that the individual viewpoints of home that I present here can inform and ground theories that consider external political and social issues and the influence they have on immigrants.

In terms of genre, *Accidental Immigrants and the Search for Home*, like its participants, is a hybrid. The book, which strives to bridge the gap between scholarly works and those intended for general audiences, is located between conventional categories. Following the advice of Biddy Martin and Chandra Mohanty, I attempt "to avoid two traps, the purely experiential and the theoretical oversight of personal and collective histories" (1986, 210).

Anna, Lisa, Shirine, and Barrett came from and have moved to a variety of places. My knowledge of the cultures of these regions is limited. The descriptions and the references to place, religious practices, and languages are based on the memories and knowledge that the participants communicated to me and, in some cases (for example, Norway, Denver, and Miami), my own life experiences. Two of the women I had known for many years before the project began, and two I had the honor of befriending as our interviews unfolded. I know them and the details of their lives well. I see them as exceptional women not only because of their personal accomplishments but also because they have undertaken journeys full of risks and have faced those risks with courage and conviction. Although the experiences of these four women may differ from those of many readers, aspects of their lives will be familiar to all—including the joys and challenges of jobs and families, which they have worked their way through with as much grace as they can. I have made every effort to represent accurately the essence of each experience.

◆

Finding language that accurately describes the layered and complex experience of immigration and that includes both the figurative and literal aspects of the journey has been a challenge. During the course of my research, I found myself on a journey of my own, which led me to a new way of thinking about the process of immigration. After completing the interviews, but before I began the writing process, I walked the Camino de Santiago, a historical pilgrimage route across northern Spain. With nothing but a basic guidebook and my backpack, I did not know what I might encounter, whom I might meet, or even where I might sleep at night. The experience deepened my perspective of life itself as a pilgrimage—a perpetual search for meaning as we walk our individual journeys.

After I returned to my writing, the metaphor of pilgrimage came to mind as I thought about how to describe the emotional lives of the participants. Though these women did not set out to embark on literal pilgrimages, I saw their experiences as mirroring key aspects of pilgrim journeys: they traveled to new locations, where they repeatedly faced the unknown, and their movement between places was about not only geographical change but also personal transition and transformation. In the process of adjusting to their new lives, they faced self-reflection. They were challenged to maintain a sense of trust and openness in the presence of fear or personal trials. They were uncertain what they might find but hopeful that their new surroundings would bring some measure of fulfillment and, eventually, a feeling of home and community.

The core of the book is the exploration of how, in the course of negotiating the demands of family and society, these four women found a way to balance the complexity of their lives, while also reconstructing their identities around the experience of immigration. Regardless of how immigration is perceived, it is a fact of contemporary life. I hope that these narratives illustrate the incredible diversity of experience among immigrants, as well as the life experiences that we all share, whether or not we ever leave home. The stories are not only portraits of individuals and how they find meaning but also evidence of how the lives of immigrants mirror the changes that we all experience through the forces of movement and globalization.

In today's world, no one is detached from the pervasiveness of global connections. Immigrants may dress or speak differently or have a distinct appearance; they may celebrate different holidays. But whether they are invisible, working behind the scenes in kitchens or in fields, or the people living next door whom we see mowing their lawns or dropping their children off at school, their stories demonstrate how resilient and brave ordinary people can be as they face the challenges of everyday life.

I

ACCIDENTAL IMMIGRANTS

From Roots to Routes

Where am I from? Well, that's a long story.

—LISA

PATHWAYS

"Where are you from?" is a simple question but one that in today's world of movement can elicit multiple responses. Behind a one-line answer there is likely a significant story. Where a person is from might mean where he or she was born, grew up, or currently lives. "Home" is a concept that integrates many levels of meaning and emotion: home can be a structure, a town, a country, and a feeling. Home can be the location of our past or our present. We can go home to visit our parents, perhaps thousands of miles away, or go home for lunch to an apartment where we have lived for only a week. Home can be a cultural, spiritual, and physical locale. Home can be a literal destination or a figurative one—"an inner geography where the ache to belong finally quits" (Zandy 1990, 1).

As an idea, home has inspired works of fiction, memoirs, and scholarly research. Here, I explore home as it applies to immigrants. The stories that follow look at how a sense of home develops, or is perhaps inhibited, when individuals leave their roots to make a home in a new country.

In Western cultures, the idea of home generally represents something static. Being rooted is venerated, while itinerancy or homelessness is considered suspect or unstable (Malkki 1997; Jackson 1995, 85–87). This myth may give us a feeling of stability, but it is not grounded in reality. Historically, both Western and non-Western populations have engaged in travel and external commerce, or have been displaced, and as a result have had to create new homes for themselves. Geographic movement has always been part of the human condition (Wolf 1992; Tucker 1994, 186).

Before modern transportation and communication, immigrants were often unable to return home. Today, however, movement is easier, and people move from region to region, rural to urban, and continent to continent on a regular basis. Immigrant workers go back and forth between their own countries and others, sometimes several times a year and sometimes even daily. In the contemporary world, whether because of the influence of media, work opportunities, environmental disasters, political policies, or even tourism, the frequency and intensity of movement has increased (see Appadurai 1996, 191–192).[1] Greater mobility, though, does not eliminate individuals' need to have a sense of place and belonging[2] (Geertz 1996, 261).

For the purposes of my discussion, I consider the concepts of home, belonging, and identity to be interconnected but not interchangeable. The feelings associated with the concepts influence and respond to one another and often shift in concert. For instance, a deep understanding of one's identity can enable a sense of belonging. Paradoxically, though, this level of self-understanding usually occurs most dramatically when there has been displacement from home (Rapport and Dawson 1998b, 9). Home and belonging can affect perceptions of identity (Sixsmith 1986), and similarly, identity and belonging create a sense of place in the world: the feeling of home.

"Home" is an emotionally laden word. Ideally, the physical location of home is a safe place that grounds us, a place from which we can go out into the world, know who we are, and to where we will return (Dovey 1978, 29).[3] Home is our territory and the location from which we learn to compare differences with others and other places[4] (Relph 1976, 40; Case 1996). Naming our home is more than locating ourselves physically. An understanding of home reflects one's individual and social identity (see Case 1996). Where or what we call home gives clues to who we are, how we view ourselves, and in turn, how we want others to view us.

Identity, too, is a complex phenomenon. The first perception of identity usually comes from our parents. They name us, tell us who we are in relation to them, and perhaps describe our family history. Our identity is internalized through stories, holiday traditions, the media, and how others perceive us. We are influenced by cultural identities, group identities, and family identities, and gradually we develop an individual identity and sense of self as we grow up and begin to separate emotionally from our parents (see Akhtar 1999). All the things that contribute to how people see themselves, as well as how they are seen by others, are internalized and influence identity: ethnicity, skin color, community, being the child of a coal miner or a lawyer, our hobbies and interests and work. An identity is not formed in isolation; it emerges from relationships of difference from others that influence who we are as well as who we are not[5] (Gupta and Ferguson 1997b, 13–15; Hall 1996a, 4–5).

Identity continues to be shaped throughout our entire lives; it changes as we move from being a child to an adult and then through the different roles we assume as adults: as we become spouses and parents, change jobs, and grow older. Identity is not something inherent, essential, or unchanging; it continues to evolve as a person's life story is constructed and reconstructed (Hall 1996a, 3–4). Multilayered and mutable, identity is shaped not only by events but also by the meaning a person makes from those events (McAdams 2006, 98–99).

Belonging is also is changeable and constructed relationally with others. To belong, a person needs to believe that his or her life "merges with and touches the lives of others" (Jackson 2006, 12). Belonging can come from bonding with locations and communities, and it shifts as our connections with locations or communities change (Eyles 1985). Belonging to a place, then, is connected to personal history and experience (Basso 1996, 55).

Many of us who remain in our country of origin frequently leave our hometown to go to a new job in a new location, marry outside of our family's circle, or for other reasons feel distanced from our roots. Moving to a new region within the same country can feel as unsettling as moving to a different continent. Region to region, people speak with different accents, eat different food, and live in distinct landscapes. Anyone who moves away from home, even if only across town, faces some personal adjustments.

For an immigrant, the question "Where is home?" can be complicated and confusing. As immigrants go through life's passages, they are confronted with added layers of identity transformation that non-immigrants seldom experience. The significance of leaving home and its ensuing effect on identity perception becomes amplified. As a result, immigration can bring ambivalence and uncertainty about the intertwined understandings of identity, belonging, and home. The effect that immigration has on any individual's identity will be unique and will be affected by what the immigrant brings to the situation, what is encountered, and how the individual responds (Deaux 2006, 130).

Like all stories, the life stories of Anna, Lisa, Shirine, and Barrett had a beginning. To understand how these four immigrants relate to the idea of home, their beginnings and the circumstances that led them to leave their countries are as important as those that came long after the decision to immigrate occurred. I have included accounts of their lives prior to immigration to provide context and greater insight into their later motivations and the choices they made as their lives progressed. While not all life stories include childhood stories, here they are relevant to the questions being asked about home, identity, and belonging (see Maynes, Pierce, and Laslett 2008, 35).

When Anna, Lisa, Shirine, and Barrett left home, they had only a vague notion of what their futures might hold. As I spoke with each of them, common issues and shared feelings about immigration began to emerge. All four of their immigrations were "accidental" in the sense that they were the peripheral result of other choices and needs: love, education, and the desire to find a place of acceptance and belonging. What was not always a shared experience, however, was when and how their feelings began to evolve and change. All four of them went through periods of transition, contentment, and dissatisfaction, as well as moments of realization, but these phases of their lives were not always orderly. The pathways of their lives evoked a sensation of ebb and flow rather than a straight line.

The structure of this book is organized around the most significant themes in their lives—their beginnings, transitions, turning points, and resolutions—rather than in a chronological sequence. The themes were chosen because they appeared in all four women's lives and best represented the ongoing process of negotiating life in a new culture. This might not seem like the simplest way to organize their stories, but neither their lives nor any of our lives are neatly wrapped for presentation; part of life is dealing with the messy parts and at some point being able to look back and see how all the pieces create meaning.

Anna, Lisa, Shirine, and Barrett have each lived as strangers in new countries, with new customs, new languages, and new families—both those they created and those they married into. Like economic immigrants and refugees, they have had to learn to adapt and to make their best attempt at creating a life that could bring them a sense of home. The transitions they have experienced are unique, but there are threads of similarity between them. For all it was a learning process: learning how to live in a new place, learning who they are, and learning what home means to them as individuals.

This is the story of the journey of their lives.

Anna

Ataahua Hakaraia's life took a dramatic turn when she was sixteen years old. This young woman, whom everyone called "Anna," was not looking for change; nor did she have any specific vision of her future. She was taking each day as it came. Then, one afternoon when she was out with friends, she happened to look up to the deck of a ship docked at the Auckland wharf. There she saw a young man, and in that moment the course of her life was altered. It sounds like the plot of a romance novel: a pretty young girl, having suffered through an unhappy childhood, meets a handsome foreign sailor who loves her. Together they start a new life, move to a place far from the pain she endured as a child, and live happily ever after. Of course, Anna's life has not been perfect. There have been difficulties and sadness along the way, but in many respects the fairy-tale plot has been followed.

A little over three years after that day at the wharf, Anna; her new husband, Olav; and their young son boarded a plane that would take them from New Zealand to Norway, Olav's native home. Anna had never traveled outside her country; nor had she traveled much within New Zealand. She had seen snow only once and had never experienced dark, cold winters.

Anna had lived in a temperate, lush climate all of her life and had spent Christmases having barbecues at the beach, not sitting by a fireplace trying to keep warm. Anna had no idea what to expect from Norway, but she was not particularly concerned, because she intended to be gone for only a year. Anna could not foresee that thirteen years would pass before she would return to New Zealand or that when she finally did go back, she would find that her perception of "home" had been forever altered.

∿

Anna, now in her fifties, lives in an attractive residential neighborhood in a seaside town in southern Norway. The outside of her house looks like any other in the area, and the interior appearance gives no indication that one of the occupants is a foreigner. The house is well furnished, with a pine breakfast table and high-end appliances in the kitchen; the living and dining room are quite large, and in addition to a dining table, there is room for two well-appointed sitting areas, each with couches, chairs, and a coffee table. While the house is usually immaculate, it is not austere, and it has a cheerful and welcoming feel, with soft colors on the walls and lace curtains. But after a more careful look around, you might notice a photo in a corner of the living room that belies Anna's history. That black-and-white photo is of several people standing outside a wooden building. Given the style of the building and the tropical vegetation surrounding it, the location is clearly not Norway. Anna is in that picture. She is just a girl at the time, and she is standing with her grandmother outside a *Marai*—a traditional Maori meetinghouse, in a small town in New Zealand.

Anna's childhood was vastly different from her adult life. She came from a family with sixteen children and lived in a small town near the coast on the North Island of New Zealand. There were no hospitals in the area, so Anna was born in her parents' home. Anna's father worked at different jobs; sometimes he was a night watchman, and other times he worked in an abattoir. In a family as large as theirs, money was always scarce, so when Anna was just a baby, she and two of her older siblings went to live with their maternal grandmother.

Her family viewed this type of informal adoption as a good way to provide for children. As Anna explained to me, "The Maoris . . . don't adopt kids—not adopt with papers, I mean, but, you know, they would give them to a family member that doesn't have any children. But why I was given to my grandmother I never knew, but I don't regret that at all." Anna was sent to a home where she was wanted and loved and where she received more attention and care than her parents could have given her.

Anna's grandmother was a devout Mormon, steadfast in her beliefs and determined that her grandchildren would share her convictions. She was also a matriarch of the small Maori community in which she lived. Both aspects of her life held equal importance, and she found a way to blend traditional Maori culture with the rigorous Mormon practices brought to

New Zealand by missionaries in the 1800s. With the other elderly women in the town, she shared the duties of arranging and participating in events at the *Marai*: "Oh yeah, all of the women around there, they are what we call *Kuia*, which means elderly woman. So all the neighbor wives or mothers, they would get together and arrange for the ceremonies; it doesn't matter what it is. They've got the key to these houses, and what they say goes."

Singing and music are an important aspect of Maori culture, and Anna's grandmother's function at the *Marai* was to "call" people to events, particularly funerals, by singing to them as they arrived: "Maoris have always been known to be good singers . . . and it's always a woman that stands outside these houses, the *Marai* . . . where we have the dead, and would be calling them to come and [give] your last wishes to this person. And it's kind of a very eerie call. Yeah."

Anna and the two siblings who also lived in the house were required to pray every night and attend church faithfully. So fervent was her grandmother in her beliefs that frequently she would wake the children late at night so that they could join her for another round of prayers before she went to bed: "She would call us, and then we would have to . . . sit up there, sit up in our bed, tired, and we would have a prayer with her. And we were falling asleep, and then you would just hear her say, 'Amen,' and then you would just say that too and lie down and go to sleep again."

Life changed abruptly when Anna's grandmother died. After eight years Anna was suddenly returned to her parents, who were now living in a larger town about a two-hour drive south of Auckland. Anna had not seen her parents or her thirteen other siblings often during her first eight years, and the transition was painful and shocking. Instead of calm days with a routine schedule of church and school, Anna was now in a chaotic environment in a house full of people she hardly knew. Everything in this new home—all the activity and disorder and people—was confusing for Anna.

Anna's mother had had a child nearly every year for sixteen years, and Anna had been born somewhere in the middle of all of them. When her older siblings began having their own children, they were brought to live in the house as well. The family home, in effect, had a revolving door to accommodate the children and grandchildren who frequently came and went. There were four bedrooms—one for Anna's parents, two rooms for the boys, and one room for all the girls: "All the kids were there! And how many we are, I don't know, because, you know, they got bigger, and then they started having their own family, and there were kids everywhere, people everywhere. You know, don't ask me how many; there were just people everywhere."

Everything about Anna's life was different now. Her grandmother had been strict, but Anna felt safe with her. In her parents' home, Anna was vulnerable:

My grandmother, she had her ways and her traditions, and I learned a lot of that. . . . I missed my grandmother when I moved back to my parents'. And as a child you know what you can do to gain love and to feel sympathy and that. But my father was very hard on me, and he would—whenever I did anything wrong like any child would do, my father would beat me. . . . I would always hide, like anybody else, and cry for my grandma, 'cause she was a hard woman too, but . . . I loved my grandma, and my parents were kind of strangers.

Although Anna's parents were members of the Mormon church and considered themselves "very, very religious," they did not actively practice the faith. Her father was a heavy drinker whose life tended to be a cycle of working, going to pubs, and sleeping. When he was home, he frequently became angry and violent, and Anna quickly learned to fear him. Her parents had intense fights: "I tell you, you know how [people] can get into fights, and they would shake the whole house when they started. But you got used to it. I mean, it's not anything that I like, but what are you going to do as a kid? . . . [Y]ou just go and hide."

Anna's mother did her best to ease the transition for Anna, and after her father's outbursts, she would take Anna aside and soothe her. But the protection and nurturing Anna's mother could provide was limited in this home where there was alcohol abuse, little money, and so many children. Anna has few fond memories of this part of her childhood.

At her grandmother's Anna had certainly not been pampered, but with only three children in the house, there had not been a need to ration basic necessities. At her parents' home, finances were so dire that the family barely had enough to feed and clothe the children. There was never anything extra, even for school supplies. Anna remembers feeling humiliated at school because she never had what she needed. The other students came to home economics class with fabric for sewing or food for cooking lessons. Anna came almost empty-handed, with nothing but an apron.

Life with such a big family also meant there were always chores to be done and few opportunities for fun. And even though there were usually more boys than girls in the house, the girls were still required to do most of the chores. While the boys could bring friends home or go swimming after school in a nearby creek, the girls were expected to come home as soon as school was out and work until the work was done. By then it was often too late to go out and play: "Compared to today, we always had chores to do—I mean *real* chores. You know . . . my sisters and I . . . we would do all the clothes washing until we'd go to school in the morning, after making breakfast and making the kids' lunches, and then we would come home after school and start making dinner and baking bread and then washing clothes at the same time. And we could wash clothes until it was black outside and hang them up so that if you're lucky, then they're dry the next day. You know, it's just the way things were."

Although Anna was raised in a Maori home, she was also required to function within the British-based culture of schools and work. While there was some social separation, Anna was never aware of race being an issue at school. She always had both Maori and Kiwi friends: "I hung out with both; they were alike. That was me. You know, there are people that only went with Maori people. But, I mean, I don't see a friend in the color; I see a friend in the person."

At school the Maori language was not particularly encouraged, and the children were taught to read and write only English. Anna's family sometimes spoke Maori at home, but Anna never learned it well. Maori was used primarily between adults, particularly when they did not want the children to understand what they were saying. In the disruptive household, there was not much emphasis on teaching the children about the meaning of Maori traditions. Other than taking one elective course in Maori culture at school, Anna had no opportunity to explicitly learn about her culture once she left her grandmother's home. Instead, Maori ways are something Anna understands intuitively, in the way we all understand the subtle rules of our culture or even our own family dynamics: "I'm a Maori; that's what they call us in New Zealand, the way we're brought up. It's so different compared to the British way . . . so Maori, it was my life."

As Anna grew up, she began to be more and more troubled by the inconsistencies within her family. She was well aware of the contradiction between Mormon prohibitions against drinking and the substantial consumption of alcohol in the house, and she was exasperated by the double standards that applied to boys and girls. As she got older, the violence she experienced at the hands of her father became more frequent and more disturbing. By about the time she turned fifteen, all of the ordeals in Anna's life had started to catch up with her. She decided to quit high school and get a job. The job helped a bit; Anna now had enough money to buy a few things. But it was not enough—Anna was now a teenager, and she needed new clothes, at least some of which she did not want to be hand-me-downs. On impulse she shoplifted and was caught.

As Anna recounted this story to me, she seemed embarrassed but made it clear that she understood the motivation for her actions: "I needed some bras! I needed some underwear! So what? Even at that age I used them!" In a sense this may have been the best thing that could have happened, because in the aftermath, the authorities took Anna away from her family and put her in a group home for girls and eventually a foster home. The rationale behind the severe consequences is not something Anna can recall in detail. Whether she was removed from her parents' home because of violence, because of poverty, or simply because of the shoplifting incident, she is not sure. But she never returned to live with them.

It was in the group home that Anna received her nickname. Unlike her real name, Ataahua, Anna was easy for everyone to say, whether Maori or Kiwi, so she decided to keep it. Away from her family, Anna was able to build up some self-confidence. When she turned sixteen and was released from the group home, she was ready to "spread her wings." Instead of going back to her parents, she moved to Auckland with some friends.

Not far from the town where her parents lived, Auckland is a major port. One Sunday, Anna and a few of her friends decided to watch a boat race at the wharf, and this is where she first saw her future husband, Olav, standing watch on the bow of a cargo ship: "You know, I was sixteen years old, and I saw this tall blond guy, and I just can't get over it. . . . [O]h my, he was so beautiful. . . . [A]nyway, he became my husband." By the time Olav's ship left Auckland, several days later, the two had already decided to spend their lives together.

For the next year or so, they exchanged letters, seeing each other only every few months. About two years after they met, the couple found out that Anna was pregnant. Even though Anna had wanted to get away from her family just a few years before, now that she was going to have a child of her own, she wanted to be closer to them, especially during the long stretches when Olav was away working. She and Olav decided to move back to the town where Anna's parents lived.

Being near her mother again was good for Anna, and her pregnancy created an opportunity for the two of them to forge a relationship apart from Anna's many siblings and her father. When there were serious complications with the pregnancy, Anna turned to her mother for advice. Anna's mother, who had a great deal of experience with childbirth, knew just what to say and how to comfort Anna when she needed it.

Luck would have it that Olav was on vacation and in town when Anna went into labor. They had their first child, Per, when Anna was just nineteen and Olav twenty-one. After Per was born and Olav went back to work on the ship, Anna's mother would stay with Anna and Per for several days at a time. When it was just the two of them with Per, they were able to get to know one another in a way that had not been possible during Anna's childhood. The bond that they shared during this time eased some of the painful memories Anna had of living in her parents' home.

Now a new father, Olav started to think about advancing his career. If he wanted to become a ship's officer, he needed to return to Norway for training. Shortly after Per turned one, Anna and Olav felt it was time to take a step in this direction. They decided to go to Norway for a year so that Olav could go back to school. Anna knew nothing about Norway except that it was on the other side of the world, but she was not concerned and had no particular expectations. She trusted Olav, felt "sure of him," and was certain that their life together was right for her, regardless of where they were. For her, going away for a year would be interesting, a way to learn more about Olav and a chance for his family to meet the new baby. She knew she would be back in New Zealand soon, and with a sense of excitement, she packed a few clothes and the essential baby things, said her good-byes, and got on the plane.

❧

Anna's childhood was a confusing mix of love and pain. In her easygoing way, Anna accepted and made the best of her circumstances, but she was never able to lose the sense of displacement she felt after she moved back to her parents' home. She felt put upon within the family structure because of her status as a female and ill at ease in the crowded family home.

Anna's memories of her childhood have become vague over the years. Why or how certain things happened, or her exact age when they occurred, have been lost in the blur of those conflicted years, and as her life has progressed, events seem to have taken on a hazy, more general quality in Anna's mind. What she remembers most clearly are the feelings of safety with her grandmother, confusion and conflict in her parents' home, and the hopes for her future that developed after she met Olav.

Now, at the age of twenty, she was leaving New Zealand for the first time. While she was gone, she would be with her husband and son, and that was all she needed for one short year away from home.

Lisa

I first met Lisa Nichols at a dance studio in Florida, where we were both taking a jazz class. We had seen each other before, but we had never had a conversation, just exchanged smiles or pleasantries as we attempted to be graceful while moving our middle-aged selves across the studio floor—something I must admit was easier for Lisa with her tall, slim build than it was for me. On this particular evening, we both happened to arrive a few minutes early, and sitting on the steps outside the classroom, we struck up a conversation. Because so many people who live in South Florida are from elsewhere, the first conversation most people usually have concerns where they are from, so this topic came up quite naturally. I had not noticed that Lisa had a foreign accent, and I expected that I would get a simple answer—for instance, "Illinois" or "Arizona." Instead, Lisa laughed and said, "Well, that's a long story!" That one question turned into a series of rich interviews that took place over the course of about a year. Sitting at Lisa's dining room table, drinking tea served from one of a collection of teapots, I listened as Lisa opened up and let me into the story of her life.

❧

In 1983, when Lisa was twenty-two, she moved to the United States from Canada. Lisa had emigrated several times during her childhood, from South Africa to Zambia to England and then finally to Canada, and she had not anticipated that she would again move to a new country. She had been satisfied with her life, enjoying her office job with an airline and traveling as much as possible. Then, on a brief trip to Miami, Lisa met Jason, her future husband. She eventually decided to move from British Columbia to Miami to be with him without much deliberation as to how another emigration might affect her.

Over the more than twenty-five years that Lisa has lived in Miami, she has certainly thought about the changes the move brought to her life—and has recognized the shifting feelings she has had about the experience, ranging from joy and contentment to anger and frustration. But until we sat down with the tape recorder, she had never evaluated the journey comprehensively, and in so doing, she uncovered the depth and meaning in the events that led her to where she is today.

Lisa's childhood was, in one sense, uneventful, stable, and happy, without the traumas that many children have of divorcing parents, poverty, or even serious family squabbles. Her parents got along, had many interests, and made an effort to ensure that their children were exposed to new experiences and ideas. But in another sense her childhood was remarkable: by age ten she had lived on three continents and in four countries.

Lisa's parents both came from white, working-class British families. They grew up during World War II and the Blitz and were accustomed to hardship. Lisa's father was trained as a machinist, and though he was generally employable, he had a hard time making a living in postwar England. Shortly after the young couple married, he suggested that they set out for Africa, which offered the promise of sustainable work. What Lisa's father wanted in his life most, besides adventure, was steady work and the opportunity to be comfortable financially. Although her mother had some hesitations, she agreed. She was interested in travel, and this would be a way to see the world.

Lisa describes her parents as a "formidable team": hardworking, strong from having suffered through the war, and having the initiative to move to a new country where they knew no one and had no resources but their own ingenuity. They took a ship to Cape Town, South Africa, where Lisa's father quickly got a job. Two children, including Lisa, were born there, and when she was two years old, Lisa's father got a better job working for a copper mine in Northern Rhodesia (then a British colony but soon to become the independent state of Zambia), and the family moved again. Not long after, they had another child.

Lisa's childhood in Zambia blended the British lifestyle with the landscape of Africa. She and her family lived in the town of Kitwe in a small brick house with a concrete floor. The backyard had a pawpaw and several banana trees and was dusty in the dry season. Although the family lived amid Africans, their social life consisted primarily of friendships with other expatriates from Western Europe. The social and political climate of early 1960s Africa did not allow whites and blacks to mix socially, and racial distinctions meant that even household employees were kept, and kept themselves, at an emotional distance—their interactions cordial but formal.

For Lisa, it was normal to be living a life that was both British and African. She played with Barbie dolls sent from England and African dolls from Zambia. She and her siblings went to a Catholic school attended by both expatriates and local children. At school their lives were intertwined, and Lisa has no memory of racial distinctions ever being made, but outside school her friendships were with only other expatriate children. In the afternoons Lisa went to ballet classes, occasionally performed in a recital, and played in the backyard. Lisa's parents maintained their British habits: pictures taken at Christmastime show a house with customary British Christmas decorations, and Lisa remembers having mincemeat pie and other English treats around the holidays. Tea was always served in the afternoon.

Lisa's parents liked to explore, and whenever her father had vacation time, they made an effort to travel in the countryside. They would load up an old station wagon, and with the children in the backseat, they would drive for days in the heat to visit the animal parks. Outside their neighborhood, Lisa was exposed to the contrast between her life, the protected life of a British expatriate child, and the local Africans. They drove on unpaved roads through vast savannas, miles from any cities. Along the way they passed lions and other animals by the side of the road and saw local women, topless, selling beads or walking between towns with heavy baskets on their heads, their feet their only form of transportation. This was not a particularly easy kind of car trip with children; in fact, it was a bit dangerous for foreigners. There were few gas stations and certainly no fast-food restaurants where they could get a quick meal and use a clean restroom. Instead, they had to stop where it seemed relatively safe and keep an eye out for snakes when they got out of the car. They slept in huts, with mosquito nets over the beds, because this was the only kind of place her parents could afford then. It was life as usual for the people from the area, but it seemed extraordinary to a young English couple and their small children.

Lisa first became aware that Africa was not really "home" when she was nine and her family took a trip back to London. After the long and expensive trip, they arrived, tired, in a dramatically different setting from the one they had left. Suddenly they were in an enormous, busy city where there were no African people and it was cold and rainy.

While in London, Lisa and her siblings were surrounded by cousins, aunts, uncles, and grandparents, most of whom the children had never met, and were taken around London to see all the sights. Lisa and her siblings were "showered with affection" by their grandparents, and Lisa felt special in the circle of this large, loving family. She began to comprehend that in Africa they were alone:

> My grandparents, I think, worked hard to make us feel we were like the rest of the cousins, their [other] grandchildren. And I remember feeling a little bit jealous that my grandparents had that daily contact with my cousins. . . . [Y]ou know, we didn't have a lot of contact, because we were raised in Africa and then in Canada, and all of our immediate family, all of our first cousins were always in England; our aunts and uncles were always in England; our grandparents were in England. So we did see them but not on a daily basis. And I always felt that loss, of not having them.

A year or so later, back in Africa, the family was at a crossroads. Lisa's brother, James, was turning twelve, and James would need to go to boarding school to get a European-style education. Lisa's parents did not want to send him away and decided that this would be a good time to leave Africa. They sold most of their belongings, and the family went back to England.

It soon became apparent that staying in England was not feasible. The prospects for work were not good for Lisa's father, and he did not want to be "on the dole." Except for the contact with grandparents and other family, Lisa remembers being unhappy: the schoolchildren laughed at her funny clothes, and she hated the cold, damp weather. Everything felt "drab and dreary" compared to Africa. Rather than bright sunshine and open plains, there were crowded city streets, rain, and a general feeling of gloom.

Lisa's parents decided to leave England again and try western Canada, where they hoped there would be better opportunities. The two parents and three children took only what they could fit into two black steamer trunks and boarded a ship for the American East Coast. Two trunks for five people meant they could bring only essentials, and Lisa still remembers how hard it was to choose what she would bring. The dolls she had carried all the way from Africa were precious to her, but some had to be left behind. Those she was able to keep are still packed carefully away in her closet. Lisa showed me these dolls, laughing at herself for saving them for so long but also remembering the emotion behind what was, for a child, a painful decision.

Canada turned out to be a good choice. Lisa's father got a job with a major Canadian airline. Her parents bought a home in a suburb outside Vancouver and settled into their new lives, making friends, joining clubs, and raising their children. As soon as possible, Lisa's father applied for citizenship for himself and the children. Lisa's mother, however, resisted giving up her British citizenship and held on to her passport for a number of years.

At age ten, Lisa was old enough to realize that she was somehow different from the other kids in her new Canadian school. She had a funny accent and did not know the Canadian playground games, like tetherball. Initially, she was teased, but Lisa eventually made friends and got used to the routines in her new school. Through primary school and junior high she took ice-skating and flute lessons and went on camping trips with the Girl Guides. She and her two siblings walked home from school for lunch every day, where their mother was waiting for them with a hot meal.

Still, Lisa never stopped feeling like an "outsider," and she remembers her adolescent years as being full of turmoil and oppositions. At home her parents saw a sweet, well-behaved girl, but outside the house, Lisa was skipping classes and hanging out in the park, trying to fit in with the popular kids: "I remember when I got to eighth or ninth grade, it was really a difficult time. I think maybe it is for all girls. Your body is changing, and you want to be in the cool group, and I wasn't allowed in because I was a foreigner. . . . I don't know whether it was that I considered myself different from them or they considered me different from them. But I was not in the cool group."

During the 1970s a social revolution was under way, and even a sub-urban high school in Canada was not immune to change. Instead of school uniforms and skirts, teenagers were emulating hippies, wearing bell-bottom blue jeans and flowered shirts. Lisa's parents did not approve. Though they had adventurous spirits, they were still conservative when it came to proper behavior and dress. Lisa's mom, now busy with another baby, was perhaps a bit out of touch with the trends. She wanted Lisa to continue to wear the clothes she sewed—clothes that might have been appropriate ten years earlier in England but were not so fashionable anymore. These primarily consisted of skirts and frilly blouses, and once, even a kilt. The adolescent Lisa was mortified, and one day she finally sneaked out of the house with her brother's jeans hidden under her skirt. She quickly rode her bike around the corner and removed the skirt before she got to school. Lisa now tells this story with amusement, but at the time it was not funny to her at all:

> Being an immigrant and coming to a new country when you're a preteen or teenager, I think you do try extra hard to fit in. And I think your parents are struggling. No matter what culture or what country you're in, those immigrant parents are struggling to find their way in that new place. And things are always different. Accepted behaviors are different. . . . I wanted to run with the wrong crowd; I wanted to dress the way I wanted to. But my parents, I think, were struggling with [the] North American lifestyle; it's not what they were accustomed to.

Lisa's parents were torn between trying to adjust to a new culture and trying to retain values and norms from their own backgrounds. Lisa was caught in the middle, trying to do what her parents wanted and attempting to find her own way: "I remember feeling like I was two people. I was this person when I was at school, and then I was this different person at home."

Even though Lisa did not feel that she fit in with her peers, in a sense she felt more at home in Canada than she had in Africa. Her memories of Christmas, for example, are of a happy, magical time, with snow falling outside. Lisa and her sisters wore matching red velvet dresses; there were parties, presents, and a Christmas tree—all the trappings of the traditional English holiday. Christmas in Canada mirrored the nostalgic stories she had heard from her parents about their own childhoods, and so this experience of the holiday felt natural to her. The settled feeling her parents had in Canada had in some respects been internalized by their children.

When Lisa was eighteen and had finished high school, she got an apartment in Vancouver and began working for the same airline as her father. The tension with her parents had lasted through her school years, but distance and independence helped ease the situation. By now Lisa was enjoying her life: dating, occasionally traveling, and enjoying the city with new friends.

Lisa has natural beauty. She does not wear much makeup or jewelry, and she certainly has no air of pretension. She is much more interested in biking or kayaking trips than she is in getting a manicure. When she was twenty-one, however, her friends persuaded her to enter a beauty pageant. Lisa did not take the contest seriously, but to her surprise she won the first round and was asked to go to Miami for the international finals.

Lisa's first glimpse of Miami was through the airplane window. The sun was shining on Biscayne Bay, the waves were cresting on the sparkling beach, and she was enthralled. The contestants, young women from all over the world, stayed in an elegant hotel in South Beach and were wined and dined by the sponsors. With a fellow contestant, Lisa drove around Miami in a convertible Volkswagen, sunbathed by the pool, and shopped for an evening gown for the pageant. This was beyond anything Lisa had ever experienced. She had lived in several countries, but Miami was more glamorous than anything she had seen before. The trip was a whirlwind of parties and events, and Lisa had a marvelous time. Although she did not win the contest this time, she did not care. Something much more important happened in Miami: at the final party, she met Jason, whom she would eventually marry.

Jason Nichols was seven years older than Lisa and already an established businessman in Miami. He was good-looking and charismatic, and he and Lisa hit it off right away. Before she left town, she and Jason discovered they had a lot in common—none of which involved beauty contests or fancy parties: "We played racquetball and discovered that we had so many things that we loved, the same kinds of things, like love of sports, love of the earth, outdoor activities."

Lisa returned to Canada infatuated with Jason, but she did not really expect that meeting him would change her life. Jason, on the other hand, was determined to pursue her and began to call and send cards and flowers. They visited each other a few times, but Lisa was not ready to take any drastic steps to be with him.

Jason finally won Lisa over when one weekend he spontaneously flew to Vancouver to surprise her. Lisa, who was not expecting him, was out with friends, so Jason ended up at her parents' home, where he spent the night. This gave Jason and her parents the opportunity to get to know one another. When Lisa saw how well they all got along and realized how serious Jason was about her, she decided the relationship was worth taking a risk. Not long after, Lisa agreed to move to Miami.

Lisa now says that when she got on the plane, she really had no idea what she was getting into. On one hand, Lisa knew what it meant to immigrate, but on the other hand, she was a relatively inexperienced young woman who really did not understand what it would feel like to be separated from family. In a way, her naïveté probably helped her, because she had few expectations.

Her parents, of course, had a better idea of how the move might affect her life, but they let her make her own decision: "My parents were really helpful . . . 'cause I think they really understand the whole experience of living away from your family and making that transition. . . . They didn't encourage me, and they didn't discourage me. They let me make my own choice. And I think a lot of that comes from them making their own choice. . . . [I]t was very hard, because I wanted somebody to tell me what to do. But I had to choose."

Being the practical person she is, Lisa did not completely cut her ties when she left Vancouver. Making sure she had a "plan B," in case things did not work out, she took a leave of absence instead of quitting her job. Her father agreed to look after her car, because she could not quite bring herself to sell it before she left. At the airport there was a tearful good-bye, and Lisa's father gave her a bracelet to remind her that she could always come home if she wanted to.

᪥

When Lisa talks about leaving Canada, she refers to an event: "when I immigrated." But at the time she left, she was not thinking in those terms. Her reason for moving was not that she especially wanted to live somewhere else; it was that she wanted to be with Jason. The circumstances of her life, in this case falling in love with a man from another country, led her to a place where by definition she was an immigrant.

The culture in the United States did not appear to be dramatically different from what Lisa was accustomed to, and she spoke the language. But as time went on, the differences between her culture and the cultures she was surrounded by in Miami became more and more apparent. Perhaps because the differences were subtle, they took a bit longer to become visible to Lisa. Though Lisa had been an immigrant before, she was just a child then and was with her parents. Now she was an adult, and the reality of living away from her home and family—of being an immigrant—would take on new meaning.

Shirine

When Shirine was born in 1955, the shah still ruled Iran, and the 1979 revolution was far in the future. Persian society at that time highly valued family history, and those who were part of the old aristocracy held central positions, both socially and politically. Shirine's parents were part of this influential social class: her grandfather on her mother's side was a member of Parliament and a well-respected businessman, and her father's family, while not as wealthy, was from the elite old guard of Iranian society. Many of her father's relatives had been politicians, including one former prime minister. When Shirine's father began his career, he followed the family path, joining the Iranian foreign ministry and eventually becoming a diplomat. Shirine's mother played the important part of the diplomat's wife, attending and holding social events and spending a great deal of time cultivating personal connections. The couple was ensconced in a political world, which, while bringing a great deal of opportunity, also brought obligations and, ultimately, risk.

By the time Shirine was born, her father had already held several foreign posts. He continued on a diplomatic career path, which required the family, including Shirine and her older sister, Fatima, to move every few years. Shirine's life, although advantaged in many ways, was disrupted by constant movement—the family usually alternated between three years abroad and two or three years in Iran. As a result, Shirine never became comfortable in any one culture, including the one she came from. She moved through her childhood feeling detached and separated, in part because of the frequent cultural disengagement but also because her parents were emotionally unavailable. Both had strong personalities and were dedicated to furthering her father's career. Their time and energy were focused on diplomatic matters, and family life was secondary.

Shirine's first experience living abroad began when she was only three months old and her father obtained a post in Poland. Her memories of this experience are vague, except for one: her beloved Polish nanny. Shirine spent much more time with the nanny than with anyone else, including her parents, and the two became very attached. Since her nanny spoke only Polish, Shirine was also more comfortable with that language than with Farsi.

When Shirine was three, the family returned to Tehran, but the nanny had to stay behind. Shirine was now surrounded by a language and culture that were, to her, very foreign. No one spoke Polish, the language that Shirine had experienced as one of comfort and love, and everything about her life—such as routines, food, and people—was radically different. Upset and confused, she spent many days clinging to her mother, crying. Shirine's first experience with her own country was one of helplessness and fear.

The family left for Hamburg, Germany, for another diplomatic assignment when Shirine was six. In Hamburg, she was enrolled in a school for international students, but she was the only child from Iran. The first day of school can be scary for any child, but for Shirine it was doubly hard. She was in a new country that looked and smelled and felt different from anything she had experienced before. On top of that, classes in the new school were taught in English, a language Shirine had never heard. Her parents seemed to be oblivious to how this might affect Shrine: "I remember my first day of school was really traumatic. My dad had to force me. . . . [I]t was scary; I mean, I didn't know the language. That wasn't very smart on their part. . . . I have to say, my childhood was just emotionally neglected. . . . I mean, none of the stuff they did was intentional, but they just were totally clueless."

Shirine had abruptly been thrust into an environment where she had to converse in three different languages on a daily basis: Farsi with her parents, German with the nanny and outside the house, and English at school.

Fortunately, Shirine discovered that she has a natural ear for languages. She picked up German and English and eventually adjusted, but she never felt at ease in Hamburg. She was already beginning to understand the temporary nature of her living situation.

After four years in Hamburg, the family again returned to Tehran. For a ten-year-old girl, Shirine had traveled extensively, but she had also been living the life of a diplomat's child, sheltered in a world of affluence. When she returned, it was as if she were seeing Iran for the first time. Not realizing the impact a different culture would have on their daughter, Shirine's parents did not think to explain that there would be striking contrasts between the Middle East and Europe. Unexpectedly exposed to a new world, Shirine was overwhelmed.

One of the most vivid memories Shirine has of returning to Iran is seeing the toilets for the first time. Unlike the typical European- or American-style sit-down toilet she was used to, the toilets in Iran essentially consisted of a hole in the ground bordered by porcelain. To use them, females had to lift their skirts and squat. A pitcher of water was used for cleaning; there was no toilet paper. While this is the normal custom in many parts of the world, it was a surprise for a little girl who had never seen or even heard of such a thing. She was shocked: "When I saw it, you know, as a child, I was afraid I would fall down the hole. . . . I freaked out when I saw it."

Even as a child, Shirine could feel how differently women were treated in Iran than in Germany. In Hamburg, she had walked down the street without any feeling of restriction or fear. But in Iran, she felt vulnerable: "You had no safety; there was so much oppression. And as a woman, if you went into the streets, inevitably some man would say something gross to you or try to [touch] you. . . . I never felt safe in Iran. . . . [I was] just living in fear all the time. . . . [Y]ou weren't safe as a woman walking down the street. . . . I just hated being in Iran."

Returning to her native country, Shirine felt bewildered and anguished. Even now, when she talks about it, Shirine's voice betrays the distress of a frightened child. While from an intellectual perspective she knows that this comes in part from her parents' lack of sensitivity, she still cannot help but feel anxiety at the thought of being in Iran.

During the 1960s and 1970s, the Iranian upper classes tended to wear European and American clothing, read European and American books, and generally embrace a Western lifestyle. Shirine's parents followed this trend. Like many others from the more privileged classes, they lived secular lives, rejecting most traditional religious practices. Although Shirine's grandmother had a religious sensibility and prayed on a daily basis, Shirine was never taught anything about Islam: "My grandmother prayed, and I just joked about it. . . . Islam meant nothing to me." What little Shirine did learn about Islam came from seeing the religious practices of the family's employees. Shirine knew when it was Ramadan only because the household staff was fasting.

In Iran, Shirine attended a private school, much like the one in Germany. The school catered to foreigners and Iranian children who, like Shirine, came from advantaged families. It was located in a compound, with the buildings and outside grounds surrounded by high walls. Classes were taught in English, the games played were American games, and the children wore Western-style uniforms. Inside the school walls, the children were allowed to run around freely and could play outdoors without fear. It was the one place outside her parents' home that Shirine felt safe.

The pattern of separation from Persian culture was reinforced to the point that almost all of the contact Shirine had with traditional Iran was framed in negativity. Although Shirine's parents had been educated in the rich culture and history of the country, they did not emphasize this perspective in the course of raising and educating their daughters. Between living abroad for many years and the trend toward Westernization within Iranian society, Shirine's parents had become in many ways more comfortable with Western than with Iranian ways of life, and they apparently saw few reasons to introduce Shirine to that history.

Sent to Western schools and without much reference to Iranian culture in the home, Shirine never had the opportunity to develop an understanding or appreciation of her own culture. She was never able to become comfortable living in her own country. Iran was always a place where the people were strange, the smells and atmosphere seemed shadowy, and the culture felt mysterious and unrelated to anything in her immediate life. Outside the protected areas of family and school, the people were different in dress, mannerisms, and language: "Iran is just so hard to describe to people; the whole experience of Iran is such a difficult thing to explain. . . . All through my childhood I couldn't ever wait, I couldn't wait to leave. . . . I really do believe that there are people that are born somewhere and they don't belong there. And I truly feel that I'm one of those people. . . . I was misplaced, from birth—wrong country, wrong family . . . and I've always felt that way."

It is no wonder, then, that Shirine never felt that she was coming home when the family returned to Iran. She had never developed a Persian cultural identity. At school, while most Persian children gravitated to other Persians for friendships, Shirine did not: "Even by then I wasn't as much relating to Persians, you know; I had no identity. . . . I wasn't seeking out Persians. . . . I've never sought out Persians as a safety net." Shirine's identity was based more on being an outsider in whatever place she found herself than on any particular culture.

Shirine was learning to adapt to change at a rapid pace, and while this was at times painful, it taught her to be resourceful and resilient. She readily points out that many children move frequently and regularly face traumatic changes in their lives. These children simply have to grow up more quickly than most and learn that they have inner strengths to draw on when they feel alone. For Shirine, the ability to function in a foreign country with ease served her well, and the skills she learned helped her adapt to many unexpected challenges as her life went on.

Three years after the family returned to Iran, Shirine's father was posted to a high-level position in Berlin. This transition was a little less arduous for Shirine because they were back in Germany, where she already spoke the language and understood the cultural norms. She had little contact with Germans, though, except those employed as domestic workers by her parents. The children of a diplomat, Shirine and her sister were not allowed to explore on their own or to take public transportation. The family had a chauffeur, and the girls were driven wherever they needed to go. They were again sent to an American school geared toward foreign students.

While the family was living in Berlin, Shirine's parents finally began to recognize just how estranged their daughter was from her ethnic heritage. Shirine was reading and writing English and German with ease, but she could barely write Farsi and used the language only when she had to, for basic conversations with her parents. Concerned, her parents eventually hired a private Farsi tutor. But Shirine, who was not particularly motivated, became more and more comfortable in English, to the point that she now considers English her first language.

Shirine has happy memories of Berlin. She was relieved to be away from Iran, and in Germany she was more relaxed. There were many American children at her school, and Shirine could relate to them easily after attending the American school in Iran. She felt socially connected for the first time: "In Berlin I had a really much better experience, because I met a wonderful American girl. And we became best friends. And we had so much fun. We hung out together; we had a good time." Shirine was also undergoing somewhat of a physical transformation, growing from a child into a young woman. By the time she was fifteen and the family went back to Iran, Shirine was feeling more self-confident than she ever had before. She accepted the transition with relative ease and actually looked forward to seeing friends from her old school.

The good feelings did not last long, however. About the time the rest of the family moved back to Iran, Shirine's sister, who was four years older, moved to Paris to study art. Shirine was now the only child in the house. Although the sisters had never been particularly close, Shirine was lonely without Fatima's companionship. As usual, her parents attended many social events, and Shirine was left on her own to do what she wished. She sometimes went out with friends, but still she felt isolated. After Fatima left, the house felt "weird and lonely . . . very lonely. . . . [I]t was an emotional barren. My parents went out every night." Shirine was beginning to realize and resent the fact that her mother was not giving her the maternal support she needed. Shirine's mother was beautiful, elegant, and always "dressed to a T." She was someone to admire but not someone who was emotionally available when her daughter needed her. Shirine's father was more affectionate and supportive, and Shirine felt a great deal of love and adoration for him. But while he was more demonstrative emotionally, he just was not around much.

Shirine began to ask her parents to send her away to school. "One night I remember, I finally said to them, . . . 'You know, this is ridiculous.'" Shirine had learned to understand herself well enough to know what she needed in her life. She did not like anything about Iran and wanted to be somewhere—really anywhere—else. Her parents hesitated, but since many of the elite Persian families sent their children to boarding schools abroad, the suggestion was not out of the ordinary. After just a year back in Iran, Shirine went to Milan to study at an international girls' school.

Moving to Italy on her own turned out to be a good idea. For the first time, Shirine was not living the isolated life of a diplomat's child. Staying in a dormitory, Shirine made friends, focused on schoolwork, and managed to learn Italian in a short period of time. She liked the school, because there she felt respected for who she was and what she could accomplish rather than because she was from an important family. Smart and motivated, she was able to graduate just a year later, when she was only seventeen.

Shirine had wanted to be an artist for as long as she could remember. There had been several professional artists in her family, and her father, in particular, had always been interested in antiques and art. He had encouraged both Shirine and her sister to paint and draw when they were young. When Shirine finished high school in Milan, her parents decided that her best alternative was to join Fatima in Paris to study graphic design and illustration.

Studying in Paris would seem like the ideal choice for anyone with artistic aspirations. But the experience left Shirine feeling ambivalent. She loved the work and in the process created a substantial portfolio. But the atmosphere at the school felt judgmental and unforgiving. The students' work was subject to public critiques and juried exhibits and was very competitive. On top of that, she was studying in another new language. Shirine had some rudimentary knowledge of French from high school but was far from fluent.

Shirine's parents had purchased a beautiful apartment in the sixteenth arrondissement, an exclusive section of the city, for Fatima and Shirine to live in. They lacked nothing: all of their expenses and material needs were provided for; in fact, they had more than they needed. But the art school was located in St. Germain, a completely different part of town, and this is where most of the other students lived. Shirine had again been thrown into a situation in which she was isolated, challenged by language and culture, and forced to make her way on her own. She felt awkward and alone.

During this time in Paris, Shirine's mother began a long-term pattern of almost daily phone calls. But speaking to her mother did not alleviate Shirine's loneliness. The conversations were dominated by her mother's stories of her social activities and personal laments. Shirine patiently listened, without demanding that her own needs and feelings be given much attention.

Shirine's parents had no idea how alone and confused she was. The two sisters had been dropped off in a foreign country, with no one to teach them how to manage their lives. In such activities as setting up bank accounts, shopping, and making travel arrangements, the girls were left to their own devices. Unlike Fatima, who made friends easily and coped by immersing herself in an adventurous social life, Shirine retreated into her studies and solitude. She felt disoriented: "You know, that part of my life was all a fog. . . . I always felt by myself, like not really connected to the rest of my family."

Shirine had been in Paris for about a year when Fatima decided she wanted to go to the United States to study. Shirine did not have any family or close friends in Paris, her parents were now stationed in Leningrad, and she was not at all interested in returning to Iran. The girls' father had studied at Columbia University in New York and loved the United States. He encouraged Shirine to go with Fatima, believing that the education and connections they would obtain there would be important for their futures. Wanting to win the approval of her adored but distant father, Shirine agreed: "So with my sister, I just kind of followed in her footsteps because it was just natural for me to do. . . . [I]t just seemed like she was doing the right thing for us." Both sisters applied and were accepted to the prestigious Rhode Island School of Design.

In 1973, before moving to Rhode Island, the sisters spent the summer with their parents in Leningrad. The visit was an unsettling experience. The politics of the time were uncertain—this was during the Cold War, and Iran was an ally of the West. Living in the embassy with her parents, Shirine felt a constant undercurrent of risk. The family's activities were restricted, even inside the embassy walls, because there were fears that the building was bugged.

When they left Leningrad for the United States, both sisters were relieved: "God, freedom. We couldn't believe the difference between being [there and being] in a free country. It just hit us so hard." The oppressive atmosphere in the Soviet Union reminded Shirine of how unsafe she always felt in Iran and how different, and more comfortable, she felt in Europe. Shirine came away from the summer with her old feelings toward Iran reinforced—she knew she did not belong in Iran, and never had, and she did not ever want to return.

❧

As a child, Shirine never felt safe whether in Iran or in Europe. She was pampered but alone. "Life was . . . none of this suburban comfort that all these American kids grow up with. On one side a lot, a lot, a lot of luxury and then on the other side a lot, a lot, a lot of fear." Her life was one of affluence and opportunity, with servants and drivers and beautiful houses. But it was also a life of insecurity, based on her mother's emotional distance and her father's unavailability.

The underlying trepidation she felt about life in general existed "not only externally but internally. Because my parents . . . nothing about them spelled safety." It was not that Shirine's parents were not concerned or did not love her, but they did not understand the need to be more involved in their adolescent daughters' lives. While they provided ample material comforts, there was still an aspect of neglect, from not paying attention to their daughters' school grades to not being aware of what the girls were doing in their spare time. At fifteen, in Iran, Shirine was sometimes staying out until five o'clock in the morning with her friends. While in high school in Milan, she once flew to London to see a friend for the weekend without her parents ever knowing about it.

During her entire childhood, Shirine had been surrounded by emotional uncertainty. Each move created a rupture that left her feeling that she did not belong anywhere. Shirine's life was a portable one. Feeling like a foreigner no matter where she was became internalized and was the context for how Shirine perceived herself in the world. Because Iran was as much of a foreign country as anywhere else she had lived, there was no sense of belonging or commonality there, nothing that could bond Shirine to Iran or create a feeling of safety or comfort. She had no emotional connection to the place her parents called "home."

When Shirine came to the United States to finish her education, it was without much thought about what would come next. She did not know where she belonged in the world, but she was willing to try something new in the hope that the next step would become apparent in its own time. In this new place she would again be nothing more than a sojourner, with no anticipation of permanence. She did not know that in the next few years she would have to face the death of her father and the reality of a political revolution that meant that even if she wanted to return to Iran, she could not do so. Coming to the United States was not meant to change the pattern of impermanency; it was to be one more stop in a series of temporary addresses.

Barrett

On a breezy February evening, Barrett Meyer arrived at my front door wearing snug jeans, high heels, bangle bracelets, and a bright red turtleneck sweater. We had spoken on the phone several times but never met. Yet when she arrived, she smiled, took my hand, and kissed me on the cheek as if she had known me for years. I was struck by both her natural poise and easygoing manner. Barrett managed to have an air of simultaneous elegance and casualness about her, and I immediately had the feeling that she is someone who knows exactly who she is and where she wants to go in her life.

Barrett's demeanor belies the fact that she is from the United States. The fluid stride with which she walks and the way she gestures with her hands when she speaks are evocative of a European or Latin American woman—someone who is not afraid to be both feminine and strong but with a softer strength than North American women seem to exhibit. It was a great surprise to learn that this woman who could so articulately describe her experiences to me was such a different person when she was young. By her own accounts, Barrett was not always the gracious, confident woman she is today.

❧

Barrett was raised in a Jewish family in a midsized Connecticut city. Both of her parents were classically trained, professional musicians. Barrett's father was the conductor of the local symphony, and her mother was an accomplished pianist. The nature of her father's job required him to frequently be in the public eye, and he and Barrett's mother became well known in the community. Symphony involvement required them to participate in society events and to entertain, and they were a popular couple. Barrett describes her parents as "glamorous," and compared to those of most middle-class North American families, their lives were unusual and somewhat bohemian. They frequently had guests, as other musicians and friends were always dropping by, filling the house with people and music. Sometimes rehearsals were held in the basement of their house, and afterward the musicians would gather in the living room and stay late, laughing and telling stories.

Though Barrett's parents were prominent members of the community, they did not earn much money, and the social requirements of their positions meant that, to a certain extent, they lived beyond their means. To avoid financial struggles, Barrett's mother worked long hours teaching piano in their home, and her father also taught private music classes on the side. Their household was a busy one, with Barrett's mother caring for three children, teaching, and in between students making family meals and helping with homework. Barrett's mother was home more often than many working parents, but that did not mean they had a typical family routine. On evenings and weekends, when most families would be home relaxing, it would not be unusual for Barrett's family to be either attending a performance or hosting company.

Barrett loved and was stimulated by her home environment, but at the same time, all the activity was overwhelming: "I remember always being kind of invisible. I would go sit on the stairs going down to the basement while my mother was teaching, and I would listen to her interact with her students. I would sit on the stairs between the living room and upstairs and listen to my father teach, or I would see him studying; he would take a score and sit at the piano. I was always observing. I had to see what was happening. I had to experience it. But I wasn't really part of it."

Barrett's family placed a high value on culture and education, and when she started school, they managed to get a scholarship for her at a private academy. While the school was wonderful for Barrett's intellectual development, it did not help her social adjustment or sense of belonging. The differences between her background and those of the other students were obvious: her parents were artists with unusual schedules and activities, her father was older than most of the other children's fathers (and almost twenty years older than her mother), they were an intellectual family, and they were Jewish. Barrett began school a year early, and she was younger than the rest of the students in her class. Most of the other children came from established New England families, had traditional households, and had roots in the community that went back many generations. The school could have come "right out of the preppy handbook." Barrett frequently · had the feeling that someone "had dropped her from another planet."

Every afternoon the feeling that she did not fit in was reinforced. When the other children went home or out to play with their friends, Barrett attended Hebrew school. Although she missed out on some social time, this was an important part of Barrett's early intellectual development; it was where she was first encouraged to analyze and discuss ideas and felt safe to think independently.

The sense that she was somehow different from everyone else was a pervasive theme in Barrett's childhood. At home, she did not quite fit in because she was outside all of the social and musical activity, and at school she did not fit in because she was younger than the other children and had an unusual background. In response, she withdrew socially, becoming introverted and shy.

Barrett's scholarship ended in fifth grade, and she had to transfer to a public school. Now, in addition to being much younger than the other fifth graders, she was also much more advanced educationally. The transition was not easy. Again, Barrett was left feeling that she did not entirely belong. She took refuge in books, reading about faraway countries, and started collecting travel brochures. By the time she was ten or eleven, Barrett was fantasizing about leaving New England and going somewhere warm and tropical. Her desire to travel was so great that more than once she called a travel agent and tried to book a trip to India or Tahiti. Throughout her childhood, Barrett dreamed of a dual life: of going away on an adventure but still staying home with her family, of being in two places at the same time. For as long as she can remember, she felt that her "essence was not totally in one place" and that at some point she would have to leave home.

Barrett had resisted her parents' efforts to involve her in music as a younger child. With the guidance of the public school music teacher, however, Barrett began to discover music for herself and learned to play the cello. She kept her school-based lessons a secret from her parents, practicing only at school, until the day she surprised them by playing with the orchestra in the annual school concert. Her musical parents were thrilled and immediately put Barrett in private lessons with a professional cellist.

Barrett quickly fell in love with not only music but also the instrument itself. The cello became a means of escape from the uncomfortable social scene in junior high school, where just as in her earlier school years, Barrett felt disconnected from the mainstream. When she sat behind the large instrument, she felt protected and safe, until the time she could fulfill the fantasy of moving away—a fantasy that was persisting through her adolescent years: "I loved the sound of the cello. I loved the fact that the cello was there; it's like this person, you know? Physically it's like your size. . . . [I]t's like having an alter ego, really. And something that would help, sort of be a shield in a way, to this fragile extraterrestrial that was stuck in this horrible [social] situation. And the only way that I was going to get through this was finding refuge in something, somehow, until I could get away. Still, and forever, there was always, 'I've got to get out of here. I've got to find [a place] where I fit in.'"

While playing the cello gave Barrett a great sense of comfort, she was unable to avoid a different kind of trauma, one that would only exacerbate her feelings of being an outsider. Shortly before Barrett turned fourteen, she was diagnosed with a serious spinal ailment. For a year her torso was in a cast from her neck to her hips. Unable to go to school, she was tutored at home. When her back had finally healed, she again went to a small, private girls' school. The atmosphere there was supportive, and there was more camaraderie between the students than in the other schools Barrett had attended. Because the school was ethnically and economically diverse, Barrett did not feel that she was the only "different" girl there.

The change for Barrett was immediate and positive. For the first time, she felt included and began to flourish. She spent four wonderful years at the school, continuing to study cello, singing in the chorus, and developing lasting friendships. She still wore a back brace, but as time went on, she could wear it less often.

Relating her story to me, Barrett did not convey that she had a miserable childhood. Yes, she had some difficult times. But Barrett does not hint at self-pity or resentment. Her biggest issue was that she consistently felt that she did not fit in either her parents' world or her own social and school world. Barrett's own illustration is the best way to understand her feelings: she asked me to imagine what would happen if a flower were dropped into the desert and did not have what it needed to survive. If the flower could have only three drops of water, it would be fine, but if there was no water, the flower could only wait and hope that someday a little rain would fall. Barrett always knew that at some point she would have to go to a place where she would be in a different environment and could get what she needed—her three drops of water. She just did not know how and when this would happen.

When Barrett was fifteen, she made friends with some students at the neighboring boys' school who were from Venezuela. Edmund; his best friend, Karl; and Barrett quickly bonded and started spending most of their free time together. The boys opened up a new world for Barrett, introducing her to the other foreign students at their school from Asia, Latin

America, and Europe. Rather than experimenting with drugs, as a lot of teenagers in the United States were doing in the 1970s, this group took their schoolwork seriously. Barrett was delighted with her new friends: "They had a totally different way of looking at things, and I began to feel like this was something where people were appreciating me differently. These were . . . people with other backgrounds and experiences. So I wasn't so totally different because everybody was different."

Edmund was two years older than the rest of the group and eventually went away to college. He stayed in touch, calling frequently and visiting when he had school vacations. While he was away, Barrett and Edmund had what she referred to as an "old-fashioned romance." Their mutual infatuation did not subside, and when it was time for Barrett to think about college, she decided to study music in New York with Edmund.

At the university, Barrett moved into a dormitory with the other freshman students. Once again, she quickly found that she did not feel comfortable with most of the people she was meeting. Edmund, who had already been at the university for two years, had become connected with other foreign students, and he brought Barrett into his network, just as he had when they were in high school. And as before, with this group Barrett felt comfortable.

Barrett's difficulty with the local students was not that she did not know how to fit in but that she had no desire to do so. Even though her family was somewhat avant-garde, her mother was concerned with social conventions and insistent that her children follow them as well. But Barrett never put much value on social propriety or tradition, and her mother's requirements felt stifling. Barrett did not necessarily want to do anything too far out of the ordinary; she just wanted to feel free to be her own person. She was relieved to find a group of friends who had no expectations of her, who were not concerned about whether she dressed a certain way or had traditional goals.

Being around people who came from different parts of the world, Barrett began to feel that the travel and adventure she had dreamed of as a child were no longer a impractical fantasy but a life she could actually pursue. To a certain extent, Barrett was already living an international life, surrounded by foreigners, adopting their attitudes and mannerisms in an attempt to project her dreams into reality: "It was just different. . . . Immediately, you find that you walk differently and you talk differently and you act differently, and the only thing you're missing is you're not living in the other country and you're not speaking the language, but, you know, it's not such a far-off possibility." Barrett's friends understood and supported her desire to move away from home, and under their influence she began to think more broadly about her future.

As Barrett became more involved in her classes, it became increasingly clear that the music program at her university did not suit her. Barrett was interested in performance and wanted to find out if she had the skills to make it as a professional musician. The program at the university was focused on music theory and composition and put less emphasis on playing and technique. Her frustration with the music program was compounded by the fact that during the first two years of college, Barrett was just as concerned with where she would end up living as she was about her career. She wanted to find somewhere that she could feel a sense of belonging and contentment, but she had no clear destination. She knew only that she wanted to be away from New England and the cold. Karl and Edmund planned to move back to Venezuela soon, and eventually her other foreign friends would be leaving too, some of them also going to Venezuela. She and Edmund were still in a romantic relationship, but they had not discussed a future together. Any reasons for her to stay at the university were dwindling, and Barrett's enthusiasm was flagging.

Barrett's nature has never been to just sit back and hope for something to come along, and she started to actively look for a way to expand her world. She was ready to take a risk and found the means to do it in a three-week summer music course in England. A renowned cellist and friend of her family would be teaching a master class there, and Barrett saw this as an opportunity for a new challenge. Attending this rather serious course would either get the idea of being a professional musician out of her system or prove to her that it was what she should do with her life. And of course there was the other motivation: she would be away from New England. Her parents could hardly afford it, but Barrett was able to persuade them to let her go. They managed to somehow scrape together the minimum amount needed to pay her way.

The master class took place at the beginning of the summer course. In a master class, a student is put onstage with the teacher and plays in front other professionals and the other students in the class. The teacher critiques the student, commenting on everything from style to technique. Almost always an anxiety-provoking situation, this is the only way that most students can have the experience of being taught by a prominent musician.

Barrett was justifiably nervous. Although she had been playing cello for a number of years, she had not had an ideal musical education. For a professional she started training late, not beginning to play until she was thirteen. Her first teacher was a choral director, not a cellist, and Barrett never learned some of the basics as well as she should have. She did not hold her bow correctly or sit with the best posture, and she was not playing at the level required for the summer course. The teacher had a reputation for being tough, but she knew enough about him to believe he could help her: "So I played, and it was awful. I couldn't play; it was like my bow was trembling so much. And there I am with this smile on my face, ever the well-brought-up young lady. And he was very kind . . . but the humiliation was already done." The instructor pointed out, in detail, all of the flaws in her technique and slowly worked her through the corrections in front of the rest of the students.

Feeling embarrassed, Barrett went to breakfast the next morning and sat by herself, hoping that no one would notice the pitiable student from the day before. To her chagrin, one of the professional musicians who had been observing the class approached her. The musician was an Englishwoman named Adele Martin. Adele had been moved by how gracefully Barrett had handled the awkward situation and seen something special in her. She offered to be Barrett's teacher if Barrett could stay and finish school in England.

Barrett and Adele were kindred spirits. Both were willing to take risks, loved the cello, and had felt the need to leave their homes and families. Adele came from an old established Scottish family whose expectations she could not live up to and from whom she had had to separate. She had what she referred to as a "smother mother"—a parent who wanted to control all her decisions and feelings. Barrett knew exactly what Adele meant. Adele also started playing the cello late and understood the struggles that Barrett was having learning proper technique as an adult.

Though Barrett's parents voiced disappointment, her three-week trip turned into two years away. She enrolled at the university in Bristol and once a week took a two-hour train journey to London for lessons with Adele. Other than her music lessons, however, Barrett's time in England can only be described as miserable. She hated the cold, rainy weather and felt lonely, not forming close bonds with her fellow students. To Barrett, the people in England seemed just as repressed and tied to convention as those she knew in Connecticut. Barrett missed the informality and ease that she felt with Edmund and the rest of the foreign students in New York. She had landed in the same circumstance she had been trying to escape: the social isolation that comes from feeling that you are different and misunderstood.

Though the feeling of being an outsider caused what Barrett describes as "psychic pain," she was able to maintain a positive outlook about the future. Barrett's spiritual makeup gave her the ability to trust that her situation would improve. This did not come from a conventional religious faith or her Jewish upbringing but more from an inner sense or intuition about her life: "There was always something inside that kept me looking for something . . . [T]here was also an absolute certainty that there was some place, some physical place where I would . . . be able to get those three drops of water." Even though she knew this place was not England, she knew that it was important for her to stay there until she finished school: "It was part of a path that [would] eventually bring me to where I had to be."

In December of her second year in England, Barrett received a card from Edmund. Things were going well for him in Venezuela, but he missed her. He was planning to visit London with his family soon and wanted to see her while he was there. When Edmund arrived they had a warm and tender reunion and some intense conversations. He asked her if she would be willing to move to Venezuela to be with him: "I knew that I had fallen in love with him when I was fifteen, and . . . this was the logical thing to do. And there was [also] Venezuela—the weather, the exoticness, the other place of it, different than England in that the people [and climate] are Latin and warm . . . versus cold and rainy, in every sense of the word." They decided that as soon as Barrett finished final exams in April, she would make a short visit to her family in Connecticut and then move to Caracas.

Suddenly all of the questions Barrett had been struggling with were about to be answered, and Barrett was ecstatic. Until then, Barrett "had not the faintest" idea what she might do when she finished school and no longer had a reason to stay in England. Her parents were assuming she would come home, but Barrett knew she did not want to do that; she just did not know where to go instead.

Now Barrett had a solution. She was going to a South American country where it was always warm, where she would be with a young man she loved, and where there were opportunities for work in the field of music. Most of their mutual friends were now living in Caracas, and even though Barrett had never been there, she would have a readymade social group in the city. Edmund's family had contacts in the Venezuelan arts world, and they were willing to help Barrett find work, maybe even playing in the Caracas symphony. Her dreams of living in an exotic foreign country were about to come true.

As is usually the case in life, the situation was not as perfect as it first seemed. When Barrett announced that she planned to move to Venezuela and would probably marry Edmund, her parents were distraught. The pressure for Barrett to return to New England permanently was intense. Barrett's parents were fond of Edmund, but the idea that Barrett might want to live her life elsewhere was something her mother, in particular, could not fathom.

Barrett held steady and refused to give in to her family's desires. Eventually her parents realized that Barrett was now an adult and would do what she wanted. Her parents' lack of understanding was painful, but looking back, Barrett now feels better able to understand them, to understand that their ability to support her decision was clouded by their desire to have her near them and their own fears of the unknown.

Barrett's decision to move to Venezuela with Edmund might not seem entirely sensible under the circumstances. She was taking a leap of faith and moving to a country she had never seen. That she would enjoy being there was something she was taking on trust, on the basis of her experience with Latin American friends and what little knowledge she had of the country and the area. She did not have much money and was not certain she would even have a job. Barrett knew that there were risks in her decision, but she wanted to go anyway. When Edmund asked her to move to Venezuela, Barrett was not thinking of immigration per se; she was thinking about an opportunity to find the life she had been fantasizing about. Perhaps even more than she wanted Edmund, Barrett wanted and needed an answer to the question of what she was going to do now that she had graduated from the university.

Barrett arrived in Caracas a few weeks after leaving England. With her were few possessions other than clothes and, of course, her cello. The instrument was the one thing she needed to bring with her, the one element of her past she wanted to accompany her into her future. She would need it for her livelihood but also for a sense of stability and grounding in the new world she was entering. When Barrett got off the plane and walked down the stairway onto the tarmac, the first thing she saw was the beautiful mountain range surrounding Caracas. Then she felt the warm air; saw Edmund standing there, handsome and with open arms; and felt a sense of relief: she knew she was home.

MERGING ROOTS WITH ROUTES

In many parts of the world, it is not unusual for young adults to leave their family homes and set off on their own. In Western cultures, asserting independence by the physical act of leaving home—whether it be by going away to college, getting married, or moving into an independent living space—conveys to the individual, and to the world, that a child has become an adult. Though not always formalized, "moving out" is still a rite of passage that is generally expected at some juncture. How and when this stage is undertaken and its effects are not matters that are separate from the other facets of life; both choices and responses to leave-taking are based on personal history, family and cultural backgrounds, socioeconomic status, and a host of other factors, including history and politics.

During my many conversations with immigrants, I have observed that while many of them share certain perspectives and feelings, some have a much harder time accepting and adapting to their immigrant lives than others. The way they think about their lives before immigration and the degree to which they express their emotions about living away from their roots, their language, and their culture seem to be based in part on the reasons why they immigrated, what kind of life they came from, what kind of life they went to, their inherent personalities, and even their appearance.

Shirine may have felt ambivalent about moving to the United States, but she was certain she did not want to return to Iran. Through no choice of her own, Shirine had been exposed, but never entirely connected, to many cultures. As a child, she was more susceptible to the vagaries inherent in her family's itinerant lifestyle. Shirine was "culturally homeless": as a result of multiple cross-cultural moves during childhood, she had no straightforward sense of cultural or geographical identity (Hoersting and Jenkins 2011, 18). She was emotionally detached from Iran and had no qualms about going somewhere new. Studying abroad fulfilled the next step in her education that her upper-class, Westernized parents expected and encouraged, and it gave her a sense of direction.

Lisa and Barrett both moved to begin a new stage in a relationship. Barrett's experience in England had already taught her that leaving home did not equal instant contentment, but she trusted herself and her decision. Her motivations, while genuinely directed toward being with Edmund, were heavily influenced by her desire to avoid a return to New England and what she felt was a suffocating life there. She left home on an existential search for self-understanding, influenced by the idea that freedom and personal growth would result from exposure to a different culture (see Rudmin 2009, 117; Madison 2010).[6]

Despite Lisa's multiple childhood immigrations, she was not "culturally homeless" in the same sense as Shirine. Lisa's parents maintained a strong orientation to their British background when they were living in Africa and had instilled this sense of identity in their children. When her father and the children became citizens of Canada, they cemented their decision to stay, but given the historical and political connections of the two countries, the children were able to blend English and Canadian culture with relative ease. When Lisa boarded the plane to Miami, she was excited about building a life with Jason, but she was unaware of the difficulties she would encounter emigrating as an adult and of the compromises she would need to make in order to enter Jason's cultural world.

Anna left home with her husband and child. She was not alone, but she was a stranger going to an unfamiliar land. She was truly a sojourner: when she left New Zealand, she fully intended to return. Anna, of all of these women, was the least prepared for what was in store for her. Her expectations were only that she would have the opportunity to meet her husband's family and have a year to experience his country. Anna identified with both her Maori and her Mormon backgrounds when she left and had no reason to expect that this would change.

Though there is some overlap in terms of feelings and reasons for leaving their countries of origin, the visible aspects of each of these women's personalities, as well as their backgrounds, are different. Whether outgoing or shy, artistic, intellectual, spiritual, funny, or serious, and for whatever combination of reasons, they all left home. Some researchers have argued that certain personality characteristics make some individuals more likely to immigrate. They suggest that a person who is a risk taker, ambitious, or lacking strong family affiliations may be more likely to take his or her chances in a new country and may be more successful economically after arrival (see Boneva and Frieze 2001; compare Deaux 2006, 144–145; Akhtar 1999, 15).

While this premise seems to apply to Shirine and Barrett, it does not apply to Anna or Lisa. Anna had a painful history of familial trauma, but she had become close to her mother and felt a strong affiliation to her culture. Unlike the others, for Anna, leaving home was not connected to any objective relating to her own desires or goals; it was a necessary practicality for her husband's education. Lisa was not particularly ambitious; nor did she tend to take substantial risks. She loved her parents and was comfortable living in Canada. Her decision to migrate was connected to her tendency to be somewhat acquiescent at that period in her life, and like Anna, she was willing to follow her partner. For them, immigration was associated more with cultural norms that endorsed moving in the context of marriage than it was with a particular personality trait.

Regardless of their motivations to immigrate, all were now separated from their roots. They would have to search for new ways or "routes" to merge their perceptions of their pasts with their futures (see Gilroy 1993, 19; McLeod 2000, 215). These routes would be affected by not only their origins but also the collateral circumstances of their lives. Considering the complex interplay of childhoods, personalities, and circumstance is more than a means of trying to understand what drew each person to become an immigrant. More important, it is an effort to understand how, once they arrived, they found the means to create a sense of identity, home, and belonging for themselves, as well as to discover the meaning of the search itself. The exploration of these questions does not end, then, in the moment that they left home but over the years that follow, as they make the winding transition from one life to another.

II

TRANSITIONS

Negotiating Identity in a New Culture

> Oh, what a lovely life it would be if you could just meet in
> between: something in the middle—the best of both worlds.
> Humans are like that; they always miss what they don't have.

—ANNA

IN BETWEEN

Anewspaper article I once read listed life events and the level of stress each causes. Those at the top of the list I expected: death of a loved one, marriage, and divorce. Farther down, but still near the top, was moving. Initially that surprised me, but then I started to remember the sense of utter exhaustion I have always felt during and after a move. Packing boxes, cleaning out drawers, and loading up the car with bags of stuff destined for a charity shop felt like giving away part of my life. The process never failed to drain me both physically and emotionally. On the other hand, new can be exciting. Enthusiasm and hope can mediate the challenges and stress brought about by a move. Regardless of how it may be viewed, moving is a major life event (Fielding 1993, 201).

Newness wears off eventually, however, and no matter where a person lands, no matter how beautiful or charming the place might be, there are still bathrooms to clean and laundry to do. The hassles of daily life do not disappear because location has changed. Once the initial honeymoon period begins to wear thin, family dynamics, bills, and everyday obligations loom just as large as they did before. Added to that are the stresses of becoming accustomed to the aspects of the new place that perhaps are not as pleasing or easy as they might have first seemed. Familiarity might not always breed contempt, but it can dull a once-shiny finish.

"Immigration" technically refers to the discrete event of moving permanently from one country to another. But the meaning of immigration is not just in the physical move itself—the airplane flight, the border crossing, or the attainment of any particular legal status. Immigrants also cross the imaginary borders of identity that are influenced by historical and political realities (McLeod 2000, 217; Bhabha 1994). The multilayered, continuous experience of migrating has more to do with navigating a life course than traversing a border.

Whether a person who has moved to a new country considers himself or herself an immigrant, and at what point that happens, is not always clear-cut. Rather than being a decision that occurs at a moment frozen in time, recognizing that one is an "immigrant," in a permanent sense, is commonly a realization that comes with hindsight. U.S. Census data indicate that for many immigrants there can be a long period, sometimes years, between the time they arrive in the United States and when they decide to stay permanently. Many immigrants cannot pinpoint exactly when they realized that they were no longer sojourners but permanently settled and would not be returning to live in their former homes (Redstone and Massey 2004, 723).[1]

In the months and years after arrival, there are constant adjustments and adaptations to ways of life and ways of thinking. During the transition an immigrant has to find a way to negotiate a new world, not just in terms of logistics but also on a personal level. The act of crossing a geopolitical border does not mean that emotional ties to the immigrant's former home will automatically be cut. Particularly in a social or cultural context, one's sense of oneself—one's identity and attachments—do not change overnight (Eyles 1985; Glick Schiller and Fouron 2001).

Living for an extended time in a different place will certainly have some effect on a sense of self, however. Perceptions and feelings about expected life events involving jobs, children, houses—the stuff of adult life—are bound to be altered when they take place under the umbrella of "foreigner" and when feelings about home, belonging, and attachment enter the picture. Anna, Lisa, Shirine, and Barrett have led different lives but have all had to find coping strategies to help them move through the transitions of their adult lives in a new country.

Anna

Young, untraveled, and trusting, Anna left for Norway. When the plane landed in Oslo, she would be in an unfamiliar country where she did not speak the language and would know no one except her husband. Completely dependent on him, she would have no income or resources of her own for the year they were to be away. Carrying her baby in her lap, and with Olav by her side, she spent nearly two days on cramped flights and in airport terminals.

Landing in Oslo did not mean the end of the journey. Olav's parents met them at the baggage claim, and the five of them spent the next three hours in a small car driving to Olav's hometown. Drained, Anna spent this first meeting with her in-laws fast asleep in the backseat of the car. This was the last time she slept for several days; between adjusting to the fourteen-hour time difference and the endlessly long Norwegian summer days, Anna's inner clock had been turned upside down. She did not know what was day and what was night. Inundated with the unfamiliar, she was disoriented, exhausted, and excited all at the same time: "Landing in Norway for the first time, it was strange . . . culture shock. Everybody asks about that. . . . [I]t is a culture shock, a big culture shock. . . . [F]irst, I couldn't sleep because of jet lag and then because it's light outside all the time, and that was a real big difference. It was terrible. . . . [T]his was new for me." Surrounded by people she did not know and a language she could not speak, Anna felt overwhelmed. Her first few days in Norway passed in a blur.

The young family had come to Norway so that Olav could attend a mariner's course and become a ship's officer. The course started less than a week after their arrival, so there was no time to rest or adjust to the un-familiar environment. They had to find an apartment and get settled in a hurry. On a tight budget, they did not have many choices, so they ended up in a sparsely populated area near Olav's school, several hours' drive from the town where his parents and siblings lived. In the course of a week, Anna went from living in a place she knew intimately and where there were lots of family and friends to the remote Nordic countryside.

Every morning Olav left at 7:30 A.M. to catch the only bus to town. During the long days that Olav was in school, Anna had no company ex-cept for her young son. Occasionally, Anna would go to town too, but since the bus left early in the morning, she would arrive long before any shops would be open. The only bus that would take her home was not scheduled until late in the afternoon, and that left her with many hours and nothing to do all day in the small village. With a young child, it was easier to stay home and let Olav do the family's shopping on his way home from school.

Anna's only real contact with adults, besides Olav, was once a week when she went to a Norwegian-language class. The class was held in the same town where Olav's parents lived, and getting there took some effort. Anna had to take Per with her on the early-morning bus, spend three hours traveling, and then wait until 6:00 at night when the class finally started. Olav's parents watched Per during the class, and at 9:00 P.M. Olav's sister would drive them all the way back to their place in the country.

This ordeal was the highlight of Anna's week. The class was for foreign-ers, so she met other adults in a similar situation and had a day out of the house. Anna did not need to take the class, since they were in Norway only temporarily, but she wanted to learn enough Norwegian to communicate on a basic level. And, perhaps more important, she was aware that so much time alone was not good for her: "Well, I did it to have something to do, too. Because when Olav was at school, I was in that flat, in the middle of nowhere."

Despite the isolation, Anna enjoyed herself those first months in Norway. She was content spending the days with Per and her evenings with Olav: "I mean, it was fun, because we were a family. Yeah, we were a young family. That was exciting." The quiet and peaceful existence she had in Norway was refreshing compared to the family life she had known in New Zealand.

As Anna settled into her new routine, the first three months passed quickly. Then, devastating news came in the form of a telegram. Anna's mother was dead. Shocked, Anna grieved deeply. Despite all of the instability of her youth, Anna had seen her mother as a protector and source of support, especially after Per was born. Without her mother as an anchor, Anna began to think differently about a return to New Zealand, and she began to go through a process of emotional separation from her past. (This major turning point in Anna's life is described in more detail in the next section.)

Like her childhood, the details of this stage in her life are difficult for Anna to remember. She was faced with not only the heartache of losing her mother but also a multitude of changes in her daily life. Everything she encountered was different, whether in the way people interacted, the food, the language, the smells, or the strange woolen winter clothing. Unlike sunny New Zealand, the winter skies in southern Norway are gray, the days last only a few hours, and the nights are long. The air is cold and damp, the streets are covered in ice, and the landscape is bleak. In contrast, the summer is green and beautiful, and everyone spends as much time outside as they can. Sleeping can be close to impossible, as dusk occurs between midnight and 3:00 A.M., and morning begins at five. Though a welcome relief from the cold, the summers were just as hard for Anna to adjust to as the winter.

Anna had few preconceptions about Norway before she arrived, and this allowed her to be open to whatever she might encounter. Keeping what she calls a "go with the flow" attitude was easier than worrying about how she would adjust to this new place: "I came here as blank as I could. [I'd] never been interested in learning about Norway . . . even though I knew I was coming here. It didn't interest me to go to the library and read about Norway at all. You know, I just thought, 'We'll take it as it comes, and I don't have any expectation or anything.' So I never said what a big difference it is, and I never really explained to people what a big difference it is coming here, compared to being in New Zealand." Because no one in Norway, aside from Olav, knew anything about Anna's personal history or culture, she could present herself however she chose. No one had to know her about her tumultuous childhood or the poverty in which she grew up. But this also meant that Anna was alone with her transitions, unable to share with anyone how she felt about all of the differences.

Before coming to Norway, Olav and Anna had saved enough money to get by while Olav was in school. When the year had passed and the course was over, the money was gone and he needed to get a job as soon as possible. He found work on a cargo ship that left from a Norwegian port and would be at sea for four months at a time. Anna would not be able to manage alone in the countryside with the baby. So, despite the expense, they had to move into town. Quickly, they took an apartment near Olav's parents, and within days Olav left.

Anna and Olav never made a clear decision about staying in Norway:

> Why we decided to stay I'm not really quite sure; it wasn't really planned [for us] to stay. After all, I said that we were only going to stay here for one year, while he went to school. And, I don't know, we just took one day at a time, didn't plan anything. We just stayed. . . . And what made it go fast was the way that Olav used to work; he would go to sea for four months and then would come home for four months. And it was just like, okay, he's going to get a job; he's going away for a while. And then it was like we were just looking forward to these four months, till he comes back again. And then we could be a family again. That was all I looked forward to; you know, I didn't think about the future here or there or anything.

With Olav away, Anna now had to take care of everything. She had to buy groceries, manage the house, and care for Per on her own. By now Anna had picked up enough Norwegian that she could have simple interactions; she could do the shopping and negotiate the bus system, and if she had a problem or question, she could call her mother-in-law.

But this was not enough for Anna; she wanted to be truly self-sufficient and realized that she had to learn more than the basics of the language: "I felt the need to be able to speak Norwegian as quickly as I can, as good as I can. I just learned and tried to speak Norwegian as much as I can, even though I had some English words in between." Others have told me that Anna became fluent in a short time. But Anna is humble about her language abilities: "Even though people say . . . , 'Oh, you learned to speak Norwegian so early' . . . and [that I] integrated much quicker than other foreigners that they've heard about, I never take credit, 'cause what I do is, that's what I am. I see it as a natural thing; I don't see it as anything wonderful. . . . The things I do, I think they're natural for me. If people see the positive in it, okay. You know, I don't see it like that. Yeah, it's just the way it is. . . . I mean, Rome wasn't built in a day either!"

Anna continued going to the language class every week, and at home she learned bit by bit. Anna and Per practiced together by reading comic books. In the late 1970s, television was not available until the late-afternoon hours in Norway, but once it was on, they watched English-language programs that were broadcast with Norwegian subtitles: "We would have breakfast, and I would just sit and read. I read a lot of Donald Duck in Norwegian, because I could see what I'm trying to read, and it explains, and it gives me more idea of what they're talking about. And we would watch TV. . . . I'd be watching it and listening to them, but then I'd be reading what they're saying, or trying to read. But by that time, I could understand quite a bit . . . because I always thought that you learn every day. And I even say that today I still learn." Anna found that she did not miss speaking English at all. She became so comfortable with Norwegian that by the end of her second year in the country, she stopped speaking English even to Per and Olav.

Anna always describes herself as a person who takes things as they come: "I am easygoing. Not that many serious things get to me. . . . I try not to let things get to me." But once she realized she would be staying in Norway indefinitely, her mellow attitude began to be eroded by the need to fit in. Learning the language helped enormously, but Anna knew that she would continue to feel self-conscious until she could think and act the way Norwegians do.

This was not easy. There is a precision to the way Norwegian society operates that Anna was not accustomed to. Norway is place where orderliness, timeliness, and a reserved demeanor are valued, and this was different from Anna's background:

> You have to think like the Norwegians. It's nothing that you can learn, how they think. . . . I mean, you just learn it and feel it by the vibes. . . . This is my way; this is how I've experienced it. . . . Don't ask me how they think, because I didn't know then, and I don't think I know now either, after so much time. . . . You know, if I think about it, I integrated, gradually, gradually, gradually. . . . It came naturally and unnaturally. It came because it had to come. If you look around and see what's happening around you, automatically you just do the same thing. I've always heard that saying that if the neighbor buys a new car, you have to go and buy a new car. And there's something in it. . . . You just learn as you go by, so what you do is what you've learned.

Norwegian society tends to be secular, but some Lutheran traditions are still maintained even in families that do not otherwise participate in the church. About two years after Anna and Olav came to Norway, they had their second child, Nora. When Anna realized that everyone expected them to have a christening, she agreed, but not for religious reasons. She wanted to do for her daughter what other Norwegian families did for their children—and she wanted to do it properly. No longer quite as laid back as she was when she arrived in Norway, Anna was worried.

In Norway, christenings are special events. There is a religious ceremony, and then the parents usually host a formal dinner for the family. Anna had never had a formal party the way the Norwegians have them, with linen tablecloths, candlesticks, and well-rehearsed speeches. Concerned that the guests would notice if the silverware was not placed correctly or the Norwegian food did not taste right, Anna turned the party over to her mother-in-law. With the pressure off, she was able to relax and enjoy the event. But she paid attention during this party and others, and over time she learned the details of Norwegian customs. After several years and holiday seasons passed, she finally did not feel the need for her mother-in-law's help: "I feel and I think, I hope, that everything that's so traditionally Norwegian, I hope I covered that and have performed it, their different things, the way the Norwegians do. You know, Easter, celebrations, decorations, and Christmas and all that. I hope so. I think so. I think I have. . . . [A]fter a while it turns into habit, you know."

Anna seems comfortable with herself, and I was surprised she had such a strong need for acceptance: "I don't know; it sounds stupid, but maybe we [immigrants] do it to fit in. It's funny—I mean, I always wanted to be accepted; let's put it that way. . . . I feel that here I had to prove to myself; I had to prove to Olav's family and the Norwegian people that I can do this. I had to prove to them that I could fit in. It would be just like them saying, 'Yeah, she can adapt.' You know what I mean? It feels like I needed to show them."

When Olav was away, he and Anna were in touch only when his ship was in a port. Depending on the ship's schedule, they might speak every day or go four weeks without a call. More than once they were separated during critical events. During the last stages of Anna's second pregnancy, she had to live with her in-laws so that she would not be alone with Per when she went into labor. Several years later, Anna was out walking with the children and came home to find that there had been a fire in their apartment building. The fire did not harm their belongings, but the damage was severe enough that she immediately had to find a new place for her family to live. Olav did not know they had moved until he returned from sea.

Anna never worried about being alone in Norway:

> I have . . . faith in Olav. I really do. Even though he wasn't here to help me make decisions on a lot of things, he would ring as often as he could, and we could discuss things. Of course, it's lonely. But, you know, there's different kinds of loneliness, but you manage, because you've got your house to look after, and you've got a child to look after. . . . I survive with my own company. I do, and I've always been like that. Yeah I don't—I don't need anybody. No, that's not right; everybody needs someone. But most of the time, I'm okay with myself. I can do things by myself, and, you know, things, they're just fine. I have no problem with myself.

Once Anna felt comfortable with her written language skills, she decided it was time to get a driver's license. Driving would mean freedom and independence. Four years after she moved to Norway, Anna felt confident enough to take the driving exam: "I didn't need it; it was just . . . wouldn't it be nice to have a car? You know, I can go and meet people and go for a drive and go and see something new. So the day I got my license I went down and ordered a rental car for the weekend, from Friday to Monday, and packed up my kids, and we went down and picked it up. . . . [It] was nice to just drive. And, you know, this car is secure, and the kids are buckled up back there, and we just drove and drove and drove. . . . Oh, it was really nice, and I thought that was a good achievement."

Eventually Olav decided to go back to school again, this time to get his captain's license. Since Olav was not working, Anna got a job driving a taxi to help out with expenses. By now both the children were in school, and Anna did not need to be home all the time. She liked being out of the house and contributing to the family income, so Anna kept working even after Olav finished his course. Anna also had another motivation to earn: she had starting thinking about taking a trip to New Zealand and wanted to start saving. There was no immediacy to her plans. What Anna wanted was the security of knowing she could go back if she needed to: "I had my own income, and I thought if I wanted to go home, I didn't feel a burden. I felt a little bit more independent."

∽

Norway was historically a sailing culture, and many of the country's young men, like Olav, still work on ships that travel throughout the world. After spending a few years away, these young men occasionally return home with a foreign wife. Norway has always had a complex society, with distinct regional cultures and dialects (Wikan 2002, 31–32). Immigrants from countries outside Europe were uncommon, though, and other than foreign spouses, Norway was relatively homogeneous until the 1970s. In recent years, as a result of globalization as well as Norway's generous refugee policies, the number of foreigners living in Norway has increased dramatically.[2] When Anna arrived in 1978, however, her appearance in a small, rural town in southern Norway was an anomaly.

Anna does not have the sharp facial features or the slim, angular shape of many Norwegians. She does not have blond hair and light eyes. Anna is tall, her build sturdy. Her hair is black and shiny, her eyes and skin brown, her nose wide. Anna's foreignness was obvious in the sea of pale, blue-eyed Norwegians. She could never go unnoticed, never be inconspicuous. As a Maori, Anna grew up as part of a marginalized population. But in her new home, she was not part of a minority group—Anna was the only person from the South Pacific for miles around.

Norwegians are not known as the most outgoing people, and most would probably acknowledge that as a society they tend to have a bashful nature. This did not help: between Anna's obviously foreign background and the Norwegians' shyness, meeting people and making friends was a challenge when Anna first arrived. Fortunately, Olav and his family could help: "They have so many friends that I got to know, and through that network it was so much easier. I felt that it was easier to be accepted here, because in Norway, you know, there's just white people living there."

Still, for a long time Anna lived with an undercurrent of fear about her foreign appearance:

People were pretty good. . . . Nobody would say [anything] or point—not that I really remember. But what I thought about was children. To be mocked by children. . . . I do remember that children I was most afraid of. The time that I took the buses when we wanted to come and visit my mother-in-law wouldn't be until in the afternoon, and that's about the time that the children got off school. So there was young children and there was teenagers everywhere. And I thought that that was very scary. The children, . . . they didn't do anything, but because of my own experience, before I came here, I know that children—it's funny, but children, they can be really bad. Like, they would tease me. . . . I was afraid of that. You know, what am I doing here, and, you know, "You're dark," 'cause Norwegians, you know, are white. . . . I was wondering, "How am I going to cope with that?" I know that kids are taught that there are dark people and foreign people and that. Kids are taught through their parents— I know that—and kids, because they're so inquisitive, they're not afraid to ask anything that they want to ask foreigners about.

Anna experienced overt racism only once. Driving the taxi late one night, Anna picked up an intoxicated woman. This woman was not just drunk; she was angry, and she wanted to take it out on someone. She swore loudly, made ugly statements about foreigners, and threatened to have Anna deported. Anna was in the country legally, so there was no basis for what the woman said, but the incident was upsetting. Years of contained anxiety about race had risen to the surface and had a profound effect on Anna: "I felt so offended; I was so offended, and I thought, who on earth was this woman to say [these things]. And I didn't want to drive [the taxi] for a while. I've been here so long; I've been here nearly ten years, I think, when this happened. . . . I was so depressed, and I was like that for a while. You know, if they want to make a fool of themselves, let them. But I've never felt so humiliated in my life, and so angry."

Ultimately Anna's strength returned. She might look different, and, yes, this might sometimes cause her to feel ill at ease, but she was not about to let those feelings control her:

Because I'm darker and I have other ideas and that, I am different, but I didn't let my color . . . make me feel [like] a minority, not at all. No, not at all. I was proud, but I am what I am. I was proud, coming here. I was proud that I was a Maori. No, I never let the color get the better of me. You know, a lot is maybe because I was stubborn and I wanted things to work, and I don't know what to expect of people, so I just go with the flow. . . . No, I don't see my color [as] different. I don't mean that's a good thing; I don't mean that's a bad thing either. It's just that I—I do what I've got to do; I do what I do.

❧

In the twenty or so years that I have known Anna, she has always had a busy social life and certainly never seemed lonely. But her life in Norway was not always like this, and in fact, during the first eight years she was in Norway, Anna had virtually no relationships outside Olav's family.

During those early years, Anna's days were occupied with raising her children and becoming accustomed to the rhythm of life in a new country and culture. There were neighbors and couples that she and Olav occasionally socialized with but no one she considered a close friend. When I asked Anna if she ever phoned friends when Olav was away, her response was that she certainly could have, "but who was I calling? I wasn't really looking for friends then. . . . I just had to adjust. I had to learn so much about Norway and where I was living." Nor was there much contact with her relatives in New Zealand. They exchanged letters, but phone calls were prohibitively expensive back then. In 1978, a call from Norway to New Zealand was about thirty-six kroner per minute—the equivalent of about seven U.S. dollars.

Although her in-laws' life experiences and perspectives are nearly poles apart from Anna's, they were there for her, especially during the early years: "That was really nice, to have family there; it was nice. . . . You know, I had only them. I had to have trust in them, and, you know, they were my foundation—because if I didn't have a good relationship there, that was really important. I just took it for granted that it's what it's supposed to be. But they didn't have to be like that. I was really lucky; he's got a good family. I got a lot of support from them, which made it easier being here."

The relationships Anna had with Olav's family were vital but were primarily based on duty and need. Their support did not translate into friendship, and Anna never felt that she could show vulnerability, particularly when it came to her feelings about living in Norway. Any uncertainty or loneliness that might occasionally crop up she kept to herself, and that meant keeping a certain emotional distance: "I thought, you know, I left my mom to make my family, and that's where I was going to be. So maybe deep down it's my own pride too, that I've got to cope with the decisions that I've made about coming here."

In 1986, Anna got a job on a ferry that traveled daily between Norway and Sweden. She became friends with a coworker who was an immigrant from the United States. The two women were from completely different backgrounds, but they understood each other immediately, having shared many of the same challenges. Both were immigrants, both were married to Norwegian men, and both had been in Norway long enough to be past the initial excitement of moving to a new country. They could see both the positive and negative sides of their adopted cultures and developed a camaraderie that Anna had not yet experienced in Norway.

Her newfound friend introduced Anna to another American who was also married to a Norwegian sailor. Through their combined contacts, they soon had a network of foreign friends married to Norwegian men. These women became her sustenance: "You know, I feel much closer to my friends than I do to [Olav's] family. . . . I get on much better with them than I do with his family. . . . And maybe that's natural, because my friends have the same [experiences]. My best friends, they're foreigners. We're just like family; we're very close. . . . [W]e laugh together; we cry together." Her friendships with fellow immigrants have now lasted more than twenty years.

❧

Pressure to fit in in Norway had its consequences. Being Maori continued to be a part of Anna's self-described identity but not an essential piece of her everyday life. Anna's past became like the faded childhood photo of her in front of the *Marai* that hangs in her living room, a memory that hides in the background until someone points it out: "I always wanted to be accepted; let's put it that way. Maybe that's why I feel and I see myself [as] more Norwegian." She wanted her children to feel Norwegian too and be a part of the world they were living in rather than her past. She did not teach them the Maori language or Maori songs or folktales or cook Maori food: "I didn't feel that need. . . . [N]o, I didn't feel that they needed to know their New Zealand identity. 'Cause they're living here now, and I don't know if they'll ever go back. But if they want to, if they want to know about it, I would try to teach them what I know."

The direction of Anna's life flowed not from deliberate decisions as much as from unplanned circumstances. Marriage to a foreigner, the death of her mother, and Olav's work all led to her immigration experience. She never felt the need to set a course for her future; she allowed her life to unfold naturally. Before she knew it, she was living in Norway, had two children in school, owned a house, was working, and had a network of friends. She had everything she needed, including stability, and she felt lucky. Thoughts of New Zealand and her family there were with her but not in the forefront of her mind. Anna had not found a way to comfortably inhabit both of her cultural identities and therefore kept them separate: "Oh, what a lovely life it would be if you could just meet in between. Something in the middle—the best of both worlds. Humans are like that; they always miss what they don't have."

Lisa

Moving from Canada to the United States might not seem like a radical change. The two countries share a border and a language, after all, and many people in the United States think of our Canadian neighbors as simply a more warmly dressed version of us. Our customs and demeanor are not all that distinguishable, and other than a slight difference in our accents, any Canadian could be mistaken for a U.S. citizen. But however subtle they may seem, the differences are real and are shaped by our distinct histories, politics, and worldviews. Lisa gives every appearance of being perfectly at ease living in the United States, and for the most part, she is. But regardless of how many years have passed and how well she has adjusted, there will always be reminders that where she lives is not the place her heart yearns for.

South Florida is a region that, from climate to culture, is an anomaly in the United States. Its semitropical environment draws people from all over the country as well as the rest of the world, particularly Latin America. Florida is a place of transplanted northerners who crave warmth and foreigners who have come either to experience the allure of South Beach or to find a better life in a more prosperous economy. Hardly anyone is "from" Miami, and on any given day, in any square block, there are likely to be people of any ethnicity, religion, or socioeconomic bracket. Both sophisticated and tacky, it is a mix of international cultures, the American South, and a theme park. Florida may be in the United States, but it feels more like a separate country, with its own special character.

Despite her immigrant history, when Lisa moved to the United States, she thought of herself as a Canadian and held a Canadian passport. Then she moved to Florida, and less than a year later, she converted from Christianity to Judaism. The language she spoke in this new place was the same, but virtually everything else was different. When she left Canada, Lisa remained on the same continent, but when she arrived in Miami, she stepped into a different world.

The actual move was not too much trouble. Lisa was twenty-two, owned little besides her clothes, and had been living in a rented apartment. Nonetheless, leaving home was nerve-racking. Excited and slightly panicky, Lisa felt she had to bring something practical with her, something tangible that would help her feel that she was not just going on a vacation. In a rush, looking around her apartment, she grabbed a set of plastic Tupperware food containers and packed them in her suitcase with her clothes. She laughs about that now: why would she carry Tupperware three thousand miles? Why not bring a memento or family pictures? Because she was not exactly thinking straight at the time, she was in a whirlwind, on the verge of making major changes in her life. Even small decisions loomed large.

Lisa's nerves did not become any calmer during the flight: "Well, I have to tell you something funny that I remember. I don't know if it's significant, but it's significant to me. I remember walking down the Jetway at Miami, having a little bit of a panic attack, with my Tupperware in tow, thinking, 'Oh, my God, what if I don't recognize him?' Isn't that terrible?" The realization that she was moving to a new country to be with a man she hardly knew was setting in. But she did recognize Jason, of course, and they had a romantic reunion. Everything was "idyllic," and within weeks the two were engaged. Aside from her relationship with Jason, however, the next few months were difficult.

When Lisa came to Miami, she moved into a townhouse Jason owned in the suburbs. The outlying areas of Miami are the epitome of suburban sprawl, and one cookie-cutter housing development follows the next. There is no downtown or city center to speak of, and it is a long drive to the beach. Like many suburbs, this is a place where it is easy to feel isolated, despite the large number of people who live nearby.

Jason was a young executive working long hours and commuting to Miami. All of Jason's friends lived in Miami, and he did not know any-one in the neighborhood to introduce to Lisa. She had no car, and public transportation in the area was practically nonexistent. So while Jason was at work, Lisa stayed in the townhouse alone. On weekends, if Jason was not working, they would sometimes drive to Miami and go out with his friends, but on many days, Jason was the only person with whom Lisa had any social contact.

Lisa is not one for parties or crowds, but on the other hand, she is not the type to depend on a partner for everything. During those first few months in Florida, however, Lisa became totally reliant on Jason for emotional support. Before long, she was in a state of torpor. Listless, she sometimes did not bother changing out of her pajamas until right before Jason came home from work. Now she refers to this time, somewhat drolly, as her "depressive period."

Lisa is not insecure or particularly shy; nor is she lazy. But Jason is a few years older than she is and has an outgoing, strong presence. Compared to him, she was, in her words, a "nonaggressive, quiet follower." Between their personality dynamic and Lisa's isolation, she became "totally con-sumed" with Jason and not at all focused on developing a life of her own in Miami: "You know, I came here, I was twenty-two years old, and I didn't know anybody, and we lived in [the suburbs]. And I was trying to find my place." Lisa realized that she was not sure where her life was going. Reality had hit—Lisa was no longer visiting the United States; she was residing there. She was getting married. She had better get off the couch and get ahold of herself.

Shifting her focus to the wedding helped Lisa come back into her nor-mal, positive frame of mind. Jason's mother, Ruby, an outgoing, loud, but endearing New Yorker, volunteered to help with the preparations. It was a mixed blessing—Lisa had no idea how to go about planning a big event, and she needed the help, but it also meant that the wedding became bigger and more elaborate than Lisa really wanted.

In the midst of all of the planning, Lisa also had to make a serious deci-sion about religion. She knew, of course, that Jason was Jewish, but that was about all she knew. Religion was not something Lisa had ever thought much about before. Her family was Christian and celebrated Christmas and

Easter, but little emphasis was placed on religion in their home. Still, she worried that if the wedding was not religious, then it might feel trivialized. The question was which religion should sanctify their marriage.

Unlike Lisa, Jason did have strong feelings about his religion. He was raised as a Jew and belonged to a temple. Since he had stronger feelings about his faith, they both felt that the wedding should be performed by his rabbi. The problem was that Jason was a member of a Conservative temple, and if the rabbi was to marry them, they both had to be Jewish. Lisa would have to convert.

Despite having lived in three different countries, Lisa had never known any Jews: "When I moved here, I didn't really know what 'Jewish' meant. What did I know about the Jewish religion? Nothing, zippo, zero. Vancouver has a thriving Jewish community; I just didn't know it. I was just totally ignorant." Lisa's concerns about converting were not based on her relationship to Christianity but on her lack of familiarity with Judaism. She had no idea how or if converting might affect the other aspects of her life. Right then, however, the focus was on ensuring that the wedding was meaningful. Lisa did not feel that her identity was bound to her religion, so giving it up did not seem like a tremendous loss: "I never really felt I had to renounce very strong beliefs in Christianity because I never had them."

In the Jewish faith, conversion is not just a matter of declaring your intent. Converts must go through a rigorous application process. First, Lisa was to study Judaism for several months. Then, there was to be an examination by three rabbis and a pledge of her commitment to the faith. In high school Lisa did well without much effort, but this was something entirely different. She could not just show up to a class and listen; she had to prepare assignments, attend one-on-one lessons, and be prepared to discuss Jewish theology. The rabbi she worked with was pleasant but intimidating, and he made it clear that he had high expectations. To her surprise, Lisa found that she enjoyed the process of learning and started looking forward to the classes. Before she knew it, the examination was over, and she was almost ready.

The week before the wedding there was one more step to take before Lisa could become a Jew. She had to participate in a *Micvah*: a ritual purification for Jewish women, during which they must disrobe and be submerged in water. The *Micvah* can take place in the ocean or other body of water, but in some communities with large Jewish populations, such as Miami Beach, there are designated *Micvah* pools. Lisa's mother had arrived from Canada, as had her favorite aunt from England, and the two of them, plus Ruby, came to the small, private ceremony.

When they arrived, Lisa was sure they were in the wrong place. The address was right, but everything else looked wrong. The building, inside and out, was old, run-down, and dark. Lisa had already been nervous, and now she was frightened. After some hesitation, she followed the instructions she had been given to go down the hallway and into a small, dank room. There she had to undress. Then a female attendant she had never seen before led her into another room with a small pool, where her mother, her aunt, and Jason's mother were waiting. The pool was built into the wall and was designed so that rainwater caught on the roof could flow directly into it. Young, modest, and completely naked, Lisa stepped into the small pool of water and went under the cold water. She submerged herself several times to complete the ritual. As she raised her head from the water to get a breath, everything was silent, except for the muted voice of a rabbi saying prayers in an adjoining room. Her apprehensions now gone, Lisa felt as if she had been through a kind of rebirth. The *Micvah* was a beautiful experience for her: "I remember just feeling, like, clean and refreshed, invigorated." The studying and rituals were finished: Lisa was now a Jew.

Lisa and Jason were married in May 1984, just a year after they met. One hundred people attended the wedding, and afterward there was dancing. As Lisa looked around at the guests holding champagne glasses and toasting her marriage, she realized that she knew fewer than ten of the people around her. The rest were Jason's family and friends, many of whom she had never seen before. She felt suddenly unbalanced. This disconcerting feeling was something Lisa would soon become accustomed to. Family events would now remind her that she was far away from her previous life, friends, and family.

꙳

After the wedding, Lisa realized that unless she took charge of her life, the depression would return. She could see that her initial difficulties had been the result of not knowing how to adjust to her new surroundings. Rather than wait for Jason to come home from work every day, she needed to get a job and find out what living in Florida was all about. Drawing on her previous experience, she went to work in the baggage claim department of Eastern Airlines.

Working in Miami was a dramatic contrast to working in Vancouver. Miami is a big, busy, chaotic city, and the pace of life is hectic. The commute was long and started every morning when Jason dropped her off at a bus station in a high-crime neighborhood. This was not the glamorous part of Miami that Lisa had seen when she went out to dinner with Jason and his friends; this was standing outside waiting in steamy, hot weather and then crowding onto a noisy bus for a long ride.

Lisa was used to multicultural environments, in both Africa and Canada, but she had never been cognizant of serious racial tension. In Miami she felt a barely suppressed undertone of hostility between all of the different ethnic groups, and it was uncomfortable. Lisa was witnessing some of the social fallout from the Mariel boatlift and racial conflicts of the early 1980s.[3]

Once she was off the bus and at work, however, the tension faded. Diversity in the office seemed to be accepted by everyone, and the work style of most of the employees, who were Cuban Americans, influenced the atmosphere. Their manner was significantly less formal than that of Lisa's colleagues in Vancouver, with a lot of joking and friendly interaction. Coming to work in Miami turned out to be fun.

Overall, Lisa was happy with the way things were going. She loved being with Jason and enjoyed her job. The only truly difficult aspect of her life was being away from her family and friends. She quietly felt their absence almost all of the time. Leaving had been her choice, however, and the best she could do was to visit and call as often as possible. Two years had passed when Lisa found out she was pregnant.

Lisa and Jason had wanted a baby, and the timing felt right. Excited but not worried, Lisa took pregnancy in stride. For her, having a baby did not seem like a big deal—she had always thought of herself as a "nature girl," outdoorsy and unaffected, and she expected that being a mother would be intuitive. All that changed once the baby, Chelsea, was born.

Any confidence Lisa had felt before the birth disappeared as Lisa was getting ready to take Chelsea home. In the clean, controlled environment of the hospital, she and the baby had been protected and Lisa had felt fine. Now she had to take this precious infant into the world, where there was cigarette smoke and loud sounds of traffic and strangers and, worst of all, germs. The photo taken as she and Jason walked out of the hospital does not show a happy new mother; it shows a sobbing woman holding on desperately to her baby, resisting even letting go to put the child in the car. Nature girl she may have been, but now Lisa felt overwhelmed, tired, and alone. She had no experience caring for an infant and was keenly aware that she would not have family nearby to teach her. The miles between Lisa and her own mother seemed insurmountable. She spent the next year as a self-described "neurotic mother."

A year after Chelsea was born, Lisa was pregnant with their second child, Michael, and in two more years, there was a third baby, named William. By the time William was born, Lisa had gotten a healthier perspective. Managing her time and caring for the children became easier with experience. Still, like any young mother of three, she was overextended and had little time for herself. Other than being a mother, she did not quite know who she was anymore.

Lisa's memories of those years are of two minds. On one hand, she was blissfully happy with her children and her husband and wanted nothing more than to be home with the babies. On the other, she felt cut off from the outside world: "When [the children] were younger, when they were first born . . . you lose your identity; you lose yourself—you really do. It's all about the babies, and then the next baby, and then the next baby. Those years, they were hard, very hard years, primarily because I had three children very close in age and I was navigating the community to find where we fit in, you know?"

Two years of living in Florida before having children had not been long enough for Lisa to adjust to her new environment completely. Now, with small children at home, Lisa did not have the time or opportunity to become any more connected to the community. Her days revolved around getting food on the table and the clothes clean and the children to bed. Arranging for child care, finding pediatricians, and choosing schools were more complicated tasks for Lisa because she was not familiar with the neighborhoods or with how the school and health care systems functioned.

Before the children, Lisa was able to set aside most of her uncertainties about living in the United States. That she was a stranger in this place that was so different from Canada was something that she noticed but for the most part could ignore. Being a mother, however, brought Lisa's suppressed feelings of being a foreigner to the surface. The problem was not the culture in Florida, although it was a busier and more stressful environment than in Canada. The truth was that having small children while being so physically removed from her parents and siblings and the place she considered home had become a heartache that was almost physical. Knowing what it is like to grow up without grandparents or other family nearby was something Lisa was familiar with. The awareness that she was raising her own children in the same situation brought feelings of sadness and doubt about her choice to leave home.

Friendships were another source of discomfort. New to Canada at age ten, Lisa had learned to tread lightly and to try to fit in. Moving to Florida brought with it the same predicament, only by this time Lisa knew more about herself and was not willing to change in order to be accepted. When Lisa arrived in Miami, Jason brought her into his "gang" of friends and their wives, assuming that they would all like each other.

Despite their best efforts to be friendly, it soon became apparent that Lisa was not going to fit in. The women in the group did not share Lisa's interest in the outdoors, and she felt awkward around them. Lisa knew she did not shop in the "right" stores or look adequately "put together." They continued to socialize as a group, but on an individual level these relationships never seemed to gel for Lisa. Friendships at work flowed much more easily but were for the most part limited to office socializing. Once Lisa had children and stopped working, these friendships eventually faded.

During the first five years or so in Florida, Lisa spent little time worrying about creating a community of friends. She and Jason spent their free time camping, canoeing, and cycling. Their relationship was still young and they were focused on each other. Once they had children, family activities kept them busy: "In those years, I didn't really pursue friendships. I think I was getting settled." Lisa had made a lot of acquaintances, but she hesitates to call them "friends," because she did not develop what she considered "deeply significant relationships" with them.

About the time their second child, Michael, was starting preschool, Lisa and Jason moved into a residential area of North Miami. Here they were closer to the city and out of the isolating suburban sprawl. They also decided to hire someone to help around the house two days a week and bought a second car. For the first time since she moved to Florida, Lisa had the time and the ability to do whatever she wanted for a few hours a week. For her, this was a "defining moment" in her life, the important moment when she recognized that it was time to expand her world. She joined a tennis league and through this connection finally started making her own friends.

Many of the women in the league were from the United States, but a number of the women were also foreigners, and these were the women Lisa gravitated toward. It was not a deliberate choice; they just happened to be the people she liked and related to: "All my friends, they come from some-where else. When you know that they've come from somewhere else, then you know that they immediately view the community and current events through two different lenses." There was an innate understanding between these immigrant women, a common denominator of knowing what it is like to live away from everything and anything that is familiar.

Lisa began to realize that this was part of the reason she had enjoyed working for Eastern Airlines so much—because her coworkers were almost all Cuban exiles. With Jason's friends she would always be on the fringe and feel that she was outside the circle looking in. With other foreigners, she could actually feel like an insider. After more than five years, Lisa finally had hope that she would eventually feel a sense of community in Miami.

◦❧

The undercurrent of dissonance that flowed through Lisa's life during her first years in the States was not only because she was an immigrant but also because she was a foreigner to her new religion. Learning Jewish customs and traditions was challenging, and it added a layer of tension to not only holidays but also her everyday life. Although Lisa did not come from a particularly religious family, her Christian background was something she had inhabited as part of her self-definition: "You know, you have a certain upbringing, including your religious upbringing; even if it's nonreligious, that's your upbringing, right? And so for you, the way you view everything is affected by that."

Converting was a choice she made and wanted to embrace, but the act of conversion and the act of internalizing a Jewish identity were not concur-rent. Moving from Christian to Jew was going to be a long-term process, based on a mental and spiritual transformation, not a ceremony or designa-tion. Conversion and immigration became intertwined, and the emotions around them inseparable.

Holidays now began to feel more like a burden than a celebration. Not having childhood memories about Jewish holidays, Lisa lacked emotional attachment to them. The symbolism and meaning felt important and real, but the songs, food, and rituals did not create the same warm, fuzzy feelings she had for Christmas and Easter. The music was beautiful, but the services were in Hebrew, which Lisa barely understood. In the fall, during Yom

Kippur and Rosh Hashanah, Lisa went through the motions without much trouble. But December, when the Christmas and Hanukkah holidays frequently coincide, was invariably harder. December found Lisa down in the dumps and conflicted. Wedged as she was between the two traditions, both "Merry Christmas" and "Happy Hanukkah" had a hollow ring for her.

Initially, a subdued Christmas was tolerable for Lisa, but as the children got older, her feelings about the holidays became stronger: "In the first few years, especially when Jason and I did not have children, it was not a big deal not having Christmas decorations. But when the babies started to become two or three years old, I wanted to have Christmas decorations; I wanted to re-create that wonderful feeling that you used to get when you were a kid at Christmas." She bought decorations and put up lights, but because there was no one to share the spirit of the holiday with, she could not get into it the way she had as a child.

Instead of being joyful, holidays now reminded Lisa of the separation she felt from her family and her past, and she gave up trying: "I've had a bit of a difficult adjustment with [holidays], because even though I converted when we married, I didn't give up my history. And for my family it was never a religious thing. We never went to church for Christmas Day or services; we just would have, you know, that festive feeling. I don't get that anymore. It's so hard to give that up. You know, it's in you."

About Yom Kippur she said, "I'm sure if I bothered to learn a little more, I would probably really enjoy it. You know, a good Jewish wife is supposed to make a nice dinner before, because you're going to fast the next twenty-five hours. It's a serious day. And, you know, I just don't bother to pull something together. It's terrible! I'm letting my family down because, like, even when we lived in Africa, we had Christmas, we had a Christmas tree. You know, my mother always pulled something together. And I find that I just don't, not for any holiday."

Over time, even nonreligious holidays such as Thanksgiving and Halloween fell victim to Lisa's ambivalence. They strike her as an excuse for excessiveness: "I think a big personality defect that I have is that I don't want to put the effort into these big celebrations. On Halloween, when the kids were little, I used to make costumes. And when they were little, it was fine, but as the kids got maybe like [to the] eight to twelve age range, they used to come home with just hoards and hoards and hoards of candy. Take my kids house to house to collect candy for what? When there are people starving in this country? So that's Halloween, and then there's Thanksgiving. Gluttony! Eat as much as you possibly can!"

Lisa readily admits that her negative attitude comes from feelings of resentment about holidays, and that, in turn, causes her to feel guilty. Still, avoiding holidays has become easier than facing the emotions they produce. From loving holidays as a teenager to hating them as a young mother, now the simplest solution is to ignore them altogether.

When it came to her children's religious education, Lisa had a different perspective. Even though she personally felt divided, she wanted her children to feel a deep connection to Judaism and to their religious community. When they were younger, Lisa made sure they attended a Jewish preschool. But when they started to grow up, Lisa realized that this was not enough. Somehow she had to find a way to make Judaism a more meaningful part of her life, too. She and Jason agreed to move from a Conservative to a less traditional Reform temple. The change made an enormous difference: "The Reform movement is much more liberal, with regard to the laws of keeping kosher and intermarriage and so many things. And it suits us really well, especially me, because I really find that I can work it into my life and still feel that we're a Jewish family, even though that wasn't the way I was raised." Instead of feeling pressured to conform to all Jewish traditions, Lisa began to feel more comfortable asking for support.

Family occasions continued to cause mixed emotions, however. Planning the children's bar mitzvahs, for example, again reminded Lisa that she is estranged from her own history: "One of the things I was thinking about is, you know, I'm planning this party, and I'm writing the guest list, and it's all [Barry's] family. And it's very annoying, you know, that it's his aunts and uncles, cousins, first cousins, second cousins, and when I get to my side, it's my immediate family, and that's it. It makes me sad. It makes me sad 'cause I have these, you know, these wonderful times of life, [and] you can't share that with your family." For Lisa, every celebration that is meant to be joyful becomes conflicted by the reminder of loss.

Jason worked for a large financial firm when he and Lisa were married. By 1994, his career had evolved to a point when he felt ready to open his own business. The risk was significant for a couple with three young children and no other source of income. Lisa had seen her parents take chances with luck and their livelihood; she also understood the potential for personal and financial rewards. She encouraged Jason to take the risk and agreed to help him in the office a few hours a week. Lisa had not worked outside the house for five years, and she was eager for a change. In the tiny, cramped office they sat literally back to back, Lisa on the computer and Jason at his desk.

As the business grew, so did the staff, and within a few years Lisa had transitioned from unpaid helper to the manager of a busy office with a large staff. Initially, managing the office was intimidating. Lisa had not been to college, and yet she was supervising an office that both employed and provided services to professionals. Her work included hiring and training staff and frequent client interaction. No longer just the boss's wife, she now ran the show.

Lisa had been living on the periphery of Jason's life since the day she came to Florida. Her place in the community had been defined by only her status as wife and mother. Her new career, though unplanned, came along at the right moment, when she was ready for some stimulation from outside the family. Working in the office gave her a stronger sense of belonging in Miami and began a reversal of some of the long-term feelings of isolation.

More than ten years have passed since Lisa went to work for Jason, and she now gets a substantial paycheck and has a retirement plan. The situation has been good for their marriage and has brought a new level of mutual respect: "He is the boss, but I will tell him if I think he's making a wrong move. I much prefer to take the more secondary role. You know, it's a respect thing. I trust his expertise and his abilities without question. But he trusts my ability to manage the administrative side."

❧

Lisa is not a planner. When she moved to Florida, she was not thinking about what might happen over time; she just knew that she wanted to be with Jason. "I don't know what it is about my personality, but I don't really plan long term. I really don't. Even when I got married, you know, when I came here, I came thinking, 'Okay, I'll give it a try. I'll just go. What's the worst that could happen? I'll go home; that would be the worst thing.' And, you know, when Jason said, 'Let's have that baby now,' I said, 'Yeah, okay.' You know, I just don't really plan." She knew that adjusting to a new country and converting to a new religion would take effort, but she had no idea how demanding the process would be.

In Lisa's life as a new immigrant, converting legitimated her religious status, and getting married gave her residency status and a green card. Feeling that she truly belonged in the United States was a long, slow process, however, and one Lisa tended to fight. Though she was frequently content, resentments were softly simmering under the surface of her busy and generally happy life. Her weapon was resistance: resistance especially to holidays or any family gatherings that were a reminder of the distance between her former and current lives. It was not that Lisa did not want to embrace Jason's world; it was that she did not know how to do that without completely letting go of the past.

Shirine

The story Shirine told of her long adjustment to living in the United States is as much about personal growth as it is about adapting to life in a new country. Trying to find a sense of belonging did not come easily. Shirine had to engage in a vast amount of soul searching in an effort to understand why she felt so adrift and disconnected even after many years had passed. Her search took her down a difficult but spiritual path. When we were introduced at a party in 1992, I was not aware of this. All I knew was that Shirine had lived in many parts of the world and was an artist.

When I met Shirine, I was not sure I was going to like her. She was cordial to me but seemed haughty. Her accent was slight but unidentifiable, and her sophisticated manner made her stand out in the crowd of Denver yuppies. Leaning against a wall, looking very stylish in expensive high-heeled boots and a leather jacket, she smiled and observed the crowd. I could not imagine that we would relate to one another.

My impression was wrong. Now when I see Shirine, I know the warmth that lies behind her smile and her generous, kind nature. I have seen the affection she gives to her children and have experienced her somewhat wacky sense of humor. Her chic style is not a pretense; it comes to her naturally from having spent her childhood in both European and Middle Eastern cities and from her artistic eye. By the time we met, years of alienation had already turned her shyness into a masquerade of detachment. Shirine had grown tired of trying to make herself blend into an environment where she would never belong. She was an exile stuck in Middle America, waiting patiently for change to come.

❧

When Shirine first came to the United States, she was seventeen. Bright and talented, she had already learned how to function in a foreign place and how to succeed in school, but she had not been happy. On her way to a new life in the United States, she felt "lost and frightened" but also hopeful that this new start might help her find her way.

The next few years would prove to be a whirlwind, both painful and thrilling: death, relocation, and revolution were interspersed with love and marriage. Shirine and her family were deluged with trauma and adjustment. Before all of the turmoil began, however, Shirine had a few months of contentment attending the Rhode Island School of Design. The school was well known and drew students with strong artistic backgrounds, many from well-off families. Shirine and Fatima were quickly noticed on campus. Dressed in the latest Parisian fashions and speaking with accents, they were intriguing foreigners, and the other students gravitated toward them.

Shirine's education was important, but she learned more from the other students than from her classes. She and her new friends spent weekends exploring New York and Boston, seeing a world very different from what she was accustomed to. Shirine's eyes were being opened by the counterculture that was flourishing in the 1970s, especially in the colleges and universities. The intellectual environment was exhilarating. The students were not just talking about ideas; they were developing new ways of expressing themselves through their art. They were "educated, creative people" who had the resources to attend an expensive school where they were encouraged to experiment: "There was a lot of very, very interesting stuff going on. . . . [I]t was a very special time. For me, it was like freedom . . . just this amazing world."

For the first time in her life Shirine did not feel isolated: "Because we were so embraced when we came and people were so nice to us, I don't feel like we ever had a hard time that way. . . . We were lucky in the way we entered the States. I never felt like, oh, you know, I'm an immigrant. Ever. And I think that's kind of cool. . . . [A] lot of foreign people come, and they don't get the chance to meet the kind of people we met."

Finally not feeling like an outsider was heaven, but that did not mean there were no challenges. Shirine's English was good from having attended international schools all her life, but she was not familiar with American slang. The other students shared familiar cultural references that went right over her head. She did not know what to make of the casual way the other students dressed. After living in Paris and Milan, cities known for their fashion, Shirine was now with young Americans who seemed to take pride in wearing tattered jeans: "The cultural adjustments! I mean, the other kids had grown up with certain TV and certain things, and we just had no clue what this was. Everybody was dressed differently. In France we were all chic, and then we come here and people are in Earth shoes. Plus, our English! Well, yes, I had gone to English-speaking schools, but I wasn't fluent. It's different when you go to English-speaking schools outside of the States."

The exhilaration ended abruptly when, without warning, Shirine's father died. Her mother, though suffering herself, was characteristically unaware of her daughters' emotional states. She demanded that there be no discussion about her husband's death and insisted that the sisters stay in school. They were not allowed to come to the funeral and were expected to continue with their lives as if nothing had happened. Numb and grief-stricken, Shirine and Fatima did as they were told. Shirine's response to her father's death played a significant role in her future decisions, and the details of that story and its aftermath are told in Part III.

Despite the shocking turn of events, Shirine continued to thrive at the college. Immersed in student life, she was able to ignore the sadness that tugged at her and pretend that everything was fine, just as her mother wanted. Within a year she had begun dating an American man she met through fellow students. Jackson Cooper was a dynamic man and completely enamored with Shirine's foreign background and artistic nature. Before long the two were in love, and in less than a year, they had decided to get married.

In the meantime, Shirine's mother had left Iran for good and settled in Nice, France, where she owned an apartment. When the spring semester was over, Shirine brought Jackson to meet her. Immediately, Shirine's mother disapproved. She did not want Shirine to stop her education or to marry so young. Shirine was disappointed, but she knew Jackson loved her and she needed stability in some aspect of her life. Everything else was temporary—she now had no permanent home, her father was dead, and in addition, her sister had developed a painful nerve disorder. The little emotional support her mother had to give was going to Fatima.

Shirine and Jackson went to Denver, where Jackson's parents lived and where he had grown up. They had a small ceremony with Jackson's family and a large reception at an old, elegant hotel, attended by Jackson's childhood friends and his parents' large social network. Getting married was joyful, but a wedding in Denver also meant that, like Lisa's wedding, the guests were strangers. In Shirine's case, no one from her family was present; she knew no one at her wedding except the groom. Caught up in her happiness with Jackson, Shirine registered, but could not directly face, the overwhelming realization that she was now even further removed from anything familiar: "But you know what? Jackson and I were really, really connected. We were so in love, or whatever. God knows what we were; I have no words for it. But I felt in seventh heaven. I didn't care where I was, as long as I was with him."

After the wedding the newlyweds packed up what little they had and, in Jackson's very old, very used Lincoln Continental, drove to Los Angeles. Jackson got a job in an art gallery and tried his hand at writing screenplays. Shirine worked for a high-end home furnishings boutique, using her design skills to cater to the tastes of wealthy Californians. For two years Shirine and Jackson soaked in the carefree Southern California lifestyle, hanging out with artists Jackson met at the gallery, enjoying the nightlife and laid-back atmosphere of the area.

Eventually Jackson became concerned about the future. His parents were pressuring him to come back to Denver, where his geologist father could help Jackson get a job in the oil business. Shirine did not like the idea. Compared to what she was used to, Denver was not particularly cosmopolitan. She worried that in the middle of the country she would feel trapped, far from anything she could identify with. She agreed to go, knowing that this was the logical choice, but inside she was "kicking and screaming" all the way.

Shirine and Jackson found an apartment in an urban, somewhat edgy part of Denver and furnished it with whatever used, and usually filthy, items they could find at secondhand stores. They started socializing with Iranian students they met through a cousin of Shirine's who was attending college in Denver. There were lots of late-night parties with Persian food, music, and dancing. Jackson loved this; he was fascinated with Persian culture and wanted to immerse himself in it. As a child, Shirine had never felt comfortable in Iran, and regardless of where she was living, she had avoided other Persians. In this group of students, however, she felt more relaxed. These new friends had lives that mirrored her own. They were Persian, spoke both Farsi and English, and had grown up as Westernized as Shirine. Though Jackson enjoyed these friends more than Shirine did, falling into step with the group was easier than Shirine expected and helped smooth the rough edges around the move to Denver.

While Jackson struggled to make it in his new career, Shirine decided to go back to school. For the next two years she threw herself into an intensive design program, finishing her degree. They had virtually no income, but instead of creating difficulty, the financial struggle gave Jackson and Shirine a good perspective on their lives and a hopeful outlook for the future. From these years come the fondest memories Shirine has of her marriage: "Those first five years were awesome, I have to say. We were inseparable. We had so much fun; we were always doing fun things, and we were young and in love and didn't care that we didn't have any money." This woman who had grown up in luxury owned nothing and did not care. She was happier than she had ever been.

Jackson soon discovered that he had a flair for the oil business, and within a few years their financial situation changed dramatically. This change of circumstance reverberated throughout their lives, and not always in positive ways. They bought a condo in a more expensive part of town and over time began to socialize with Jackson's work associates. These new friends were professionals and lived a very different life from the one that Jackson and Shirine had shared with their student and artist friends. Slowly, their older friendships began to "kind of fade away, because we changed, our status kind of changed. . . . [W]e got into that yuppie group." Her connections with other Persians were short-lived too, but for Shirine this had been an anomaly anyway and not something she felt the need to preserve.

Socializing with businesspeople was important to Jackson's career, and Shirine felt she needed to support him. She liked these new friends well enough, but she could never really relate to them. Few of them had traveled or had had much exposure to the world outside Colorado, and they did not understand Shirine's more international perspective.

She was a fish out of water in this western U.S. city, dominated by major league sports and suburbs: "I put myself kind of away, in order to live here. . . . I'm not saying anything bad. . . . [I]t's just so vastly different. I mean, it's almost like speaking a different language . . . [t]heir interests and their experiences and the way they related to us and to each other. It's just different than what I knew. . . . It's hard to explain because we're all human beings and we're all equal, you know. And that's a fact. But what I had already experienced and what kind of life I had had and what I knew and what I had seen and all that, these people had no knowledge of and could not even comprehend."

Shirine indeed came from a different world. The way she grew up was not the way she was now living. This was not about money or living extravagantly; it was about being around people who had similar backgrounds. As a child, Shirine had lived and traveled all over the world. She had seen the extremes of both abundance and poverty in the Middle East, the repression of Eastern Europe, and the art and culture of Paris and Milan. Now she was living in an insular region of the United States, where few people had seen or experienced even a fraction of what Shirine had.

Five years after coming to the United States to study, Shirine decided to become a citizen. Even though she still did not feel attached to Denver, she hoped that by making a commitment to the country she might gain a sense of security and permanence in the United States: "I wanted to do it because it made me belong here. . . . [I]t just seemed like the natural thing to do. I was excited. I had a new home. I had a husband; you know, I was excited about being married and having a new country. We were happy; we were having fun, and I really felt . . . that we were building a really great life together, and I really believed that."

The swearing-in ceremony was touching, and during the pledge of allegiance she cried and held tight to the little American flag she'd been given: "I was thinking, 'Oh good, finally I have stability.' Little did I know." Shirine now had the security of citizenship and the right to be a part of American society, but this did not lead to the sense of place that she was hoping for.

Shirine was now working with a well-known decorator, designing for prestigious offices in downtown Denver and fashionable condos in Vail. Between work and socializing, her life with Jackson was busy. But as time went on, Shirine slowly began to realize that her relationship with Jackson had changed and that neither of them was satisfied with their life together. The daily business of life kept her absorbed, and since her worries seemed nebulous, she tried to ignore them and continue moving forward.

In 1983, their first child, Francesca, was born. Becoming parents was the happy and expected next step in their marriage. Shirine quit working, and they bought a large, old, charming home in a beautiful part of central Denver. Several years later, their second child, Louis, was born. Unfortunately, at the same time, weaknesses in the marriage began to surface. Conflicts prompted the couple to try both conventional therapy and alternative, spiritually based healing. The effort was incredibly slow and intense and required both Shirine and Jackson to take a hard look at themselves and why they had married. Their personal growth was substantial, but in the process they realized that divorce was inevitable. After ten years of marriage, when Louis was one and a half, Jackson moved out.

The split left Shirine feeling rootless and confused again: "I can't even tell you; I just don't have words for it, how hard it was. I had absolutely no base to go to, no one to hold on to. . . . I felt very alone. . . . I was just a wreck. . . . I had no support, no home. . . . Jackson had been my home, my base, and all of a sudden I have nothing. I have no one that I can rely on 100 percent. A mother who was over there in France doing her own thing. My sister, she had her own stuff going. And basically I didn't have anyone." Except, of course, she had responsibility for two small children.

No longer married, Shirine did not know what she wanted to do or where she belonged. In the big house, Shirine "felt imprisoned." Shirine spoke to her mother on the phone virtually every day and visited her in France once a year, but instead of getting support, she was giving it. Since her father's death, Shirine had felt like her mother's emotional caretaker.

Shirine wanted to leave Denver and start over, but she did not know how:

No, I couldn't go anywhere. First of all, I didn't think it was healthy for the kids not to have a father. . . . I thought, "Okay, I can pick the kids up and go." But to whom? My mother? You know, that was not an option. And then I thought, you know, I would rather do the extra work and raise them all by myself without having anyone to tell me how to do it, because I knew—that's one certainty I've always had, is that . . . I have an innate sense of how to be with children. And so I thought, "Okay, I'll do this alone. I've made a commitment to these two, and I'm going to do it alone, and I don't want anyone participating and telling me what to do." I wanted to bring them up to a point and then start my life.

Shirine's life now revolved around raising her children. Jackson was providing for her financially so she did not have to work, and she spent as much time with Louis and Francesca as possible. Growing up with emotionally absent parents had hurt her, and she was resolute that her children would have the opposite experience. Though Shirine never truly felt at home in Denver, she did her best to ensure that her children did. She decorated the house in a way that was eclectic but comfortable. There were antiques, a big comfy couch in the living room, and both modern and traditional art, and the walls were painted a soothing periwinkle color. Shirine was a wonderful cook, and the house was always filled with the scent of French and Persian dishes on the stove. Friends were welcome, and her relationship with her children was open and relaxed.

Shirine also continued on her journey of self-exploration: "All this was a catalyst to bring about huge amounts of change within me. I had to fix myself. It's too hard to even explain how hard. Just—just hard. Just exhausting and, you know, I was trying to figure out who the hell I am; I knew that I had to work on myself. If I had any chance of happiness, it would take many, many years to clean up my garbage. And I was right. . . . [I]t took about fifteen years for the change to come about."

Jackson would continue to financially support the children, but Shirine knew that his obligation to support her would eventually end. In a few years, she would need to go back to work, but she did not want to go back to interior design. She resisted the advice she got from friends and her mother to take any job that would pay the bills. There had to be a way to make money and also find some kind of personal fulfillment. Stressed, but trusting that something would come along, she waited for an answer to appear: "All of a sudden one day—and, God knows, I have no idea how this came to me—all of a sudden I woke up and I said, 'You know what? I'm going to paint. I'm a painter.' I don't know when this came. I mean, it was one of those godly things."

The idea was impractical, and no one she knew gave any encouragement. Yes, Shirine was artistic, but she had never painted. Her experience and education was in interior design, graphics, and a little photography. How could she make a living as a painter when she had never even taken a painting class? Relying on her intuition, Shirine began to paint every day when the children were at school, setting up a studio in her basement.

Not knowing the basic techniques, even how to stretch a canvas or mix paint, did not prevent Shirine from having high aspirations. The fear of being a mediocre painter was intimidating, but it was not enough to stop her: "I just started painting. At the beginning it wasn't good . . . [but it] developed and developed and developed and developed. And it's a struggle, but you have to love it; you have to know, because it's against all odds."

The motivation to paint came from more than a desire to be creative. It bubbled up from a spiritual source that had always been there but that she had not yet learned to tap into: "Honoring this path was important . . . in order for my work to grow. . . . As I did more work on myself, then I opened up." Every day was an experiment. Without a conscious plan or idea about the subject matter, Shirine would sit down in front of a canvas and allow herself to channel her creativity from within. Sometimes what emerged on the canvas was a surprise. Her paintings varied from small and detailed to enormous canvases with broad splashes of color and emotion. They were all abstracts, and even when she included figures, there was little realism.

Being a painter was harder than she expected, because the artwork had to be not only created but also sold. Promoting herself in the art community was a challenge. Shirine seems quite at ease socially but nonetheless carries shyness from her childhood. Selling her art required putting aside her fears of rejection and failure and taking big emotional risks. After a few years of painting, Shirine was ready to put herself out on a limb. A friend who owned an upscale clothing boutique began to hang Shirine's paintings in his store. A few pieces sold, the exposure helped her make some contacts, and eventually Shirine was exhibiting paintings in local galleries.

Finally, Shirine was engaged in work that had depth and meaning. Earlier design work had required creating what other people wanted, not what came from her own heart: "I have to say, I like interior design only on the creative level of it. When it comes to actually doing it on a professional level, I really hate it because I hate paperwork—not that I'm not organized; I just hate all that it entails. The ordering and the this and the that. So to me, I realize I'm just more of a hands-on person. It should be between me and the piece of paper or the canvas." Finding her true vocation made an enormous, and positive, difference in Shirine's sense of herself. She saw her work improving and being appreciated.

 ❧

Divorce had finally led Shirine to the realization that for years she had been living someone else's life, always allowing her own needs to be obscured.

The pattern emerged from a childhood spent moving back and forth between countries, with parents who were unable to provide an emotional refuge. As a child Shirine adapted, at least outwardly, to wherever she was. During her marriage, she had ensconced herself in Jackson's world. In an attempt to create the belonging she craved, Shirine had to subtly transform herself to fit in wherever, and with whomever, she was. She could now see that in order to survive in Denver she had put on a mask. "I feel like I compromised myself . . . in order to relate . . . and I think it was not so great for me because I put myself down doing that . . . and that's been—that has always been my issue here." With the loss of her marriage Shirine also lost the little security she had. With no solid ground to stand on, the emotional difficulties of living in a foreign country became painfully apparent and rose to the forefront of her consciousness.

The result was a growing sense of isolation. This was not a matter of not having people who wanted to spend time with her—over time Shirine made new friends and had plenty of invitations. Shirine's loneliness was internal and came from the ongoing feeling that the people she knew in Denver would never be able to understand her. Her ability to feign assimilation created a situation in which her friends were not aware of how out of place and foreign she actually felt and therefore could do nothing to ease her solitude. Keeping a positive outlook "took a lot of grace."

Despite her pervasive loneliness, Shirine had several true friends while she lived in Denver. These friendships did not develop until after she had been there for more than ten years, though, and because of circumstance, their support did not last. One close friend died, several others moved away, and some friendships just seemed to run their course. Her closest friends were a Swiss couple who eventually returned to Geneva. There were always people to get together with, but this was not enough for Shirine to feel grounded or develop a sense of belonging in Denver.

For the most part, Shirine was able to deal with her feelings of disconnectedness; focusing on the children and her work helped. Holidays were harder. When Shirine had been married, she had learned to love both American holidays, such as Thanksgiving and the Fourth of July, and Christian holidays, particularly Christmas. Once Shirine and Jackson were divorced, however, holidays became a reminder that she had no base of support in the country where she lived: "I loved [the holidays] when I was married, and then after that I hated them. I was married into [an] 'all-American' family, and, you know, that's what we all did. I learned a lot of things; I mean, you learn a lot. It's all around you. I had to jump into it with the rest of them. I still did all those things when I was divorced, but I hated it because I was lonely . . . and it wasn't because I was longing for my country or my culture or my holidays, no. It's because I was lonely and I hated being lonely."

ॐ

Shirine did her best to build a clientele for her art. She made a name for herself in Denver, but she was not making enough money to rely on painting as a sole source of income, and this seemed unlikely to happen in Denver. Other cities had more active art scenes where she might make more money, but staying put was the only acceptable option while her two children were in school. Stuck in Denver, she "felt like the whole world was moving around" while she was there. In a state of suspension, her life on hold, she waited for her children to grow up. Then, at around the same time that her alimony tapered off, Shirine suffered a large loss in the stock market, and the combination of these two events created a dramatic financial crisis. Shirine quickly had to find a way to earn a living.

There were not many options. Shirine had not planned to go back into design, and over time she had lost her connections in the business. She had to take what she could get and ended up working in a design showroom sorting fabric, setting up displays, and selling to walk-in customers. Calling everyone she knew, she put out the word that she was also starting a free-lance graphics business designing business cards, logos, and stationery. Putting in as many hours as she could, she scraped by.

Her children, now in their early teens, were becoming more independent, but they still spent a great deal of time with Shirine. They stayed at her house more often than their father's, and Shirine did most of the parenting. Between work and family, painting was now relegated to something Shirine could do only when she had a little extra time. Putting her art on the back burner was difficult, but there really was not much choice. Her older house was expensive to maintain, and there was a mortgage to pay. Shirine would have to wait before art could again be her primary vocation.

❧

Shirine never felt contented in Denver. She had tried to connect to the United States, even becoming a citizen. But the outward appearance of a fulfilled life disguised a continuing dissatisfaction. Like a small but heavy stone hung around her neck, her discontent was invisible to others but was always within her field of awareness. Time was unable to provide a feeling of belonging, and Shirine never stopped feeling like an eternally misplaced outsider. She would ultimately find clarity and the strength to face the fact that Denver, and perhaps even the United States, was not where she wanted to be. The question that remained was what Shirine could do about it.

Barrett

Pulled as if by a magnet, Barrett prepared herself to move to Venezuela. She had never been to the country but felt sure that regardless of the consequences, she needed to take this step: "I didn't have a wedding date or anything like that, but the whole thing was that I was going to go to Venezuela and see how it was going to work, because, anyway, I was finished with school, there was a job opportunity, Edmund was there and my friends were all there, and, you know, I had to do this. I was moving to Venezuela because I couldn't conceive in my head of anything else happening to me. . . .

[T]his was a chance to live in this nice place, in an exotic foreign country where it's never winter." Moving to this place that she had never seen felt more like dropping into a safety net than like stepping off a precipice.

Nevertheless, contained in her excitement was also a small seed of apprehension. Edmund was calling regularly, encouraging her and giving the support she needed to resist her family's continuing opposition to the move. But he had also mentioned, perhaps a little too casually, that he was going through some internal battles of his own. Details were not important now; he would tell her all about it when she arrived. Barrett heard the edge in his voice and this raised a red flag, but she suppressed her concern. Excited about the move, she chose to trust that whatever the problem was, it could be worked out.

Falling in love with Venezuela took only moments. Arriving in Caracas on a cloudless, sunny day, Barrett felt something that was completely new to her: "When I got to Venezuela, I breathed such a sigh of relief; there was something about it. . . . [T]here was something that said to me, 'This is it.' . . . You don't feel like going anywhere; you don't want to get on a plane. There is something here that [makes you] you feel like your soul has finally found a place where you want to be."

Barrett spent the first few days exploring the city and reuniting with friends from her university in New York who had also made their way to Caracas. Her expectations about Venezuela had been vague; she brought only her own certainty that she would feel comfortable there. Barrett was not disappointed. From the beginning she felt that people were receptive and outgoing, and walking down the streets of the city she felt free. The sun was shining, flowers were blooming, and in every way it felt like spring. The heavy sense of alienation that had always accompanied her seemed to float away.

Within a week, however, Barrett's elation at finally being in Venezuela with Edmund was shattered. First came the news that the Caracas symphony was on a long-term strike. No firm offer had been made to Barrett, but the symphony had an opening for a cellist, and Barrett's chances for getting the job had been good. Now, her best hopes for serious employment as a musician had disappeared.

Next, Edmund finally mustered up the nerve to tell Barrett what had happened to him. Since they had seen each other in London, he had met someone else. He had not intended to get involved and had initially thought the relationship would run a short course. He still loved Barrett and wanted her to be in Venezuela, but he had realized that his feelings for her were more brotherly than romantic. His new relationship was passionate, and he could not give it up.

All of Barrett's hopes for a new life in Venezuela had evaporated. She had received two crushing blows and had no idea what to do. Should she get on a plane and get as far away as possible, or wait to see what might happen? She understood that no matter how much she loved Edmund, he would probably never return the same feelings. She also knew Edmund well enough to know that despite appearances, he had not meant to hurt her and was himself conflicted and confused.

Turning around and going back to Connecticut might have been the safer choice, but Barrett was not ready to give up. She was disillusioned and hurt but still wanted desperately to salvage the situation: "Well, you know, it was not okay with me, but I was not the kind of person I am now, that I could—that I would have fought and said, 'Okay, I'm leaving on the next plane.' . . . I was just so totally unprepared, because I was in this la-la land of romance. You know, like this was going to happen to me like in one of the books that I've read."

Shaken but not deterred, she continued to believe that moving to Caracas had been the right decision. The first thing she needed to do was find a place to stay. A friend knew a family that would take a boarder, and she moved in. Instead of the romantic situation she had imagined for herself, Barrett was now living in the spontaneous and hectic household of a large extended family.

From the moment Barrett arrived at the house, she felt welcomed. The family did not just include her for meals; they invited her to join in on all of their activities. On the weekends the family, plus various friends and cousins, including Barrett, would all jam into cars and go off to the beach. There was always a crowd of people around, and Barrett drank it in. She started to finally feel that she was getting those "three drops of water" that she had been missing. What started out as a disappointing solution to a painful problem was turning out to be a wonderful opportunity:

> I loved being in Venezuela. It was a very strange thing. I didn't have the job, and I didn't have the boyfriend, and I wasn't getting married, but I was staying with this . . . big extended family, with the grandmother living there and the parents and seven children . . . and one of the daughters was married, and so she and her husband, everybody, was there for lunch every day, for dinner every day . . . on the weekends the cousins, the aunts, and the uncles—a totally different brand of family. [There was more] togetherness and interaction than [in] my big family that also was always together but [with] just a totally different brand of interaction . . . a Latin brand of warmth . . . which felt much better to me than, than the U.S. brand.

Growing up in Connecticut, Barrett had always felt pressured to conform. Now, in Caracas, she felt a sense of relief and ease in just being herself. No one had any expectations and accepted her without question. The feeling of belonging was immediate. After seven years of longing and fantasizing about Venezuela, Barrett was finally living her dream. For the first time in her life there was no need to call a travel agent and make plans to leave, no need to fantasize about the next place, the next adventure.

Barrett found a part-time job teaching English and occasional work playing her cello. For six months she stayed with the family. She saved the little money she made and kept her eyes open for an apartment. Eventually she found something affordable in a ten-story building in an urban neighborhood.

Rather than being intimidated or overwhelmed by being alone in a foreign country, for Barrett living in Caracas was exciting:

> You know, first of all I think I embraced Venezuela so immediately that nothing was foreign for very long. And I was just so happy to be there. And when I was living with the Venezuelan family, who were just the most wonderful people, I learned what foods you eat, and so I [ate] Venezuelan style, basically. You know, it's very simple but very tasty food. I missed M&Ms and apples and peanut butter . . . sometimes, maybe sometimes, missed a fall day. But it was certainly not enough to go back to the States. Whenever I would go anywhere, I would always just try things. . . . I just figured it out. I never found it to be a trauma; I never found it to be difficult. You do the best with what you like, and you don't deal with what you don't.

Although when Barrett arrived in Caracas, she did not speak more than rudimentary Spanish, she picked the language up quickly. Having a trained musical ear helped her grasp the language, and she had studied French, which helped with the grammar. Instead of taking classes, she practiced on her own: "I would go on these long walks because I didn't have a car, and I would have conversations with myself in Spanish, which is, I believe, how I became fluent fast. And I had this little notebook that I would write things down [in]: this means *carro*, car; *casa*, house." Getting laid up in her apartment with the flu helped too: "I got a horrible virus, and I ended up spending two weeks in bed. And I had an old television that the owners of the apartment had left for me. I just watched TV all day and all night. It was on all the time. What I do know is that I got out of that bed totally fluent—totally, so totally immersed that after that, it was just a question of adding on to my vocabulary."

Money was tight, but between teaching and playing the occasional concert, there was enough for rent. Barrett eventually developed a network in the Caracas musical community, which at that time was thriving. As a foreign musician, she was seen as someone who had international experience and influence, and she was sought after. Constantly playing with different musicians and in different venues, Barrett was visible in a way she had never been before in her life, and not just professionally: "There was this whole group of international people; there were Germans and Austrians and French and Venezuelans and me and whoever, and we had this whole group of young, unattached people." Every weekend was spent with these new friends and colleagues, exploring the nearby beaches or taking advantage of Caracas's nightlife.

After being in Venezuela for around a year, Barrett was asked to help found a classical music ensemble. The group was successful and before long was touring the country every weekend. Not long after she joined the ensemble, she was offered a part-time job teaching music at a small, private academy. The owner of the school was a Jewish immigrant from Prague, Adam Klein. Though the school focused mainly on the sciences, Klein held strong beliefs about the power of music and wanted all the students to have exposure to musical learning in order to "educate the soul." This philosophy was something Barrett could believe in, and though the salary was low, she took the job.

Almost overnight, Barrett's life had changed dramatically. From an emotionally shattered young woman with no plan and no job, Barrett had been transformed into a busy, popular musician. She had two part-time jobs and plenty of friends, and she was enjoying her life in a dynamic, vibrant city: "I was living a totally Venezuelan life in a very exciting time when all of the cultural activity was well funded, lots of things happening; there was just plenty to do. Somehow I've always gotten connected with friends who are actors; I have lots of friends who are musicians. . . . I know a hell of a lot of people."

A year and half after she came to Venezuela, Barrett went back to the States to see her family for the first time. Instead of going back to Connecticut, she met her parents in South Florida, where her grandparents had a home. Nothing seemed right to her there:

I remember feeling how weird it was to be standing on my grandmother's front porch and there were no mountains. [In Caracas] I could see the Avila, this beautiful mountain range on the northern side of Caracas, which is what defines Caracas, this beautiful mountain. You're aware of it all the time, every day, all day; that's literally your north. And [in Florida] there was just nothing. It was just so weird to be in a flat place. The other thing is that I hadn't spoken very much English, except when I spoke to my mother on the phone, during that first year and a half, and it was just a very strange feeling because I couldn't express myself totally in English anymore. . . . I just couldn't understand why nobody understood me if I was speaking Spanish.

The visit did not produce a single feeling of homesickness or a desire to leave Venezuela; nor did it inspire Barrett to visit family more often. In spite of the distance, she never felt too far from them: "My mother never gave me a chance to miss anybody, miss her or them, because she would call all the time, which she still does after thirty years. I guess, what I missed more was the fact that home didn't seem to miss me." Barrett had been in touch with her brothers and extended family on occasion, but they did not call or write often. Hearing about Barrett's life through her mother seemed to be enough for them.

Barrett's family seemed to think she was just going through a phase. The life she was leading in Venezuela was a wonderful experience, but it was not something to be taken seriously. Barrett would become significant to them again when she returned to the States and finally started her adult life. For Barrett, the opposite was true. Living in Venezuela had not turned out to be an adventure or a temporary stop but a place she might stay forever. She had become a legal resident of Venezuela, was involved in work and a social life, and had no plans to leave. She had a sense of permanence and stability there, and it felt good.

Time passed, and Barrett became more and more ensconced in her life in Caracas. Venezuela was making a mark on her: no longer awkward and uncomfortable with herself as she had been when she was younger, Barrett now had much more confidence. She had absorbed outward Latin American mannerisms and now dressed and carried herself like a Venezuelan woman, not an uptight, scared girl. Friends involved in television taught her how to wear makeup and jewelry. Now possessing a "sense of style" and obvious self-assurance, she fit easily into image-conscious Caracas.

Barrett's job at the Klein school had worked out well. Like Adele, Barrett's teacher in London, Adam Klein had immediate confidence in Barrett's abilities. He believed she would be able to develop a love of music in young children and teach them in a gentle and encouraging way. She stayed at the school for seventeen years, developing many close relationships with students and their parents. Along with teaching cello, she conducted the children's orchestra, published the school newspaper, and eventually formed and managed a visiting artist program.

The friendship between Barrett, Klein, and his wife turned out to be one of the most significant in Barrett's life. Though she was never paid much, the Kleins treated her like family. They had her over for meals, took her on an annual trip to New York, and even loaned her money once, when she needed to put a large deposit down on a new apartment. Barrett had asked her family in the States for help first, but they refused to make the loan, not understanding the Venezuelan rental system or trusting Barrett's judgment. Klein responded differently. Without asking any questions, "he just wrote me a check, because he trusted my instincts—at all times. He never, ever doubted what I knew; it was the only thing I had ever asked him for." Barrett insisted that she would pay him back out of her salary, and he agreed, but no papers were signed or formal arrangements made. Their relationship was based entirely on trust.

The Kleins became Barrett's substitute parents in Venezuela: "It's just this incredibly beautiful relationship with them. They gave me so much; I can never repay them, what they gave to me. I did so many things at that school; I became the mother of so many kids at that school. I mean, I never had any money, but I got so much more." From the beginning, the

Kleins took Barrett seriously and assumed she was in Venezuela to stay. The same is true for the many friends who embraced Barrett like she was family. Though Barrett never had children of her own, many young people in Caracas call her *Tia*, Spanish for "aunt": "It was wonderful to be at a school, because you saw kids at every age, through high school. And the teachers were of every age—I mean, a wonderful school community."

Around eight years after coming to Venezuela, Barrett decided it was time to address some unfinished emotional business. Feeling supported by her friends and coworkers, she found the strength to begin seeing a therapist: "I realized that, no matter what, no matter where I was and what I was doing, there were things that were not happening in my life that should have been happening in my life, in anybody's life. And I needed to understand. I didn't · want to be in this pain anymore." The conversations with her therapist took place entirely in Spanish, which, for Barrett, created a buffer between her present and the difficult events of her past. Looking back at all that had happened—the trauma of her childhood back injury, her suffocating relationships with her family, the breakup with Edmund—was incredibly difficult but worth the effort. When Barrett ended therapy three years later, she had found a level of stillness and peace that she had never known, one that would carry her through future challenges.

In 1993, when Barrett was thirty-nine, her father died after a long illness. During the last six months of his life, Barrett traveled to see him every month, and she spent the last ten days of his life at his bedside. Her father's death did not cause Barrett to have regrets about leaving New England—in fact, just the opposite. The ability to deal with her emotions in a healthy way, learned through therapy and the years away from home, reconfirmed for Barrett that Venezuela was where she was meant to be: "If I had not gone through therapy, through analysis, I would never have been able to deal with this. And if I had lived in the States, I doubt . . . that I would have been able to deal with it, because . . . I don't know how I could have had the distance."

During her years at the Klein school, Barrett experienced both an internal and external transformation: "Toward the end of that whole experience, I realized that I was born in the States and my parents brought me up for seventeen years, and then I went through a process to be able to get here, so I could be at the school for seventeen more years and finally grow up to be me. And, you know, very often I will tell people I feel that I'm an alumni of the school. My feelings for the school are as if I had gotten there in nursery school and I graduated seventeen years later. . . . [T]his was a place where I was able to grow up to be me."

Barrett's job at the Klein school was always part time, and so for eight years she continued to play with the classical music ensemble. Being a professional musician meant that weekends were frequently tied up with performances and travel, but for her this was as much fun as it was work. She also started representing and managing other musicians, finding gigs and arranging concert agendas. When she left the ensemble in 1987, it was because she had become so busy as an agent that she no longer had time to perform. Weekends continued to revolve around work, attending concerts and events and otherwise developing connections. Cultural activity was still well funded in Venezuela then, and there was no shortage of work for an agent. Just as when she had first started looking for work as a performer, Barrett's status as a foreigner added to her visibility, and this did not hurt her business.

By the 1990s the economy in Venezuela had slowed down considerably, and as a result, less money was directed toward the arts and music. Finding work for clients became harder, and Barrett decided to try something new. During the school's summer break she applied for a job with the Latin American affiliate of a large U.S.-based cable television company. The job was supposed to be temporary, and Barrett had every intention of returning to teaching in the fall.

But when Barrett began working at the station, she realized that in many ways the job suited her: "There was something about the whole programming thing which was not so far away from organizing a concert. You have a concert, you want the overture, you want to see what the symphony is, then you see what the soloist plays, and then you have the encores. This is a program of listening. And what I do is a program of viewing and listening at the same time. So it was really very easy for me to fall into, or to learn the craft, because the concept was already there. [It was] totally natural to me."

Having what she calls "*gringa* knowledge" was an enormous asset as well. The cable station's shows were based on the culture and history of the United States. Raised there and having a superior education, Barrett was familiar with anything that is intrinsic to the North American psyche, and that applied to much of the programming content. People who knew basic historical facts about the United States were rare in Venezuela. For the first time in years, Barrett was valued for her skills with the English language and U.S. culture. With her background, she could also communicate easily with and understand the needs of the "mother ship"—the corporate managers in the States. Having already spent almost twenty years in Venezuela by that time, Barrett was the perfect cultural broker, able to sort out misunderstandings and miscommunications between the North American–based and Venezuelan divisions of the company.

At the end of the summer, the cable company asked her to stay, and Barrett had to make a painful decision about leaving the school. At forty-two, Barrett was going to start a brand-new career. The decision was bittersweet, but Barrett recognized that it was time to move on. She needed to leave the nest, just as she had needed to leave her parents' world. The cable job was "something that has helped me in the next stage of my growth process. If I had stayed at the school, I probably would have been stifled in a way; I wouldn't have continued growing. Life has been very good to me; it always has shown me the way. And I probably had gotten to the point at the school where I could not grow any more. The school still loved me, I loved them, but it's very clear that I was not going to just be a cello teacher."

~

Barrett is a grounded, intellectual person, but she also has a spiritual side, one that influences every aspect of her life. In Venezuela she has found comfort and support from Jewish friends, such as the Kleins, but she has never felt drawn to any formal or group religious practice. She maintains her Jewish identity, but she does not object to joining friends in Christian celebrations, although she participates in these in a festive, secular rather than a religious way.

Finding a community of friends, or in Barrett's case, several communities, was always more important than organized religion:

> The search that I had begun from the time that I was very small, with my astrology and tarot and spiritual stuff, all of these things indicated to me that my spiritual development was something that was internal. It's something for me alone. It's not something that's done in a community way. It's not something that needs to be inside of a church or a synagogue or [needs] the blessing of a rabbi or of anybody. It's just me and God, and that's it. You know, my communities are like the community . . . of the Klein School; my community is the community of my friends at work now, the community of my friends who are actors and the community of friends who are musicians. I have lots of communities, but they are not something restrictive. . . . [T]here's no boss in the communities; there's nobody saying, "I'm God."

The other three women who were interviewed for this book all married native-born men. Barrett did not have this connection to Venezuela; she was there completely on her own. There were boyfriends along the way but never a romantic relationship that would qualify as a partnership. But being single has not been an impediment to Barrett's social life in Caracas. Her social connections came fairly easily, first through the friends she had known in college and then through contacts in the music world and in the Klein school. Her line of work brought with it a lifestyle that opened social doors that might otherwise have been closed: "There has never really been any activity that has stopped, that I haven't done because I'm single. The only times that I stay home and don't go someplace is if I'm feeling—just feeling particularly lonely. I don't want to go to a Christmas thing if I really wish I had somebody to share it with—somebody in particular, not just my friends. You know, there are times when you don't want to be number seven or number nine or number five at the table."

Her single status actually feels more comfortable in Venezuela than when she visits the United States: "I find that in Venezuela my personality is much more sure of itself than it is in the States. If I'm in the States and I'm in a [social] situation, it's very hard for me to be as me as I am." The way people in the United States tend to date feels awkward to Barrett. She does not want to go to bars or use an Internet service. In Caracas she feels no pressure to be part of a "singles scene"; she feels accepted as she is and included all situations, whether she arrives alone or not.

❧

While growing up in New England, Barrett was haunted by the fear of becoming trapped in a world where she would always feel ill at ease. She dreamed of a future in an unknown location and felt the longing for a home she could not name. Barrett's desire to escape her past was part of a search for an understanding of herself, and of a spiritual quest that required her to trust her intuition. Edmund's offer of a new start in Venezuela came at the perfect moment and provided legitimacy to her vision. And while the relationship failed her, Venezuela did not. Rather than feeling displaced in a foreign country, she felt in her element, finally able to be who she wanted to be, with no pretense.

Barrett's past did not evaporate the minute her plane landed, of course. She had to work hard to come to terms with who she is and what she wants her life to look like. The combination of physical distance from her past and the fellowship of the Venezuela cultural environment allowed Barrett the opportunity to face and move through the tough issues. Barrett made it clear that her love of the Venezuelan "brand of warmth" isn't a disparagement of the United States but an awareness that for whatever combination of reasons, the North American way of relating is "a brand that has never felt . . . like it was my home brand or my home market." In Venezuela, she found a place where her nature, her way of thinking and responding to people and circumstances, was a good fit.

VISITOR, SOJOURNER, IMMIGRANT?

Although there is much research about the rationales for and causes of migration, in the end leaving home is a personal as much as a practical decision and has personal ramifications. How those outcomes would manifest for Anna, Lisa, Shirine, and Barrett was not something they could have predicted. They left home uncertain about how a new country and culture might shape their lives: their goals, outlooks, and personal relationships. The physical journey was only the start of a long and arduous process.

Cultural adaptation was once considered a linear process of exchanging one cultural identity for another, a view that assumed assimilation was not only inevitable but also desired (Fortier 2000, 19; see Phinney et al. 2001, 505). In the 1990s the analytical focus shifted. Anthropologists began to explore the concept of transnationalism, which suggested that, in sync with globalization and technological development, migrants were able to maintain closely connected ties to their first homelands. Because of these continuing economic, political, and social connections, migrants were now leading dual lives across borders, moving easily between different countries and cultures.[4]

With the acceptance of transnationalism, longstanding explanations of how immigrants negotiated adaptation, in particular assimilation, began to be questioned. The inevitable separation from former identities, cultures, and homelands was no longer assumed to be the only, or best, option. More recently, though, researchers have suggested that earlier models are not incompatible with transnationalism and that immigrants can live transnationally connected lives while also assimilating and finding a sense of belonging within host cultures.[5]

Regardless of which theories of adaptation apply, adjustment to a new culture requires immigrants to go through a process of learning. The nuances of language, traditions, and invisible social mores must all be acquired to become comfortable in a new environment (see Masgoret and Ward 2006; Rudmin 2009, 110–111). The field of psychology has generally referred to this experience as acculturation, which, with regard to individuals (as opposed to groups), is defined as the change that occurs from exposure to a new culture. Acculturation is the process of incorporating the new culture's values, viewpoints, and behaviors (Sam 2006a, 14).[6]

The first few years these émigré women lived in their adopted countries were by far the most intense in terms of learning and adaptation. As new immigrants, they were faced daily with the task of trying to understand what was expected of them. Countless unwritten rules and cultural references exist in every society, and not knowing them quickly marks a person as a stranger. These rules can run the gamut: how bread should be sliced and served, whether it is appropriate to wave to a passing car, how a line is formed in a crowd, and what is appropriate to wear to a party. Discovering these details can take years and involve a steep learning curve.

How acculturation occurs and the challenges it presents varies considerably. Personal motives for immigration, personality, and cultural preferences affect the ease with which immigrants learn and potentially accept differing aspects of a new culture (Akhtar 1999, 6–7; see Kosic 2006 and Lechuga and Fernandez 2011). Acculturation can be affected by how dissimilar the first and second cultures are, past experience moving between cultures, the individual's positions in both the sending and receiving societies, and how the host culture receives the immigrant (Berry 1997, 21–23;

Portes and Rumbaut 2006, 201). The attitudes and characteristics of immigrants and the response of receiving societies are therefore interactive in terms of how any one person adapts to a new culture (Berry 2008, 331–332; see Phinney et al. 2001).

The process of adjustment is affected by not only individual situations but also the larger contextual forces such as socioeconomics, politics, history, and gender and ethnic pressures (Bhatia and Ram 2009, 147–148; Brettell 2008, 136). All of these factors can, on one hand, buffer or, on the other, exacerbate the stress that comes with acculturation (Lueck and Wilson 2011, 188). Social support, gender roles, education, economic status, and discrimination, in particular, played substantial roles in the immigration experiences of Anna, Lisa, Shirine, and Barrett and are discussed next.

෴

Many immigrants, especially those who move for economic reasons, go to a location where there is an enclave of other people from their first culture (Brettell 2008, 129–131; Deaux 2006, 109–110). Districts, such as "Chinatowns," are in many large cities worldwide, but even suburbs and rural areas now have ethnic social networks. Newcomers join these enclaves because they provide connections and information about jobs and residences. Social networks help new immigrants discern the subtle cultural rules that surround them from the moment they arrive. But in addition to practicalities, ethnic enclaves link immigrants to people from their same background who speak the same language and understand the experience of migration (Portes and Rumbaut 2006, 40–42).

What about immigrants who do not have an ethnic enclave? Anna, Lisa, Shirine, and Barrett were all in this circumstance. None of them had the benefit of an immigrant community that could help them adjust to their new lives or provide a sense of affiliation with their past. They had to forge new ways of relating to their social environments on their own.

A common thread that runs through the lives of these four women is that their most significant friendships in their new countries are with other foreigners. Their friends may not share a culture of origin, but they do share the experience of immigration. This commonality bridged cultural differences: whether or not they shared a language or ethnicity, they did share a deep understanding of what it is like to live in a foreign country. This particular kind of support was something that no one else could provide.

Although they did not consciously set out to do it, Anna, Lisa, and Barrett gravitated to other foreigners and created their own enclave of immigrant friends. While over time they made close friendships with locals, their immigrant friends have been the ones who filled the void left by the absence of family. Shirine, however, never had the equivalent of an "enclave" of immigrant friends during her transitional years. Virtually all of her friendships remained tenuous because she never stopped feeling different from everyone else. Most of those with whom she did have enduring relationships, however, were also foreigners. Of the four, Barrett alone would have had the opportunity to find an enclave of sorts in with the U.S. expatriate community in Caracas, but as she once said to me, why would she want to belong to a group of "expats" if she had never been a "pat"?

Learning a new culture is also complicated by language, and language learning is a long road. The difference between the skill needed to order food at a restaurant and to have conversations about layered or nuanced topics such as values, family dynamics, and moods is dramatic. A lack of language skills reminds everyone that you are an outsider. Even a fluent speaker of a foreign language does not easily understand humor or subtle cultural references and can usually be identified by accent. Learning a new language is not just about words—it is also about learning to think in a new way, a process that changes the individual (Agnew 2005b, 44–45). Learning to "think like a Norwegian," for example, is something that Anna says she still has not completely mastered, even after more than twenty years. Anna chose to master Norwegian as soon as she could, but realistically she had no other choice. Anna was fully aware that if she did not learn the language, she would be socially isolated, especially in the years before she made her foreign friends.

During Shirine's childhood migrations, language was an enormous obstacle. Like Anna, her choices were limited, and learning languages became an expected part of her life. By the time Shirine came to the United States, she already spoke English well. Despite her need to learn the nuances of American English, her language skills made the transition much simpler than it was when she moved to Germany, Paris, or Milan.

Once she arrived in Caracas, Barrett consciously immersed herself fully in the Spanish language. The lack of participation in an English-speaking enclave was related to her strong motivation to be a part of Venezuelan culture. Lisa did not have language issues when she moved to Miami, but as she pointed out, learning how to be Jewish was as difficult as learning a language.

Many studies have found a relationship between gender and the stress that comes with immigration. Women are generally faced with inferior status and in addition must negotiate the differences that exist between their first and second cultures for the multiple roles of mother, wife, and employee (Lueck and Wilson 2011, 188). Whether gender status has a positive or negative effect will most likely depend on how women are treated in each culture and how they individually respond (see Berry 2006, 49).

Only Anna and Shirine mentioned gender as an influence in terms of their immigrant experience, and both related positive responses. In Norway Anna was able to escape some of the traditional expectations of females that negatively influenced her childhood. Shirine described being uncomfortable with the way women were publicly treated in Iran and, like Anna, appreciated the different attitudes she experienced in Europe and the United States.

Regardless of whether they addressed the issue in the telling of their life stories, the trajectory of each woman's life post-immigration was undoubtedly affected by her gender. The underlying patriarchal norms of the sending and receiving cultures supported each of the four women in her choice to move to or remain in her partner's homeland rather than her own. Lisa, like Shirine and Anna, wanted to be a mother, and all three accepted the role of homemaker in their immediate families; Lisa also elected to convert to her husband's religion. These choices, too, were compatible and probably encouraged by each woman's culture, both pre- and post-immigration. None of their decisions were simple ones but were based on complex and varied situations. They themselves may not have been aware of how their internalized cultural values affected their choices.

Pressure to become a part of their new countries and cultures existed for all four women, whether that pressure was self-induced or a result of family circumstances or external factors. While individual immigrants place different levels of importance and value on ethnicity as an aspect of their sense of self (Deaux 2006, 103–106), female immigrants tend to be expected to take on the role of "culture bearers" in their families. They have the added pressure of passing on ethnic traditions and language as well as guiding their children through the maze of two cultures (Sam 2006b, 409–410).

For Anna and Lisa, these responsibilities became increasingly problematic. They not only lacked the support of an enclave; they were married to men who were members of the dominant culture. As a result, they were completely isolated in their efforts to preserve or pass along their own cultural identity. Attempting to do so required a level of determination and emotional energy that was difficult to maintain. (This is not unusual. My nephew Thomas refers to his parents' efforts to maintain each of their different holiday customs as a contest to "outculture" one another.)

Lisa's situation was particularly difficult, as she had committed to raising her children in the Jewish faith and was therefore doubly conflicted about passing along her background. In the initial years of her immigration, Lisa tried to celebrate both her own traditional holidays and those of her husband, but she eventually found it too taxing. Though Canadian and American cultures are similar, Lisa still struggled in Florida, especially when it came to giving up Christian holidays and the link they provided to her past. And though she was not as well versed as her husband in Jewish traditions, as a woman she accepted the role of holiday planner without question, a circumstance that clearly added to the challenges of her immigration.

Anna never consciously decided to keep Maori culture from her children. She assumed they would eventually learn, perhaps by asking questions or when they were able to visit New Zealand. Her priority was making certain that her children felt in all ways Norwegian, even though their mother was a foreigner. This burden, plus taking care of a family, learning how to be Norwegian herself, and working, was enough to consume her days. Culturally and linguistically isolated from New Zealand, she found it simpler to allow a Norwegian identity to infuse her consciousness as well as her children's. Anna's Maori identity did not disappear, but over time it became absorbed into her Norwegian existence.

Given that Shirine had never felt a sense of belonging in Iran, she did not feel burdened to teach her children about Persian or Muslim holidays. In Denver, Shirine was surrounded by American traditions, and she was willing to incorporate them into her family's life. Still, Shirine tried to retain the European aspects of her cultural identity because, like Lisa, she knew that doing so was a matter of self-preservation: if she did not hold on to some of her past, she would lose herself completely.

Barrett did not have the concern of passing on her culture or religion to children. Letting go of U.S. culture happened without much struggle, because Venezuelan ways of being fit her so well. The pressure Barrett experienced came from those she left behind: her family in the United States, who did not understand why she would want to give up any part of her cultural identity or belong anywhere else.

Of the four women profiled, only Anna's appearance was different enough from the dominant host culture to be immediately and consistently apparent, and she was the only one who related feeling discrimination. Looking physically different from the dominant culture can mean that the perception of being an "outsider" may never be eliminated (Gullestad 2002). It is not possible to fit in simply by changing attire or behavior. No longer an insider, someone who by virtue of birth or personal history has a "right" to be in a place, the immigrant has become a interloper and may continually feel the need to justify her presence in her new location (Croucher 2009, 171). Significant anxiety can result (Deaux 2006, 84–86; Lueck and Wilson 2011, 188; Mak and Nesdale 2001) and may either create pressure to outwardly abandon the immigrant's first culture and language or alternatively cause a reaction against the receiving culture (Phinney et al. 2001, 494; Deaux 2006, 153, 155).

Anna did not attribute her desire to fit in with Norwegian culture (and with Olav's Norwegian family) directly to her appearance, yet she did acknowledge the emotional devastation she felt after suffering a verbal attack in the taxi and her worries about being teased by children. Notwithstanding her pride in her Maori background, the awareness of standing out must have affected her. She chose quite deliberately to ignore any potential discrimination or awkwardness that resulted from her ethnicity and tried to internalize Norwegian culture as best she could.

Though the trauma of being different could easily have been undermining, Anna was eventually able to respond with resilience. The stress of the taxi incident, rather than disabling Anna, ultimately led her to a stronger sense of self-determination. She was clear that she would not allow racism to control her.

Without minimizing the difficulties these four women faced as immigrants, it is important to point out the buffers that shielded them from some of the trauma other immigrants suffer. Unlike most migrants, these women had the opportunity and means to leave home under circumstances that were not physically or financially threatening. None immigrated as part of a social or economic underclass, by virtue of background or marriage to a native. The respective governments involved sanctioned their migrations, which allowed them to travel and work without fear of deportation. Education and economic circumstances, in particular, have been found to correlate with lower immigrant stress (Berry 1997, 22; see Bhatia and Ram 2009).

Education was an enormous advantage for Shirine and Barrett. Lisa and Anna did not have university educations, but both are perceptive and astute. They also had the benefit of being married to men who were educated and able to financially provide for them. All four women also had social buffers. Lisa and Anna knew they were going to a place where their partners had family and friends to support them, and Shirine left with her sister and went to the protected environment of the college. Barrett, though not married, had social buffers in the form of the Venezuelan friends she knew prior to arriving. The emotional support of these networks did not eliminate all stressors or provide the comfort of a cultural enclave, but they certainly provided a cushion between cultures.

Though Shirine's and Anna's first cultures were dramatically different from the new cultures they encountered, both had learned to flow between traditions as children: Shirine between Persian and Western, Anna between Maori and Kiwi. Lisa and Barrett had also experienced moving and were aware, to some extent, of the trials they would face as immigrants. The United States and Canada, as well and Christian and Jewish cultures, have similar roots, which provided some familiarity and ease for Lisa.

◦❧

Perhaps even more important than cultural learning, by living in an environment in which every small difference between themselves and the majority is underscored, immigrants learn about themselves. Alienation and estrangement from the familiar becomes a resource for self-knowledge (Rapport and Dawson 1998b, 9). In other words, as immigrants begin to see themselves through a different lens, they may begin to view their identities in a new way.

The route through identity change leads immigrants to what can be referred to as an "in-between" or "liminal" state, during which time they move beyond former cultural barriers and allow themselves to adopt hybrid identities. Existing in the space between cultures, they are neither inside nor outside, neither foreigner nor native (see Bhabha 1994, 2–5; Gilroy 1993, 19).[7]

From one perspective, the "in-between" position in which migrants find themselves has the possibility of being a creative, transformative location. Without former cultural restrictions, immigrants have the opportunity to view themselves and both their first and second cultures from a new angle and to actively decide which of each to incorporate into their current lives. Open to new ways of thinking, they have the advantage of being able to reinvent themselves (see Hall 1992, 311).

Barrett and, during her first years in the United States, Shirine felt a tremendous sense of personal freedom living away from cultures they found stifling. Barrett abandoned many of the North American social rules she felt were restrictive; Shirine felt liberated by the open-minded attitudes at the arts college she attended. Having immigrated to locations where few people knew them, all four women could present themselves, including their cultural and familial backgrounds, any way they chose.

The possibility of a hybrid identity should not be romanticized, however. For Anna and Lisa, and for Shirine (once she was married and living in Denver), the pressure to belong overshadowed any desire to maintain bicultural identities. Regardless of whether this pressure was self-imposed or external, it was still powerful. Comfortably interweaving their cultural identities was a process that took time. How these four women found a way to cope with this aspect of their individual route is discussed further in Parts III and IV.

Being disconnected from one's history, whether cultural or geographical, often brings with it a new awareness and appreciation of the meaning of "home" (Case 1996, 11–12). A sense of home, then, is dynamic and processual (Case 1996, 11–13), as is identity. In a new and different environment, individuals tend to see places more self-consciously. Comparisons to home provoke memories and emotions of which the person may not previously have been aware (Basso 1996, 55).

The desire for an idealized sense of home may not correspond to a geographical place but instead may represent a quest for personal fulfillment. The search for home then becomes analogous to a religious pilgrimage (Tucker 1994, 184). The experience of immigration, like pilgrimage, is a journey of transition between places (Casey 1996, 23–24). Similar to those of someone on a spiritual pilgrimage, the migrant's senses of personal and cultural identity are affected by the process of learning to survive in an unfamiliar setting. Along the way, there are "in-between," liminal stages when immigrants feel both at home and not at home.[8] Every aspect of life is influenced by the immigrant experience, from consequential decisions to simple daily rituals. The journey begins with movement, but the transitions do not end simply because the physical journey may be complete.

On their own journeys, Anna, Lisa, Shirine, and Barrett left behind the familiar, not knowing what they might encounter or how they would feel after arriving. They hoped to find meaning in their lives in a way that was different and perhaps more satisfying than before.

Regardless of whether changes in identity and perceptions of home are seen in the long run as constructive or painful, the kinds of transition they require are life-altering. Belonging in a new culture is unlikely without letting go of at least some of the old, and this can create a sense of loss or confusion. With one foot in each location, migrants do not entirely fit in anywhere and must find a way to balance the pressure to assimilate with the need to hold on to the past. For some, the ability to move forward from this twilight or liminal region of time, space, and identity requires more than the practical aspects of learning but also a spiritually transformative process to occur,[9] a process that leads to new levels of self-understanding.

Lisa experienced this in a dramatic way during the conversion process and later when she began to recognize how arduous it had become to let go of Christian holiday traditions. Shirine was led to personal and spiritual exploration as a result of the strain in her personal life, a circumstance that was inextricably connected to her immigration. The realization for Barrett that she had "grown up to be me" in Venezuela was emotional, but the process also had a deep spiritual aspect, one she readily acknowledges.

෴

Like the imaginary lines that are drawn to create borders between countries, the divisions in lives are also imaginary. Events or circumstances can be used to demarcate the chapters of life: this was how life was before children and after children, before taking a new job and after, before immigration and after. This does not mean, however, that the moment an event occurs a person immediately has a new definition of home or identity.

Living in a different country and culture for more than twenty years changed the perceptions and feelings all four of these women had about home. Their stories support the idea that finding a sense of home is a fluid process during which immigrants move back and forth between belonging and unease, making their way along a continuum of feelings that change over time.[10] The changes resulting from both typical life events and by the exceptional event of immigration most certainly brought a measure of ambiguity to these women's lives. Accepting situations fraught with ambiguity, though difficult, was to their benefit, because ambiguity forced them to improvise as they learned along the way (Bateson 1989; 1994, 235). In doing so, they could find ways to connect to and have continuity with both their pasts and their futures (Clandinin and Connelly 2000, 7).

III

TURNING POINTS

Realization, Transformation, and Commitment

All of a sudden I got the strength. I went to France, and all
of a sudden I got the strength. I thought to myself, "That's
enough. I'm getting old. . . . I want another life, and I'll
never live a life if I don't give myself a chance."

—SHIRINE

CROSSROADS

"Adaptation," "acculturation," "assimilation," "transnationalism": these are some of the words social scientists have used
to describe how immigrants navigate their lives. These words,
however, do not address how, or whether, an immigrant might stop feeling
like an outsider. The ability to function within and to understand a new
culture is vital for survival and social ease. But adapting does not mean
being well adapted (Berry 1997, 20), and functioning is not the same as
belonging. This vocabulary helps us gain understanding of the process of
migrant adjustment, but it does not fully address the depth and complexity .
of emotion that surrounds the ideas of place and home.

Home as a structure becomes important when it is permeated with
memories and experiences (Sixsmith 1986, 292), and whether good or
bad, these memories create continuity and ties to a place. The locations of
childhood continue to feel like "home" because of the cyclical memories of
holidays and annual routines. Childhood locations become symbolic homes
even for adults who may be physically far removed.

In a new place, however, no such memories yet exist. Finding a sense of
belonging requires whatever time must pass before new meaningful events
occur and become indelibly written in our consciousness. Watching our
own children growing up and having their first day of school or spending
holidays with our spouses and friends can eventually take on as much significance as memories from our childhood. A place is unlikely to feel like
home until we have stored some memories there.

The physical structure a person lives in is only one aspect of home. As a concept, home is better defined as the place where there is a sense of grounding, from which we can go out into the world and know who and what we are. It is the place we choose to return to when we want to feel safe and welcomed. Our homes and our identities are tightly wrapped. Like it or not, where we call "home" also defines us to the world, and others will make assumptions about us on the basis of that affiliation.

Creating a new home does not require that old bonds be let go or that affection for an old home suddenly disappear. Like any other human connection, people's relationships with places take time to develop. Strong bonds do not appear overnight; nor do they disappear in an instant. Sometimes connections grow quietly, until one day their existence rises to the surface of consciousness. But if a move is perceived as impermanent, then investing emotionally in a place and creating connections with the people who live there might feel like too much trouble and be resisted. Feelings of stability and continuity, on the other hand, tend to support a movement toward commitment and belonging (compare Relph 1976, 38; Akhtar 1999, 94).

Life's turning points can directly affect emotions about belonging and home (Gurney 1997, 383). At critical moments in life, questions may be raised about where and to what we are committed. The definition of one's home is therefore often connected to the tension that exists between commitment and separation (Bammer 1994, xiv). The recognition that the meaning of home may have changed can be a catalyst for a new self-definition and new ideas about the future.

Births and deaths, the beginnings or ends of relationships, and job changes are all events whose effects radiate throughout our lives. The moments described in this section are certainly not the only turning points in these four women's lives, but they are the ones that pertain most directly to their acceptance of where they belong and where, as immigrants, they now call home.

Anna

New Zealand was Anna's home for the first nineteen years of her life. Though leaving felt strange, Anna was not distraught, because she believed the good-byes were only temporary. Like most nineteen-year-olds, Anna gave no thought to the possibility of unexpected outcomes. Anna and Olav went to Norway in good spirits, looking forward to the year to come.

Life in Norway began to take on an easy rhythm within a few weeks of their arrival. Other than learning a new language, Anna's life was mostly domestic. The routine of caring for the baby and cleaning kept her occupied most of the time, and she hardly noticed she was in a different environment.

After about three months in Norway, Olav came home from school early one afternoon with a telegram. Olav never missed class, and his unexpected arrival was concerning: "I got a fright. 'What are you doing home now?' And after a while he just told me my mom's dead." Stunned, Anna could only keep repeating, "No, no, don't say that; don't say that." Anna's mother was fine when she left New Zealand. What Olav was saying made no sense to her. The conversation seemed dramatic and unreal, as if they were reading the script of an old movie.

Anna was racked with remorse and sorrow. All she could think of was an odd conversation she had had with her mother shortly before leaving New Zealand. Driving around town while running errands for the trip, they started talking about the upcoming year. Her mother was upset about the long separation, and though Anna was anxious too, she thought it would be easier if her mother was not aware of it. Pretending to be stoic and nonchalant, Anna told her mother matter-of-factly that there was nothing to worry about. In fact, if anything bad should happen, even if her mother were to become ill or die, Anna would not come back early. What would be the point? There would be nothing she could do to help anyway.

The memory of that prescient conversation still haunts Anna: "I don't know how much I hurt her by saying that, but, you know, we had gotten close by that time; from when Per was born, I had her a lot in my house. And I felt a very close, very close connection with my mother, more than ever earlier. But then I still managed to turn around and tell her that if something happened or she died, I'm not coming back for the funeral."

Anna tried desperately to call her many brothers and sisters but could reach no one. They had all gone back to their mother's hometown to mourn, and in the small village there was no phone service. Returning to New Zealand for the funeral was not an option, because there simply was not enough money for the plane fare. Anna felt as if she were living in a vacuum, trapped with no information about what had happened to her mother and no one from home to share her grief.

To make matters worse, a few days after the news of her mother's death, Anna received a letter from one of her sisters. Sent the same day their mother died, the letter suggested that Anna write more often. Their mother was missing her terribly, crying whenever she thought about Anna being so far away. Still trying to protect her mother, Anna had deliberately written only a few letters. Unfortunately the attempt to keep her mother from worrying had backfired: "I thought, you know, that's my way of hoping that if she thinks [I don't miss her], it's easier for her to cope with me not being there. But I'll never know. No."

Concerned about Anna, Olav took a few days off. He and his father took Anna out on the fjord. On a little boat, they spent hours together fishing and talking, helping Anna take her mind off her mother and family back in New Zealand. Away from the house and her routine, Anna could see the dramatic panorama of the Norwegian landscape. Grey autumn skies, the rocky shoreline, and rippling water helped Anna find some calm and a semblance of peace.

For a time after her mother's death, Anna wanted desperately to "pack up and go back to New Zealand." She wanted the year to be over so that they could leave. But gradually, the realization that her mother would not be there when she returned began to sink in. Anna's perspective about her life was undergoing a sea change.

Where Anna belonged was now indeterminate, and the idea of staying in Norway slowly slipped into her consciousness:

> 'Cause I thought, you know, my mother's not there anymore. I don't really have anything to go back to. . . . [T]hen I started living for myself, after my mother died. I started living more for myself. And we just took one day at a time, but I felt that I was going to be [in Norway]. I didn't have anything to go back to. My family would always be there but not my mother. I don't know, the mothers, they're the pillars of all creation; let's say it like that. I'm sure they are. So when she wasn't there anymore, I just accepted that I'm here and why should I move? What am I going to go back to, a grieving family? After so long, they've got their own lives, and I've got my life.

Anna did not return to New Zealand for thirteen years. She eventually settled into a life that had little resemblance to her childhood. She stayed in touch with several of her brothers and sisters, but for the most part, New Zealand became a part of the past, not the present. Her memories of that period were something that she kept to herself. Bounded by distance and difference, the worlds of her past and the present had no connection.

In 1991, Anna's siblings finally decided to have a traditional Maori unveiling ceremony for their mother's tombstone. Anna felt she had to go. After all the years that had passed, she would finally have the opportunity to grieve with her family and to make amends for missing the funeral. Nora, Anna's younger child, was then eleven years old, and Anna decided to take her along. Nora would have a chance to meet her relatives and see where her mother came from. Per would stay in Norway with his father: "At least Per can say he's been there, even though he was just a child. He's been there; he was born there. And now Nora can say she's been there. I just had to give her the chance."

The first thing Anna noticed when she walked off the plane in Auckland was the smell of New Zealand, the smell of home. "I had lived in Auckland, so I know the smell. I imagine and I still imagine that. Yeah, it's sweet, like a bakery smell."

Her sister drove them to the town where their parents had lived—and to the house that Anna had lived in after the death of her grandmother. One of Anna's brothers now lives in this house, and when they arrived, all of her fifteen siblings and their children were standing in the front yard waiting. Dressed in Maori costumes made of woven flax, they began to sing a traditional Maori welcoming song, calling Anna and Nora to come home.

Seeing her family again and hearing the melodies of her childhood threw Anna off balance: "It was spooky. It was my sisters and my nieces; you know, they stand on one side and all the singing and calling us, calling us and walking with us to their home, and we went in, and there was people everywhere. . . . [I]t was so touching that I just cried my eyes out . . . because, you know, I'm in my mom's house for the first time since I left."

Once inside, everyone lined up to greet Anna individually. Seeing all of these people again was not how Anna had imagined it: "I was very excited and, oh, you know, wondering how they are, my family are, and what they look like. But I was expecting to see everything the same as when I left; I really was. That's stupid, but, you know, I always just pictured them the last time I saw them, [that] that's what I'm going home to. And I remember asking one of the girls, you know, 'Who are you?' and 'Do I know you?' And she said, 'Yes, because I'm your younger sister.' Oh, and that was bad. You know, I'll never forget that." That sister had been only eight years old when Anna left, and now she was a grown woman.

Anna then began to notice that everyone around her was primarily speaking Maori. After all the time away and no contact with the language, the words sounded strange. She could not understand what people were saying. Within minutes Anna knew that the snapshot image that she had held in her heart was no longer an accurate depiction of her family. They had changed, and so had she, and how she fit in the picture was suddenly and disquietingly unclear.

When the greetings were over, Anna and Nora watched while a small group began to perform the customary Maori welcoming dance. Originally intended to intimidate enemy visitors, the dance is intense and frightening. Sticking out their tongues, taking on aggressive postures, they moved about brandishing long clubs while making loud, ferocious noises. Frozen in place and staring wide-eyed, Nora had her first glimpse into her mother's past and her own Maori heritage. She had never seen people greet one another by gently pressing their noses together or watched loud, frightening dances. The experience was strange and extraordinary, and after the initial surprise Nora began to enjoy it.

Everyone then filed out to the backyard. A feast had been prepared for the whole family, using the time-consuming Maori method of burying food in an underground pit or *hangi* and cooking it with hot rocks. Everyone helped themselves and sat down on long benches or the grass and ate with a plate in their lap.

Adjusting to the once-familiar surroundings, people, and food, Anna began to unwind. Someone began to play the guitar, and everyone sang along: "It's so lovely. If you ever should go to New Zealand, meet a family and go to a Maori party. They've got lovely voices; they just love singing and playing guitars, and oh, it was so wonderful." All of the time and distance between Anna and her family evaporated for a few hours.

As the night wore on, the party became rowdier, and more and more alcohol was consumed. Now sitting inside the house, Anna could hear her brothers arguing and the sound of things falling to the ground. The atmosphere began to remind Anna of events in her childhood, when drinking led to arguments and violence. Her happiness dimmed as old and much-too-familiar feelings of fear crept in. Anna was exhausted from the long flights and the anticipation of coming back and used this as an excuse for herself and Nora to go to bed.

Anna and Nora spent three weeks in New Zealand. After Anna decided to avoid late-night parties, the rest of the trip went well. Nora played with her many cousins and went horseback riding, and they had barbecues on the beach. Anna was having a wonderful time, yet she could not stop feeling conflicted. She felt pulled in two directions, missing her husband and son but pleased to be back in New Zealand. Seeing her roots through a new set of eyes, she was confused. Living away for so long, she had become used to the Norwegian way of life, their habits and attitudes. She found herself observing New Zealand with a new and critical viewpoint, comparing and weighing it against the positive aspects of Norway.

Ironically, Anna had done the opposite for years. When in Norway, she had thought the people were uptight and too concerned about outward appearances. Houses were always kept immaculate, with even the ceilings washed, in case someone might drop by for a visit. No one in Norway would have a ceremonial party where the guests were expected to eat sitting on the ground, even if it was outside. Anna now noticed that her siblings did not bother much with the upkeep of their property. If their houses were not cleaned today, they could be cleaned tomorrow or the next day. She saw that they were more concerned about enjoying their company than worrying about appearances.

Anna had changed. She could no longer understand why things went unrepaired and the yards were untidy. On the other hand, she knew that once she was back in Norway, her thinking would reverse: "I thought, 'Oh, there's more to life than just cleaning up dust and doing this and doing that.' I would just go backwards and forwards comparing. New Zealand is too much on that laid-back side. And Norway, the days aren't long enough to do everything you feel that you need to do."

The emotional connections Anna had presumed would still exist with her siblings were weaker than before:

> It took thirteen years before I went back to New Zealand again. It was really weird, the brothers and sisters that I didn't know that I should have known; you know, if I'd met them on the street, I would have just gone straight past them. It's like with this family bond that I had before I left New Zealand, and family memories.

I was expecting to see that when I came back again. But it's just not like that. People just go on with their lives and do what they're expected to do. So that quite shocked me in a way. And after the first time I visited New Zealand, I knew it wasn't for me, [that] I didn't belong there. Believe it or not.

The alienation Anna was feeling was exacerbated by a renewed sense of sorrow for the loss of her mother. Away from her childhood environment, Anna had been unable to mourn fully until now. The return brought back raw feelings of grief. Her family, on the other hand, had healed these wounds long ago. The tombstone unveiling was poignant, but they were past the agonizing feelings that come with recent loss.

Not wanting to spoil the visit, Anna felt obligated to keep her feelings hidden: "My family saw this as a happy event. But I didn't. For me it was a sad occasion. But then again I had Nora with me, so it was a lot that I kept in because of her. I didn't want her to see my reaction to things while I was there. I just wanted everything to seem happy. I didn't want her to experience the sadness in this occasion through me."

Anna and Nora returned to Norway at Christmastime. In contrast to the New Zealand summer they had just left, Norway was cold and snowy. They walked into a house full of candles and holiday decorations, and waiting for them was a traditional Norwegian Christmas meal that Olav had arranged. The next few days were hectic with holiday events and parties, but despite the dramatic change of both scenery and people, Anna was happy to be back. It felt surprisingly good to be in Norway for a winter Christmas.

Anna's first visit to New Zealand was a bittersweet mix of joy and sorrow. While positive in many ways, it did not bring the emotional replenishment that Anna had hoped for. The years away had been transforming. A young woman when she left New Zealand, Anna was now in her thirties. Moving through early adulthood, marriage, children, and work, she had grown up while she was gone and had forgotten how different her present life was from her past. Anna still loved New Zealand, but Norway was now her safe haven in the world.

Lisa

Miami is a city of great diversity, both ethnically and economically. Neighborhoods built both near the beach and in the western suburbs can range from the superrich, with lavish mansions and manicured lawns, to middle-class suburban, to rows of semiderelict homes interspersed with strip malls and loud freeway overpasses. In Miami, there is everyone and everything, from the most refined to the most garish, from the richest and the poorest of America, and everything in between.

The economic diversity in Miami appears to be somewhat seamless. Driving to Lisa's house I traveled in just minutes from an eight-lane freeway to an incredibly crowded main-artery six-lane road and suddenly into a peaceful neighborhood built on a wide canal. Unlike more recently developed South Florida areas, this neighborhood has been around long enough to have larger trees and flowering bushes. It has a sense of permanency, of being inhabited by long-term residents and families rather than part-time snowbirds.

When I went to Lisa's house for our first interview, she answered the door and immediately apologized for the mess I would soon see. Having lived in the house for fifteen years, Lisa had decided that it was time to give the 1970s-designed kitchen a facelift. In the family room dishes were haphazardly stacked on the floor, and measuring tapes, tools, paint chips, and tile samples were scattered around the countertops.

Lisa's four-bedroom house is large, and the back terrace directly overlooks the canal. The main rooms have an open design and picture windows, and at that time they were furnished with good-quality but older mismatched furniture. Only one small, formal sitting room seemed to have been decorated with any real intention. In contrast, the other rooms immediately revealed that a busy family occupied the house—the most obvious clue being the bicycles stored in the dining room.

As our interviews progressed, so did the remodeling. Within a few months, Lisa had a custom gourmet kitchen, with new stainless steel appliances, granite countertops, a built-in wine rack, and a hand-painted Italian tile splashboard. A year later there was new matching furniture in the living room, new curtains, a redecorated guest bathroom, and new furniture in all of the bedrooms. There were no bicycles to be seen, and the dining room now had an elegant chandelier hanging over the table.

Remodeling the house was not an issue of economics; instead, it reflected Lisa's feelings about how long this house would be her "home." After living in Florida for twenty years, raising three children, and becoming a citizen, she had finally accepted that her stay in Florida was not temporary: "Well, I guess I finally decided I was staying here. I told Jason, 'If we're going to stay here, we need to fix up this house.' I finally realized that I live in this house, and I'd better start acting like it. It's the new, post-forty Lisa!"

The "new, post-forty Lisa" is a woman with a new attitude, no longer willing to passively let her life unfold. This revised version of Lisa is more decisive and confident than she used to be. Her newfound self-assurance is about more than just household decisions; it is about her identity and her place in the world.

Through all the years of marriage, motherhood, making friends, and working in Miami, Lisa had always felt she was living a transitory life. As a sort of permanent sojourner, she had never entirely accepted the United States as her home. Moving to Florida and getting married had certainly been significant as far as her immigration, but Lisa had never assumed the move was forever. A big piece of her heart remained in Canada. Visiting there still felt like visiting "home."

For at least the first fifteen years she was in the United States, Lisa regularly broached the topic of moving with Jason. If not Vancouver, maybe they could live in Washington State; it made little difference, as long as they would be nearer to her family. That was the primary reason that she never paid much attention to the Miami house. Why make the financial or emotional investment in improvements, if their attachment to the area was only provisional?

The reality, however, was that leaving Miami would be difficult. Jason was entrenched in a business they owned and had built from scratch, and his elderly mother could not be left alone in Florida. But these obstacles did not prevent Lisa from fantasizing about leaving: "For a long time I didn't want to make it home, because I was kind of hoping we would go 'home,' where family is. But then something strange happened, [a] pivotal moment with my family." That moment catalyzed a reevaluation that allowed Lisa to see her situation with more clarity than she ever had before.

Since moving to Florida, Lisa had managed to visit her parents in Canada at least once every year. Jason and the children often came as well, and frequently her parents visited Miami. When she was in Canada, Lisa and her parents had a habit of not planning activities. They preferred to spend time relaxing together around the house, talking and having meals. Lisa loved having this restorative time. At her parents' house there was no hectic schedule, no errands or work. Surrounded by her parents' furniture, books, and pictures, she was sheltered by the objects of her childhood, and this unfailingly brought her a sense of comfort and safety: "These trips, for me, it's great. To go up there, drive that familiar road to my parents' house, and just sit in their house. . . . [I]n the morning, my dad brings me tea in bed, and we have wonderful conversations, or I go crawl in my mother's bed, and we have these wonderful conversations. And then it'll be lunchtime, and then we'll eat lunch, and then all of a sudden it'll be dinner, and we'll eat dinner, and then it's bedtime. You know, that's the routine."

Lisa's husband was not as enthralled with these trips. Relaxing at home was fine for a few days, but it did not have the same appeal for Jason as it did for Lisa. British Columbia is a mecca for outdoor sports, and he always wanted to get out and explore. Lisa tended to feel slightly conflicted when Jason came along to Vancouver. She wanted him there but was forever torn between her own needs, the needs of her parents, and those of her husband.

In the spirit of compromise, Lisa and Jason began to plan side trips when they came to Vancouver. The typical pattern was to spend several days with Lisa's parents and then spend a day in one of the nearby national parks or recreation areas. This seemed to work, and for a number of years they managed to both have quiet time with Lisa's parents and explore the beauty of British Columbia.

Then came the crucial moment and an epiphany for Lisa. Over the millennium-year holidays, on New Year's Eve 1999, Lisa and Jason were in Canada for their annual visit. That year Lisa had arranged for their side trip to be a visit to the Olympic Peninsula in Washington. It was a beautiful day, and the drive around the peninsula was magnificent. Not wanting to rush, and misjudging the distance of the drive, they did not get back until ten o'clock that night. After eight hours in the car, they were tired and not in the mood for a New Year's Eve celebration. Unfortunately, they picked the wrong night to be late. The entire family, including Lisa's siblings and their children, had agreed to meet at seven o'clock that evening for an ice skating party. The ice rink had been rented, and everyone was there except Lisa and Jason, who had broken their promise to be back in time to come.

Lisa's parents, usually reserved, were furious and showed it. As sometimes happens in families, years of emotions seemed to burst out of everyone at the same time. Lisa's parents did not hold back in expressing their disappointment. They were hurt that every time Lisa visited Vancouver, she left the family to go off alone with Jason. Lisa was angry that they failed to understand her need to be with them and also have some holiday time with her husband. There were harsh words between all of them—unusual in this quiet, proper family. Underlying the argument was a feeling of loss and sadness that their time together was always limited, and this awareness made the situation all the more difficult and appalling for everyone.

Lisa was devastated. She felt responsible for everyone's pain and for ruining the family's celebration. As they all stood there glaring at each other, she quietly walked away, put on her skates, and went on to the rink alone. Frustrated and incredibly sad, she skated around and around the empty rink. In the dark, with tears running down her face, her thoughts circled around the choices she had made in her life. On a beautiful winter night, with stars above her, snow on the ground, and surrounded by people she loved, Lisa felt no joy. The thrill of the millennium New Year had disappeared, as had the warm feelings of being with her parents and having had a romantic day alone with her husband. What was supposed to be a special family event had turned sour, and she was in the middle of it, feeling guilty, confused, and frightened about what this flare-up might really represent.

The difficult evening was not over yet. Lisa's brother, James, was married to a conservative Christian, and they had invited the family to attend their church's midnight service. Though no one else in the family belonged to the church, they had all agreed to go. Lisa rarely went to churches since her conversion to Judaism and had become less and less comfortable in them, particularly those with a more fundamentalist outlook. Jason's presence only added to her anxiety.

The service was held outside. Clouds had rolled in, and now instead of starlight they were sitting in freezing rain. The air was cold, and the speaker's New Year's Eve message was one of sin and redemption. Even though this was not the kind of Christianity that Lisa was raised with, the minister's words still evoked in her a sense of separation between her own family, their religious heritage, and the Jewish faith that she had finally begun to internalize.

The estrangement Lisa felt from her parents and siblings was all the more heartbreaking since it had been so unexpected: "I felt such a division between me and my family; it was so painful. And, you know, it was raining, and we were standing outside in the rain, listening to this guy preach to us about how we're not doing the right thing, and I'm thinking I'm like a foreigner in my own place. It was horrible. And I really think that was a pivotal moment for me, because I could not wait to get on the plane and come back to Florida to my house—back to my outdated, outmodeled, disorganized life. I was thrilled to come home."

The rift with Lisa's parents was over by the next day, and no long-term harm was done to their relationships. But Lisa's way of thinking about her life had changed. If her home was in Florida, she should appreciate and make the most of it. Now it was time to move forward, and within a few months after returning to Florida, Lisa decided she should finally acknowledge her commitment to the United States and submit her application for citizenship.

Lisa was a naturalized citizen of Canada. Still, the idea of giving up that citizenship was disquieting. Her parents had worked hard to give her a good life, and by formally abandoning Canada she felt that on some level she was betraying their efforts. Holding on to her Canadian citizenship was also a personal safety valve and a hope for the future. When times were hard in Florida, knowing she could go home had given her security; when she missed her family, she could hope that someday she, Jason, and the children might move closer to them.

Months went by between the time Lisa applied for U.S. citizenship and the ceremony. Mounds of paperwork were required to be submitted, and then she had to study for and take an exam. When she finally received the notice for the swearing-in ceremony, Lisa felt ambivalent. The emotional decision had already been made, and the rest just seemed like a formality. Out with some friends the week before the ceremony, Lisa mentioned that she was about to become a citizen. They expressed surprise that she had not asked anyone to come to the ceremony, not even Jason or the children. One of them insisted that Lisa could not go alone and asked to come along.

Once she was there, Lisa was thrilled she had someone to share the experience with: "We were a group of three thousand. And you know what? They do this every couple of months. Thousands and thousands and thousands of people at a time. You go into a big hall, in the convention center, and they have an area for the audience, and everybody's there with their family, their kids, and they're waiving the U.S. flag. And I was crying because I felt my kids should be here. It was a very big deal; it was huge. But why didn't I take my family? Was I crazy?"

Though in hindsight Lisa wishes her family had come, at the time she did not feel it was worth the effort. The three children would have had to be taken out of school, and her husband would have had to reschedule business meetings. Having them attend the ceremony would have been a complication requiring more than the usual juggling of time, so she barely mentioned it. Now, she realizes that downplaying the event was a mistake. This was a meaningful moment in her life, but until she was confronted with her feelings, Lisa was not really aware of how deep they would run.

The ceremony was much more elaborate than Lisa had expected, with speeches by community leaders, live music, and a videotaped messaged from the president. The new citizens were instructed that during the ceremony, the names of all of their countries of origin would be announced. When they heard the name of their country, each person was to stand up. That seemed fairly uncomplicated, but as they began to call the names of the various countries, Lisa suddenly realized the dilemma she was in—should she stand up when they called Canada, South Africa, Zambia, or England? Suddenly she was uncertain where she was "from." While quickly trying to sort this out in her mind, Lisa heard "Canada" over the loudspeaker. She stood up. Identifying herself as South African or British did not feel quite right, and she was afraid that if there was no one else there from Zambia, they would not announce that country. She did not want to miss her chance to stand and acknowledge her past.

The situation was a perfect allegory for her life. During all of her years in the United States, Canada had felt the most like "home," but in actuality she had lived there only half the number of years she had spent in Florida. When she was a child, her parents referred to England as home, but she had lived there for only a few months. Though born in Africa, she had been away for many years. Africa is now another world for her—a place from long ago and quite far from her current life in more ways than just geographical distance. Canada was the obvious choice, but that a choice even had to be made brought a clear insight that the years of nostalgia and longing for her Canadian "home" had not been altogether grounded.

❧

The following year, when the winter holidays were approaching, Lisa and Jason agreed that instead of visiting Lisa's parents, they would take the children on a skiing vacation to the Canadian Rockies. They rented a condo in Whistler for a week and invited Lisa's family to join them there. Her brother and sisters, their families, and Lisa's parents all came for a few days. Being on vacation together and literally not on anyone's home territory helped dissipate any leftover tension from the past year. Everyone relaxed and enjoyed spending time together, skiing and taking in the holiday atmosphere of the resort.

While they were there, the perfect answer to a looming annual problem unexpectedly appeared with the purchase of a time-share condo: "Jason figured that out. I don't know how he did it; it's brilliant. We were walking through the village . . . and my husband said, 'Let's go look,' which is so strange because he hates those things! They showed us [a condo] high on a hill. It's beautiful, and we can get the view of the two mountains. And then at night it's all lit up. There's all the lights, and it's on the ski lift with the beautiful, real Christmas trees, covered with snow." Less than a two-hour drive from Vancouver, Whistler is easily accessible to Lisa's family. Now, for one week each year, they can all get what they want: Jason and the kids can both ski and visit Lisa's parents, Lisa's family can join them in Whistler if they choose, and Lisa can spend time with her parents in either location.

When they are in Whistler, Lisa does not entirely experience the "festive feeling" of Christmas that she yearns for. Though they are in a beautiful place, she is unable to fully come to terms with the fact that these holidays will not be like the Christmases of her childhood. Still, the atmosphere of the ski town, winter weather, and family visits are a vast improvement over having no Christmas or one that is filled with stress and disappointment. As Lisa observed, holidays for many adults are laden with wistful memories and only rarely produce the magic feelings that children are able to experience: "Maybe that's just part of growing up."

Recounting the 1999 New Year's Eve story and the story of her change in citizenship still raises strong emotions for Lisa. For fifteen years she had been living between her past and present, uncertain about what she should hold on to or let go. What was initially a painful and frightening moment in her life she can now, in retrospect, see as a positive, almost liberating, turning point. Though painful, the crack in the illusion of unrealistically perfect memories permitted Lisa to let go of some of her attachment to Canada and to embrace her life and commitment to the United States: "I'm an American now. It's sad and hard to say, but it's true . . . because my family's not; my family is Canadian."

Shirine

Early in Shirine's life, a pattern had been established of moving to a different country every few years. Alternating between Iran and a new place, with new rules and a new language, became normalized. None of these mini-immigrations were intended to be permanent. Time parameters were assumed, and as she grew up Shirine understood that getting too settled or too attached was a futile undertaking. She learned at a young age not to become emotionally involved in any particular place or person.

As an adult, Shirine wanted to ensure that her own children were not repeatedly uprooted as she had been. Their world would be stable and constant: it would provide comfort and safety, and the location of home would never be in doubt. Accomplishing this was her primary goal, and she was successful. Her children lived in the same house from the time they were small until the youngest was sixteen and the oldest eighteen. For herself, the goal was less easily reached. Try as she might to feel at home, after living for more than twenty years in Denver, Shirine felt trapped, not safe. The connection and belonging she hungered for made only temporary appearances.

Immigration was not Shirine's motive for coming to the United States. Choosing the United States had more to do with pleasing her father by getting an American education than deciding where she wanted to spend her life. After Shirine moved to the Eastern Seaboard to attend school when she was seventeen, her vision of the future was still vague and extended only as far as obtaining a degree. Then she might return to Europe.

The first semester started out well. Attending classes and making new friends occupied the two sisters. Then their lives suddenly and dramatically turned. A few months into the term, Shirine and her sister received a phone call from the Iranian embassy in Washington, DC. They were told to leave school and come to the embassy right away. That no explanation for the sudden invitation was given caused a foreboding in both sisters.

They did as they were told, dropped everything, and managed to arrive in Washington later that evening: "So we packed our stuff and we went, and we were in that house; it was cold and dark, and the envoy comes in the evening, and we've never met him, but we've heard his name. So we're sitting in the huge room, and he's like, 'Well, nice to meet you guys; I have bad news for you. Your father's dead. You can stay here for a week, and you can stay at my house, and you will have a driver, and the servants will take care of you,' and then good-bye. He's gone. And, I mean, where the hell was my mother? I think she was just so overwhelmed she didn't know how to deal with anything."

Now alone in the formal embassy living room, the shocked sisters sat on the couch, unable to speak, not knowing what to do next. Finally reaching their mother a few hours later was not comforting, as she was on the verge of hysteria. She instructed the girls to take some time in Washington to collect themselves and then go back and finish the semester as if nothing had happened. Going to Iran for the funeral was not an option. The situation was much too difficult, and their mother could not take on any additional complications.

When Shirine woke up the next morning in the unfamiliar embassy bedroom, she looked around and felt that "the world was now a bizarre place." Disoriented and bewildered, she felt that she had lost the only anchor in her life. She was eighteen years old and living far away from anything resembling home. Her mother had never been a source of much security, and even as a child Shirine had felt the family's dependence on her father's strength as an iconic family figurehead; his presence was powerful and reassuring. Though at times both emotionally and physically unavailable, he had still been a symbol of safety, and "the only thing that counted" for Shirine.

The unexpected death of Shirine's father occurred in the context of immediate prerevolutionary Iran, when the country was in a state of flux. The political climate had become unfriendly to aristocratic families, mostly supporters of the shah. Shirine's mother, suddenly alone and vulnerable, had good reason to be alarmed. The reason for her husband's death was a mystery. Having become ill without warning, he had fallen into a coma and died five days later. She feared that his death was politically motivated.

Shirine's mother realized that if she did not act soon, she would not be able to get out of Iran safely. Quickly and quietly, she withdrew money from the bank, got jewelry and papers out of their safe-deposit boxes, sold or shipped furniture, and slipped out of the country. The family house and everything else that could not be transported was left behind. The financial losses were significant. Fortunately, her husband had been aware that Iran was changing radically, and he had bought property in France. At least her mother had some resources and a place to go.

Absorbed in her own grief and panic, Shirine's mother was distracted and left her daughters to fend for themselves. There was no one to nurture or support them as they dealt with the loss of their father. In retrospect, Shirine can understand how frightened her mother must have been and why she behaved the way she did. But at the time Shirine felt completely abandoned: "And so she's trying to get her jewelry out, because it's dangerous; you can't do that. I mean, she did some finagling work. She was good. She had a lot to do; she had to sell a ton of antiques before she could leave the country. She crated things and sent them; she did a lot. I have to give credit to her, except that we were lost in the shuffle."

They did not see their mother again until the following summer, more than six months later. At the end of the school year Shirine and Fatima flew to Nice, where their mother was now living. Again trying in vain to mediate everyone's distress, their mother decided that they should not speak of her late husband or his death. Silence only made the atmosphere worse. The three grieving women spent the summer in a shadow of pain, ungrounded and confused. How life would unfold from here was unimaginable now.

Their apartment in Nice was beautiful, but there was no comfort in these new surroundings: "It was horrible. We were so depressed. Meantime, I didn't have any reality. I didn't belong anywhere. Where was my father? Where was I going? Who was I?" At least the insulated environment of college gave her some kind of purpose. At the end of the summer, Shirine gladly went back to the United States. Shortly after her return, Shirine met Jackson. Like her father, Jackson was interested in the arts, outgoing, and smart. Without question they loved each other, but with hindsight, Shirine believes that her attachment to him was inflated by her need for security.

Meanwhile the revolution in Iran was imminent. The country had never pulled Shirine emotionally, never provided the refuge of home. Home was an ever-shifting consequence of where her father was assigned. But knowing that she could never return and what her family had lost created an unsteady sensation. There was no floor beneath her feet: "There was no home. After the revolution not only did we lose our country but then all this land and all this money that my mother had was lost too, because [the new government] claimed everything." ·

So Shirine married Jackson: "He was the only person that came to me and said, 'Okay, I'll take care of you.' Nobody else was [there]. I was too young and too scared. I didn't even know the States. I was scared to death! What am I going to do?" Getting married provided the answer.

❧

By 2002, Francesca had left home to go to college. Louis, seventeen, seemed to need more male influence and began spending more time with Jackson. Shirine could see the writing on the wall—it wouldn't be too much longer before both children were independent. Though she had been waiting for the time when she would have the freedom to leave, being faced with the choice was not easy. For years her life had revolved around her family, and now she needed to carve out a new kind of existence for herself.

In April, Shirine went to France to visit her mother, as she did almost every year. These trips prompted both excitement and apprehension. They gave Shirine a break from her routine and helped her reconnect with Europe. On the other hand, returning to Denver inevitably brought with it a sense of dismay and a strong reminder of Shirine's dissatisfaction with her life.

Francesca was on her spring break from school that year and came along. Together they drove around the area, enjoying the spectacular scenery of the south of France. Sitting in a café in the old part of the city or walking along the esplanade, Shirine imagined what it would be like to have an art studio in Nice. She loved the Mediterranean surroundings and the outdoor restaurants and felt inspired to work there. A vision of the future was emerging. Though her relationship with her mother had always been fraught, Shirine now understood her mother better. Unresolved conflicts had not disappeared, but Shirine had learned to accept the past and move on. Maybe Nice was the answer. Her mother was getting older, and living near her would give them one last opportunity to become closer.

Shirine returned to Denver with high hopes. But soon she realized how intimidating the prospect of moving actually was. She worried that she was leaving her children too soon, and this was exacerbated by the reactions from not only Jackson but also her friends. But Shirine has never been one to listen to others' opinions or ask for advice: "I never make myself available for that, because they don't know what's right for me. Here I am: Louis has a social life of his own; I hardly see him. What am I doing here? The reason I've been here is for the kids, [and now] the kids don't need me. So I decided that it was time for me to go. I thought to myself, 'That's enough. I'm getting old, and I'm never going to have a life. If I don't do it now, I'm not going to do it.'" Francesca and Louis agreed and encouraged her to stick with her plan.

Leaving Denver was an enormous undertaking. For seventeen years Shirine had lived in the same house, longer than she had been in any one place. Everything she held dear was in there: her children's belongings, drawings, and childhood toys, as well as Shirine's furniture and artwork, dishes, clothes, books, and years of collected family photos. Now she had to face the prospect of selling the house and evaluating every possession. Important things would be packed and stored, and the rest would be sold. For the time being, Shirine would go to France with only a couple of suitcases and her cat—the rest could wait until she established herself.

The physical and mental effort of moving out of the house took all of Shirine's strength. The effort she had put into healing her emotional wounds during all those difficult years was now paying off. With her old fears conquered, she knew she could do this on her own: "I was [a] very fear-ridden person, and I've gotten rid of my fear. It's been a long haul. I turned from victim to victor. I would never have had the courage to move by myself if I hadn't gotten over my fears. It seemed like the most insurmountable, huge project that I could never do by myself—all these years I dreamt about it and I had so much fear that I never thought that I could accomplish it on my own."

Though Shirine believed that moving was the right decision, she still worried about the effect it would have on her children. Nor was she sure how easy it would be to live near her mother after all of the years of unspoken tension. Still, having her mother there would be good for Shirine; she would not be moving somewhere all alone but going to family. Though Shirine had never lived in Nice, she had been visiting her mother there for twenty-five years, and the regular visits had brought the area a comforting familiarity. Moving there was as close as she could get to returning home.

The death of a parent is a major life event for most people, particularly when both parent and child are younger than is generally expected. For Shirine, the death of her father and the coinciding revolution in Iran caused any illusion of stability she had to abruptly disappear. Feeling lost, she grasped on to marriage to keep herself afloat. This decision changed everything. Once married and with children, she was tethered to a locale she had little affinity for. Visiting France with her college-age daughter, Shirine was finally able to see a solution to the questions about her future. With her children's blessing, Shirine could now follow her abstract yearning to be on the other side of the Atlantic and could finally move forward with anticipation.

Barrett

Feelings of alienation and fantasies of tropical climates persisted throughout Barrett's childhood. Even her earliest memories included an awareness that where she was living might sustain but would never satisfy her. The consistent internal nudge to leave home became a burning need to find a place where she would belong. The question was not whether she would leave; it was how and when. The answer was provided when she left for Venezuela.

Caracas became a familiar anchor as time passed. What was at first new and exciting eventually became normal. Barrett created a physical home for herself, bought furniture, made friends, adopted cats, and held a job. Her day-to-day life revolved around her location and the relationships that existed in that place. When she went on vacation, she left from and came back to Caracas. Every year she visited family in the States but always returned to Venezuela.

Barrett's North American family was never able to accept the idea that she was staying in Venezuela. Even after more than twenty years, they still thought that her need to live away from home was a phase she was going through. Some day, when she had her fill of excitement, she would come home to New England and settle down. Time moved ahead, but their perception of Barrett did not move with it. They continued to disapprove of Barrett's choices and never understood why a highly educated and capable woman would choose to live in a so-called third world country. There was little appreciation of the culture or lifestyle of Latin America and no comprehension of why Barrett wanted to stay.

❧

After Hugo Chavez's rise to power in the 1990s, the disapproval expressed by Barrett's family began to turn to concern for her welfare. They began pestering her to look for a job in the States and move back. Barrett generally tried to placate them but in fact ignored their advice. When the political turmoil in Venezuela escalated in 2002, the nightly U.S. television news broadcasts showed a country in the throes of chaos and instability. Her brothers, fearful that Barrett was somehow in danger, began to insist.

As part of her job with the cable television company, Barrett sometimes traveled to Miami for business meetings. She happened to be there during one particularly tumultuous episode when the political circumstances were bad enough that the airlines canceled all flights to Venezuela. To make things worse, it was mid-December, when the airlines were busy with holiday travelers. Barrett was stuck in Florida, uncertain when she might be able to get back.

Barrett decided her best option was to stay in Florida for a week or so and wait the situation out. Her mother had a condo near Miami where she spent the winters, and Barrett could stay with her, rent a car, and work at the station's Miami office until things calmed down. In the meantime, her brothers, one with his wife and children, were all on their way to Florida to spend a few weeks at the condo. What started out as a hassle might have turned into a happy family reunion. But all together in the small condo the family felt cramped, and the unexpected gathering quickly turned into a pressure cooker. Barrett was anxious that she could not get back to Venezuela, and her family argued, forcefully, that she should never return.

Barrett thought they were interfering in her life, unreasonably expecting her to discard everything she had worked for: "I was miserable because I wanted to go back; I didn't know what was going to happen. I was worried about my life there. It was pretty bad, basically because they were all pressuring me not to ever go back. They had to understand: I had to go back; of course I was going to go back. This is my life; this is my house, my cats!"

Several tension-filled weeks passed before Barrett could get a flight. Her family had no choice but to accept her decision to return, but their fears continued. On the phone and through e-mails, her brothers continued to argue that this was the time for Barrett to leave Venezuela. Now, in addition to the political crisis, they began to express concern about Barrett's financial future. She had a well-paying job, but the instability of the Venezuelan economy made the future of the currency questionable. Barrett should get a job that paid in dollars so that she would be able retire in the United States. Time was passing, and as Barrett neared fifty, her chances of getting a decent job were narrowing.

Their perspective, though realistic, only added to Barrett's frustration. Her brothers' assumption that she was not aware of the economic circumstances was insulting. The greater injury was that Barrett's family was again presuming that one day she would wake up and realize that staying in Venezuela had been a mistake. They still did not have confidence in her judgment.

Over and over Barrett implored her brothers to believe in her choices. But the continuous pressure started to erode her confidence. Absorbing her brothers' fear, she finally agreed to think about leaving. Torn, Barrett waited and considered her options but could not bring herself to plan a move. Regardless of where she went in the United States, Barrett would be starting over. In Caracas, Barrett constantly has invitations to birthday parties, christenings, and holiday dinners. She is not alone or lonely. Her friends, unlike her family, anticipate that she will stay in Venezuela, and they include her in their most intimate family events. In the United States, Barrett would be disconnected from all of this. She would once again have the painful feeling of being a foreigner in her own country.

In the middle of the conflict, an old friend in Caracas reached out to Barrett for help. She needed to move out of the city, but her seventeen-year-old daughter, Maria, who is Barrett's goddaughter, wanted to stay and finish high school. Barrett immediately offered to let Maria live with her and took on the role of Maria's surrogate mother.

Any thoughts of leaving Venezuela were put on hold. Barrett could not consider leaving for at least a year, until Maria no longer needed her. Nor could she leave her job at the cable channel just yet. In the middle of several significant projects, this was not the right time to quit. Barrett was not going to walk out on either her personal or her professional commitments. She told her brothers to give her more time to think and to wind up her obligations, and they agreed to back off.

The truce did not last long. Two months later Barrett was in the United States for business again and went to see her brother Greg in Chicago.

Unable to hold back, he brought up the topic of moving once again, this time insisting she set a date to return. These conversations had always been aggravating for Barrett, but this time it was excruciating, and she stood her ground, refusing to mollify Greg. Barrett and Greg finally had it out:

> All of a sudden this thing sort of boiled up inside of me, and I said, "You know, I just feel like you're forcing me to jump off a cliff. I feel like you're saying to me, 'It doesn't matter what you've done for thirty years; throw it all away, out. Don't even take a suitcase with you; just leave everything.' And maybe I'll end up in a grassy meadow. But maybe I'm going to be on these rocks being tormented by the sea. I don't know what's at the other end of that cliff, once I jump off. And I really don't want to jump off that cliff. You are asking me to leave my home, my love. And you're asking me to go to a nothing."

Barrett and her brother parted, both of them angry and disappointed.

Despite the love Barrett's family has for her, their ability to understand her needs and choices has not increased as time has passed. The picture they hold in their mind's eye is that of an insecure young woman searching for something that does not exist. They cannot accept that, living in Venezuela, Barrett has thrived. She has worked hard to forge both a career and a strong sense of herself. Barrett has become a part of the Venezuelan culture, country, and community.

Venezuela is not a vacation spot for Barrett; it is where she is living her life: "I think [my family] has been slightly in a time warp for the years that I've been in Venezuela, thinking that I would come back. And I think that they never really understood that I really did immigrate to Venezuela and embraced Venezuela with my heart and soul. They thought that this was a lark. They only see that it would have been better if I had stayed in the States, but I know for sure that it wouldn't have been better."

The argument with Greg was painful, but it was also valuable. Barrett had been on the fence for months, stressed about the future and uncertain which path to take. The pressure from Greg and the rest of the family forced Barrett to look back and remember why she stayed in Venezuela so many years ago. Barrett had always known the importance of following her own instincts, but in the midst of her own concerns and the political upheaval she had forgotten to trust. The crisis brought back to the surface Barrett's intuitive responses, and she was reminded once again that she alone knew what she needed.

Barrett initially came to Venezuela hoping to marry Edmund but instead found herself committed to the country:

> I didn't marry who I thought I was going to marry, because I ended up married to Venezuela. I ended up married to the country and

knowing that this country, this husband of mine, you know, poor thing, my husband is in such a bad way. And I don't think he's ever going to get better. But he doesn't mistreat me; he doesn't beat me and starve me. And being who I am and how I am, I basically ignore everything that's not positive, although I know it exists. . . . [W]hat I do is I just squeeze every bit of happiness out of everything that is good. And so it's like the typical wife with the husband who is just a good-for-nothing. You must have been very much in love, and you stay with that person, you stay with this country, you stay with your project. And, you know, the children are all of the things that you've done and your family and your extended family and your work and all of this stuff. And I realized [that] I really totally felt married to Venezuela.

Strikes and protests continued in Caracas. One day Barrett looked out her office window and thousands of people were marching in the streets, spread across a six-lane highway as far as she could see. The only person in her office who had not joined the protests, Barrett watched the television news alone, waiting until the demonstration was over to leave. Though her adopted country seemed to be falling apart, Barrett was calm: "I was in the office, and I was seeing this whole situation, and there's something about it. I cannot leave here, no matter what people say; I cannot go. Why am I not leaving here; why am I not frightened? Why am I not angry? Why, with so much pressure from my family to get out of there? I can't tell you, but I know that it's not time for me to go."

Barrett went to Venezuela looking for a refuge. She was not running away from New England as much as she was reaching out to a new place. Although neither her relationship nor her anticipated job materialized, she chose to stay, knowing that in Venezuela she would have the chance to find a deeper understanding of herself. Her life unfolded there in ways she could not have predicted, and over time her attachment to the country moved into a profound relationship—a love affair that she could not abandon.

⁓

Barrett looks at her life through a spiritual lens. She is a practical and levelheaded person, but her decisions always include a consideration of divine intent. Barrett does not rule out the possibility that she might leave Venezuela one day, but she hopes that if she ever does, leaving will be based on a choice to go toward something positive rather than escape something negative:

I just have to go with what life is dealing me. Life dealt me a situation, the family and the city that I was born into, the country where I was born, and I think that I was put there with this challenge: What are you going to do about it? I didn't have a situation like

Nazi Germany that I had to leave. I had something internal that said I had to leave. And there was no looking back. If I pray or if I talk to fate, I say, "Please don't let me have to leave Venezuela running away; I don't want to run away or be in a political situation where I have to be a refugee and flee. I don't want to flee from Venezuela."

There is too much of Venezuela in Barrett for her to leave without a backward glance. She does not rule out the possibility that something might appear one day to draw her away, but until then, Barrett will stay in Venezuela, confident that this is where she belongs and open to whatever the future might bring.

FROM TRANSITION TO TRANSFORMATION

The most painful aspect of making a choice is frequently the agonizing process that leads up to it. Once a choice is made, the stress and strain of uncertainty lifts, and rumination can give way to peace. Moving through personal turning points and resolving long-standing conflicts can be likened to a personal version of a paradigm shift:[1] the individual's overall view of how the world operates has changed. For an immigrant, this can mean that the conceptual framework of her identity has been reconfigured. After relocation, but before a home-related paradigm shift, there is likely to be ambiguity or conflict about belonging and identity. In choosing to set down roots, her conflict about belonging may be resolved—or at least recognized and therefore easier to accept.

The initial events that influenced these four women to stay in their adopted countries were in some cases dramatic, like the sudden deaths of Anna's mother and Shirine's father. There were also happy events, like Lisa's marriage and the feeling of acceptance Barrett felt in Venezuela. Regardless of why those early decisions were made, they were followed by a long process of transformation and, finally, another turning point that prompted reassessment of the direction their lives were taking.

Some of the incidents that provoked these reevaluations might not seem like critical events. A family reunion or disagreement is not usually expected to initiate a personal crossroads or an important juncture in one's life. In the case of the four women profiled here, the specific event that prompted the reassessment was as critical as what had preceded it: the culmination, on one hand, of years of living with ongoing grief and loss and, on the other, of establishing new, joyful attachments to spouses, friends, and communities. The turning point was a moment of realization, the acceptance of a circumstance that had already existed for some time.

Fusing temporary plans into long-term intentions was not immediate for any of the four women. To some extent, perceiving their moves as impermanent hindered them from fully seeing the reality of their circumstances. Deciding first to move and then to stay was only the beginning of the slow process of creating a home and community. Their later turning points were the acceptance of what moving had meant to their lives.

ﻬ

In the United States, many tend to assume that when immigrants arrive here they immediately cut ties to their first home and adopt an American identity. There is little awareness that there may be overlapping feelings of belonging or loyalty to two countries (Glick Schiller and Fouron 2001, 7), and dual allegiances are often looked on as dubious (Croucher 2009, 198–200). But our pasts do not disappear in an instant. We are the sum of all of our experiences, a cumulative whole of an entire life's worth of memories. Some are good, some are bad, but all shape who we become as adults. Our pasts create us and remind us of who we are and where we came from. They influence our choices and the way we feel about a multitude of things: politics and childrearing, work choices and mate choices, why we love to travel or hate it, why we like comedies or drama. Everything about us that makes us unique individuals is shaped by our past.

Though the past is an important piece of identity, focusing on memories can lead to a painful nostalgia. The memory of a former home can be like an anchor, providing a feeling of stability. But memories that are tinted with nostalgia do not always paint a realistic picture of the past. Memories like to be shared, but if no one is around to share them, they can become distorted—either unreal and ghostly or larger and more vibrant than the actual event. Memories can then create fictive, "imaginary homelands" in the minds of immigrants (Rushdie 1992, 10).

Visits home can be a mixed blessing for immigrants. They inevitably reawaken memories, both positive and negative. For some, revisiting the past can be a wonderful, rejuvenating experience. The psychiatrist Salman Akhtar describes immigrants' visits home as an opportunity for "emotional refueling"—an important time when immigrants can renew ties to loved ones (1999, 10–11). Although phone calls and Internet communications are beneficial, it is difficult to have meaningful relationships without occasional face-to-face contact, especially when it comes to significant family events or ceremonies. Visits home, then, can be a means of cementing commitment to those relationships left behind after migration, as well as reinforcing ethnic identities (O'Flaherty, Skrbis, and Tranter 2007, 820).

At times, however, returning to a childhood home can be fraught with conflict. Immigrants visiting home may recognize that they no longer fit in the environment of their past. Whether the physical surroundings of home have changed or not, relationships undoubtedly have. Those left at home learn to live without the missing immigrant and as time has passed have gone through their own personal transformations. The life left behind has not remained static, but memories do not acknowledge this (Glick Schiller and Fouron 2001, 84; Relph 1976, 31). The returning immigrant is now a spectator in a place where he or she used to belong. Going "home" can bring on culture shock in the same way that going to a completely unknown place did before (Glick Schiller and Fouron 2001, 84).

Lisa and Shirine both looked forward to their visits with parents and hoped that being "at home" would bring a sense of renewal (for Shirine, I refer to her mother's home in France, which was the closest representation of home she had). But for each of them, the annual visits sparked an internal struggle about where they were living and reminded them of what they were missing by living so far away. For Anna and Barrett, visits home reinforced the ties with their adopted countries, not their original homes. Returning to New Zealand also forced Anna to acknowledge that her family had undergone change, just as she had, and what she had held in her memories had not waited for her.

Some research suggests that immigrants who are satisfied in their new environments and are culturally assimilated tend to visit home less often (O'Flaherty, Skrbis, and Tranter 2007, 834). Barrett's story supports this idea. Happy in Venezuela, she tended to resist her family's attempts to draw her back to her "home" in the United States.

The experiences of Anna, Lisa, and Shirine suggest that perhaps there is an analogous connection between the ability to visit home and the propensity to be satisfied or become assimilated in a new environment (compare Akhtar 1999, 9–11). Regular visits, rather than helping, seem to have hindered Lisa and Shirine from releasing the past and emotionally connecting to their new country. For the two of them, visiting home was a conflicted source of emotion. On the positive side was the joy gained by reconnecting with their pasts; the downside was reinforcement of emotional distance from their new home.

Unable to visit New Zealand for thirteen years, Anna had no choice but to throw herself completely into her new community and look ahead to her future there. She certainly suffered from this loss, but on the other hand Anna's creation of a new home was less complicated than Lisa's or Shirine's. This is not meant to suggest that anyone should, or would want to, be deprived of connections with family or visits home. But if an immigrant's goal is to move toward belonging and identification with her adopted country (and it legitimately may not be), then social networks and attachments need to be given the space to form there.

Regardless of whether return visits were generally a source of renewal or distress, for each of these four women, a visit to her former home triggered a long-brewing conflict involving belonging and identity. Reentering her former life catalyzed an emotional reassessment of her attitudes and visions for her future. A crucial visit home reminded each of the women of the changes that had occurred in her life and helped foster the realization of who she was and where she now belonged.

Being well adjusted in their new countries did not prevent these women from carrying a conflicted understanding of home in their hearts.

A relatively innocuous event caused the conflict to rise to the surface, and the realization that an inability to form an attachment to place was coloring their lives. Now, an essential shift in perspective would allow them to stop struggling with the past and more peacefully visualize the future. For Anna, Lisa, and Barrett, going back to their first home proved to them that their new home was where they now belonged. For Shirine, going back to France verified that no matter how long or how hard she tried, Denver would never be home.

◦♥

Adjusting to a new life can be distressing, even traumatic, for immigrants, especially if acculturation happens quickly (Portes and Rumbaut 2006, 199). Many immigrants suffer from depression and anxiety (Berry 1997, 20; see Walsh and Horenczyk 2001, 502), but there can be other emotional shifts as well. Eva Hoffman, in her memoir, refers to a period of time when her primary emotion consisted of "immigrant rage," kindled by the constant feeling of being an outsider (1989, 203). That immigrants might suffer emotionally does not suggest pathology or maladjustment, however; it suggests only that the dramatic changes in a person's life brought about by migration are likely to evoke strong emotional responses at some point (Madison 2010; see Tsuda 2003, 122).

Like other aspects of adaptation, immigrants' emotions are linked to a variety of factors, including the context of immigration, the reception of the host society, and whether immigrants have support from co-ethnics (Portes and Rumbaut 2006, 179–181). Feelings of emotional distance or closeness to a new home can vacillate, initial feelings of infatuation for a place can shift to dislike or ambivalence, and there can be a tendency to avoid focusing on the present and to focus instead on either the past or the future (Akhtar 1999, 78, 105).

One family therapist and immigrant I spoke with compared the adjustment process to the emotional phases of dying famously described by Elisabeth Kübler-Ross (1997): denial, anger, bargaining, depression, and acceptance. Though Kübler-Ross's theory does not adequately address the complex process of grief, it does illustrate the changing nature of emotions that immigrants experience (Susan Schwartz Senstad 2001, pers. comm.). When I mentioned this to Lisa, she suggested that while the process might involve the death of an identity, the final result is not just acceptance but a newfound happiness.

During the years of adjustments and transitions, guilt, resentment, and mourning arose at times for all four of these émigré women—guilt because they left their families behind, and for Anna because moving to a more affluent life in Norway involved crossing not only geographical borders but also class borders. While these women had more choices than many immigrants, this could not protect them from the feelings associated with leaving home. Having the choice to return in fact may have added layers of complexity to feelings of guilt or responsibility.

Anna, Lisa, and Shirine felt resentful because they lived in their husbands' countries, close to his relatives but not their own. Barrett was weighted with resentment because the family she left behind did not respect her needs and choices. Despite conflict and dissatisfaction in their pasts, they all still missed their families and friends and mourned those losses. Conflict grew out of the feeling that their lives were on hold, lived in an unending pause, until the day they might finally have some resolution about what home meant to them. This does not mean that they were unhappy or disillusioned for all those years; in fact, all experienced joy and love in their new countries and were for the most part living fulfilling lives. Grieving the loss of their first home and culture was needed, however, even if the past did not always hold carefree memories.

Our culture is a part of who we are. Changes in routines, surroundings, friendships, and even food are stressful. Having to let go of these pieces of ourselves is often painful. Lisa had her "depressive" period early and it soon lifted, but she revisited those same feelings every Christmas. The other three had periods of sadness later, but their feelings were equally significant.

Anna, Shirine, and Barrett went through what might be called a "honeymoon phase," during which the euphoria they held for their new circumstances obfuscated any pain associated with leaving home behind. For them, excitement and anticipation for their future enveloped them and helped initial obstacles and frustrations melt away. Anna's joy with her young family overshadowed her grief for her mother and what had been left behind. Her ultimate mourning would come later, after she came face to face with her first culture once again.

Shirine grieved the loss of her father and the family possessions left behind in Iran, but the excitement of college life and then marriage kept grief at bay for some time. It was not until her marriage was over that she began to understand the toll that not having a sense of belonging had taken. Much of Barrett's grieving took place before she ever arrived in Venezuela, during all of the years she dreamed of leaving Connecticut. She was able to acknowledge and finally cease grieving by living the life she wanted and through hard work with her counselor.

Whatever form these emotional phases took, they were not always separate or clear-cut. They progressed at their own pace, depending on the circumstances that existed for each person. A realignment of belonging does not follow an outline or plan; it is fluid, and it takes place over years and frequently a lifetime (Bhatia and Ram 2009, 147). The emotional "learning curve" involved in creating home and community in a new place is more like the movement of the tide: it is a continuous, ever-flowing presence that sometimes is as smooth as glass, peaceful and clear, and at other times swells with discord and contradiction. Ripples, however small, will never completely disappear.

❧

The ability (or inability) to commit to a place is often related to the ability to connect to it. The process becomes circular: if there is no connection, there is no commitment; if there is no commitment, then detachment prevents connection. Most commitments, even big ones, can be broken. Marriages break up, jobs change, and houses are bought and sold as they become less suitable for our circumstances. People move from city to city or country to country. Obviously the making of a commitment does not translate to literal permanency. Human beings, however, seem to need at least the idea of permanency in some aspects of their lives, even as they are aware that it may be nothing more than an illusion.

The transition from sojourner to immigrant does not necessarily require a defined commitment, such as acquiring citizenship. Citizenship, however, is one way that migrants attempt to gain belonging, whether from an emotional or political perspective. Citizenship provides formal membership and belonging and offers an officially sanctioned identity (Faist 2000, 203). In many instances, citizenship is necessary to obtain important rights and benefits, and so the commitment is made out of practicality; in other situations, becoming a naturalized citizen can be a significant symbol of dedication to a new country, tied with nationalistic emotions (Magat 1999, 137–138).[2]

An immigrant's citizenship (or other documented) status certainly legitimates her presence, but the legal right to be in a particular location does not necessarily lead to a feeling of belonging. Legal status is not a requirement for personal transformation. Akhil Gupta has questioned whether, in today's globalized and transnational society, citizenship is a sufficient basis for assuming belonging or nationalism. He suggests that citizenship should instead be considered as only one of many forms of imagined community that lead to the creation of home (Gupta 1997, 193).

None of these four women was in the position of having to choose her national loyalty. They did not need to become citizens of their new countries; they were catalyzed to do so for personal reasons. In this way they are more fortunate than many other immigrants. For Shirine and Lisa, the decision to change citizenship was a reflection of their need to belong. When Lisa realized on that critical New Year's Eve that her future was in Miami, not Canada, she became motivated to change citizenship partially as a way of validating her commitment but also so that she could vote—something that would give her a sense of contribution and bonding with the country. Shirine's attempt at finding belonging through citizenship was not as successful. Shirine feels loyal to the United States and grateful for the way she was welcomed there. She values her ties to the country and says that she would never give up her citizenship. Nevertheless, becoming a citizen did not create for her a feeling of "at-home-ness" in the United States.

Research on citizenship change indicates that the prospect of return migration diminishes the desire to naturalize. In other words, if migrants hope that they can someday return to their countries of origin, they are less likely to commit to a new country (Portes and Rumbaut 2006, 146). When Lisa decided to become a U.S. citizen, she was acknowledging that her hope of returning to Canada was unrealistic. Shirine did not have Lisa's conflict about transferring citizenship. She could not go back to Iran and did not want to. For her, there were no feelings of turning her back on her country or her family by becoming a citizen of the United States.

Neither Anna nor Barrett has become a citizen of her adopted country, and it is unlikely that they will. Because Anna is married to a Norwegian, her connection to Norway is legally and socially authorized, and she has access to social benefits. She has had no impetus to change her citizenship; nor does she want to. Anna does not believe that she will return to live in New Zealand, but she wants to continue to feel that her ties to that country are secure, if only for emotional reasons. Nevertheless, she feels attachment and loyalty to Norway.

Barrett emotionally committed herself to Venezuela soon after arriving there. Though her intentions to stay in Venezuela are clear, she acknowledges the political benefit of having a U.S. passport and is reluctant to give up that privilege. Unlike the others, she has no external validation of her decision to stay in Venezuela. There has been no citizenship ceremony, and she has never married or had children in Venezuela. The possibility of returning to the United States remained a point of contention within her family, because in their eyes Barrett has no legitimate roots in Venezuela and no apparent reason to remain.

❧

Relationships with place are not so different from relationships with people. The more time that passes in a place, the easier it is to become involved with it, to develop a love for the physical environment and for the people who inhabit the place. Connection and belonging grow out of an unselfconscious commitment to a location—an ability to identify with it. Also referred to as "existential insideness," belonging to a place includes an acceptance of imperfection: unpleasant weather, uncomfortable communication styles—whatever makes up the grind of life in any one particular place. As attachment increases, so does a sense of rootedness (Relph 1976, 41, 50). And our roots help to center us, to orient us in the world. They are a point of reference for our identity (Relph 1976, 38; Dovey 1978).

For some immigrants, such as Shirine and Lisa, committing to a new home was a struggle and the subject of resistance. For them, resisting attachment was a means of defending against an identity shift. Gupta and Ferguson contend that while resistance can lead to identity transformation, it can also have the effect of reinforcing existing identities (Gupta and Ferguson 1997b, 19). For Lisa the struggle was eventually resolved, and she was able to accept a certain level of identity change. For Shirine resistance was not a phase—though she tried, she could never form a strong attachment to Denver, and her identity as a foreigner was strengthened the longer she stayed in the United States.

Living with an underlying conflict about belonging, identity, and home caused all four women to feel that their lives were fragmented. Like a jigsaw puzzle with a few missing pieces, they always felt incomplete. They were eternally searching, forever trying to grasp something familiar that was just out of reach. Familiarity is comforting, even if it is flawed, because it does not need to be interpreted through language or culture.

Finally, there was a moment of clarity when each one realized that she no longer belonged to the past and could begin to let go of her "imaginary homeland." The feeling of comfort and familiarity they each needed was not behind but in front of them. Their turning points were moments when they consciously accepted that certain facets of their identity had changed as a result of immigration. This critical realization gave them the courage and the power to act and to assert agency for the construction of their identities. They were then able to take control of how immigration was going to shape their lives and how they were going to find meaning in their experience of home.[3]

When Shirine surrendered to her intuition and desires, she was able to move forward with her life in France. Barrett surrendered to her love for Venezuela and gave up trying to please her family with a compromise she could not believe in. Lisa surrendered to her desire to belong to one place, her love for Jason, and her commitment to Judaism, and Anna surrendered to the knowledge that feeling at home in Norway was right for her and that she no longer needed to feel guilty for leaving her family.

Though the turning points were painful ruptures, at their essence they were more of a relief than a wound. Acknowledging them allowed the inner turmoil created from living an in-between life to begin to ease. Finally understanding where they belonged meant a better understanding of their own identities. For both Barrett and Shirine, this understanding amounted to a spiritual "immigration." Anna and Lisa were able to accept how much they had changed after living for many years in a new country.

Displacement may produce alienation, but it also facilitates new ways of thinking and new ways of envisioning one's life (see Kaplan 1987). Whether faced with loss of love, culture, religion, or death, all four of these women were able to find the strength to look forward rather than turn back. They share this experience with many other immigrants who must also leave behind their familiar pasts and try to face an unknown future with hope rather than despair.

Reaching a point of acceptance about identity shifts does not mean transition is over or adjustment complete. But acceptance of change can be a line of demarcation for the beginning of a more comfortable existence. It is unlikely that every immigrant will experience a clearly identifiable turning point such as those described here. None of the preceding discussion is intended to suggest a negative judgment of those whose lives (including mine) are spent more in a state of transience than permanence. "Being grounded is not necessarily about being fixed; being mobile is not necessarily about being detached" (Ahmed et al. 2003, 1).[4] Sometimes a full commitment to a specific home is not possible, too painful, or unwanted. For some, a dual belonging is preferable to the alternative of losing either home, and this is becoming increasingly common in today's globalized world. How immigrants realize harmony rather than dissonance in maintaining bicultural and transnational identities varies enormously. The next section illustrates how these four women integrate this experience into their everyday lives.

IV

LEJANÍA CERCANA

Living "Closely Far" from Home

I think everything about my life is close distance or distant
closeness. I'm as close as I can be, but no matter how close I
am, I'm still far away.

—BARRETT

INTERSECTING IDENTITIES

Translated from Spanish, *lejanía cercana* means "close distance" or
"close but far away." The deeper meaning of this phrase, however,
has more complexity than a direct translation can provide. The
words embody feelings of wistfulness and longing and connote the paradox
that results from feeling emotionally close to a place when it is physically or
geographically far away. For the four women whose stories are presented
here, the consequences of emigration have at times been both positive and
painful, but all have been left with the feeling of being *lejanía cercana* from
home.

The passing of time has led to new and creative ways of approaching
the challenges that resulted from deciding to move to a new country. But
each person eventually wanted more than to cope. They were searching for
contentment. To find it, they had to learn not only to accept but also to
treasure where their choices had led them. The search has not been a simple
process. Finding contentment has meant striking a balance between their
sense of self, place, and purpose and learning to live with the ongoing feeling of being "closely far" from home.

Each woman, then, has had to find her own way of understanding her
immigrant experience. Each has lived on the margins of belonging, trying to find a state of equilibrium somewhere in the confluence of various
identities. Like many immigrants, they were searching for a personal sense
of place and peace within the continual longing for a physical refuge. Not

entirely part of any one place, they have had to look for stability in the middle ground, straddling their feelings of loyalty and commitment to each place. Sometimes more weight was placed on one side than the other; to maintain steadiness there was a constant need to lean gently back and forth between the two. The balance was not just between the status of outsider and insider but also in the desire to shift between categories of belonging. Underlying that was the fear that letting attachments form in one place might preclude belonging to the other.

Away from their roots, the lives of Anna, Lisa, Shirine, and Barrett became, to a certain extent, fractured. Pieces of their first homes were lost along the way, if for no other reason than because they were not physically present to maintain relationships with both place and people. Connections with old friends, siblings, and parents may be better or worse, but they are undoubtedly not the same as they would have been without the distance of time and space.

The difficulty these immigrants faced is common to many of us who leave our roots: home changes, just as we do. Our memories, however, remain, and sometimes we long to feel we are inside them once again. We want to feel the ambience of the past: the smells, the feel of the air, the sounds. Though we can sometimes feel close enough to reach out and touch this world in our minds, in reality we cannot, because what we are trying to reach has no current dimensions. It is a memory, not something that is living and breathing. The challenge is in discovering how to move beyond the eternal searching for home and to understand that it is with us all the time, despite how distant or close it might feel.

The reasons for leaving home and for staying in their adopted countries affected how and when each of these four woman came to a sense of resolution about the issues of home and place. It is to each woman's credit that she has learned to understand herself and where and how she fits in the world.

As a young mother, Anna moved to Norway temporarily. She never imagined that she would spend the rest of her life away from New Zealand or that she would become more comfortable sitting by a warm fire, looking out the window at the falling snow, than having a party in her brother's backyard. The decision to stay in Norway came gradually. The death of her mother and her desire to release elements of her past, along with the positive reinforcement that came from having her own family, smoothed the way. Lisa's reasons for moving, like Anna's, revolved around love and relationship. Never returning to Canada to live was not an issue in her mind. Immigrating as a young adult, she could not foresee the grief that distance would cause. Because this move was not as geographically distant as her childhood moves, Lisa did not realize that she would feel quite so foreign for so long or that changing her religion would cause such tension within her own psyche.

The timing of Shirine's decision to leave Iran and study abroad was fortunate in that it saved her from the trauma of sudden political exile, but the rejection of her culture did not prevent adjustment difficulties or protect her from a free-floating sense of estrangement. Barrett adapted to her new country more readily, without the feelings of resentment or discord the others experienced. But the lack of a ritualized passage, such as a citizenship change or marriage, kept both Barrett and her family from drawing a firm line between her past and present.

From friendships and community, through work or raising children, each woman has found her own special way to make sense of a life lived in the in-between spaces. Incorporating multiple and overlapping identities, each has recreated herself. None wanted to fit into someone else's mold, and instead each worked hard to be true to herself while taking the best from each culture and family to which she was linked. Reconciling the conflict between intimacy and distance, insider and outsider, is what these stories are ultimately about. Sometimes deliberately, sometimes not, each woman has reconstituted herself within the dichotomy and has developed a new frame of reference for her future.

Anna

Every May 17 at precisely 8:00 in the morning, large national flags appear in the front of homes all over Norway. It is Norwegian Constitution Day. The festivities start with an early-morning parade of schoolchildren. Streets along the parade route are lined with townspeople cheering, clapping, and waving smaller, handheld flags. In schoolyards and town squares, parents sell strong coffee and waffles to raise money for activities and clubs.

Later in the day, the aroma of cooking waffles changes to that of hot dogs and sausages as the afternoon parade begins. All kinds of organizations put together a group for the parade. Children who were in the morning parade march again, this time with their sports teams; adults march with their dance class or rowing club. Bands play, and town leaders make speeches. Later in the day, when the parades are over and there has been time for a rest, the parties begin, and family and friends gather for a long night of celebrating.

The point of this national day is not to show military strength but to show national pride. Though filled with fun and celebration, the day is taken seriously. Both adults and children dress carefully; this is not a day for jeans or shorts but for suits and ties for boys and men and dresses for women and girls. Many adults wear a traditional costume, called a *bunad*. *Bunads* are elaborate, with complicated embroidery, pewter fasteners, and decorative pins. For women they include a long skirt, vest, blouse, and small matching purse, and for men, knee-length breeches, vest, jacket, and hat. An authentic *bunad* should not be purchased but handmade, and this is not a simple task. Special patterns and fabrics are required and difficult to get unless a special class is attended. Traditionally, teenagers are given a hand-sewn *bunad* that they continue to wear throughout their lives, not only on May 17 but also for weddings, christenings, and holidays. The specific design of each *bunad* identifies from what part of the country a person's family originated.

Anna sewed a *bunad* for her daughter, Nora, when Nora was fourteen. But Anna does not wear a *bunad*. For more than twenty-five years she has participated in the celebrations, watching her children march and marching herself with one or another of the clubs she has belonged to. She has sold waffles at the school and carried the Norwegian flag around all day long, just like everyone else. But over the years, the fact that she does not have a *bunad* has been a small but noticeable reminder that she is not a native Norwegian.

The first few years that Anna lived in Norway, May 17 did not mean much to her. She did not feel Norwegian, barely spoke the language, and did not have any childhood memories of the celebrations or parades. When her children started school and were marching in the parade themselves, the holiday began to have more significance for her. Not surprisingly, that is when she also began to enjoy it: "When you see your child go in the parade, then the Seventeenth of May is for you. . . . I think, for a foreigner, you have to have kids to feel with the Norwegian people on the Seventeenth of May. And I'm proud of the Norwegians that way—you know, the big turnout they make of it and all their lovely costumes."

In fact, Anna is so proud that after all this time, she is thinking of making her own *bunad*. She has some hesitation, though—she wonders if her Norwegian friends and family would accept an immigrant wearing the national costume: "I thought to myself, 'I've been here long enough that I could wear a *bunad* with pride.' I mean, I've [thought] this for a few years, but what do the Norwegians think? And I just started hinting around. 'Of course you can wear it,' they would say. 'After all, you've been here longer than you've been in New Zealand.' So I have a bond to, I think, to be able to wear it. But who am I to ask? Is there a right answer or a wrong answer to that? No, I don't think so; I think it's your heart."

If Anna feels Norwegian enough that she wants to wear a *bunad*, does that mean she is no longer a foreigner in Norway? The answer is no. Anna will always be a foreigner there, no matter how much she has changed: "I'm a foreigner because I'll always have a New Zealand passport." But literal truths regarding her political status as a New Zealander do not correspond to Anna's feelings: "I say I'm a foreigner—I am a foreigner—but I don't know; maybe I'm a foreigner on the outside, but I feel Norwegian on the inside. . . . Even though I—I am a foreigner, but this is my home. You know, black and white, I am a foreigner."

❧

Of Anna's two children, Per reminds her most of her Maori family. He is outgoing and relaxed in social settings. When there is company at the house, Per is always the one who is welcoming guests, making sure they have enough to eat and drink, and engaging them in conversation. Though born in New Zealand, he left when he was just a baby and did not return until few years ago. Then, in his early twenties he decided he wanted to visit, and he asked both his girlfriend, Bente, and Anna to come with him.

Anna was excited but also a little worried about the trip. How would her son, who was raised as a Norwegian, see her Maori family? What would he think about both the good and the bad parts of their lives? There was a piece of her that wanted Per to see only the best of Maori life, but then he would not really understand his mother's history or his own roots. Her pleasure over the prospect of her son finally coming to her "territory" and learning about his mother's culture overcame her fears: "I'm not ashamed of it. But, you know, oh, sometimes I was a little bit afraid of his reaction. . . . I wanted Per . . . to see my family; I want him to see them the way they are, not the way they want to be because we're there." Before they left Norway, Anna made a point of describing what her childhood home would look like, preparing him for the material along with the cultural differences.

The first few days were spent with family in Auckland. Given the size of the family, there were plenty of cousins to show Per and Bente around the city while Anna spent time with her siblings. After a few days, they traveled to the town where Per was born and where Anna lived as a young girl. Anna showed Per her mother's grave, the family home, and the places she used to go. The three of them drove around the North Island to see the sites and to visit other cousins.

While they were in New Zealand, Anna's family took the opportunity to arrange a celebration in their hometown. The entire family—aunts, uncles, brothers, sisters, and many children—met at the *Marai* for a traditional Maori gathering. For three days, Per experienced Maori culture, with all of the customary music, dancing, meals, and sleeping taking place within the three buildings that make up the *Marai*. Being with him allowed Anna to see the *Marai* through new eyes: "In there they've got paintings on the walls, on the ceilings, and everything has got their own meaning, and they've got carvings, and they mean different things too. And it's so wonderful." The ceremonies were elaborate, with songs and dances in honor of the Norwegian guests, including a special call sung by the *Kuia* when they arrived.

The family spoke with one another in Maori, except when addressing Anna, Per, and Bente, but they made sure that during speeches and performances someone was always on hand to translate. Anna did her best to follow the Maori, but it was difficult after all these years to understand a language she scarcely remembers. During the many hours of music Anna could only listen—the words to the songs had long since escaped her memory:

They would start playing music—you know, New Zealanders, Maoris, they love their harmony. . . . [A]nd then [there would be] a sing-along in Maori, of course. . . . [W]e could do whatever we want together. . . . [W]e could just sit in this *Marai* and talk and read and sing. . . . I started talking and explaining everything in the family, telling about their lives and their family and my mom. . . . I wanted to show them what I think was important. . . . [O]h, it was so nice.

When her daughter, Nora, had visited New Zealand years before, she had been too young to fully appreciate the experience or to understand the depth of feeling Anna has toward her first country. But on this trip Anna was able to see one of her children engaging as a adult with her family and her culture: "He made good friends with them, which is nice, because he's so easy to get along with. . . . [H]e's like an easy-come, easy-go guy; he can adjust to anything."

Per loved New Zealand and wants to return, perhaps to live for a time. Anna realizes, though, that Per's experience was only that of a visitor. It would not be possible to have a deep understanding of her history and culture in a short visit. Her family naturally had wanted to put their best foot forward for Anna and her son. To Anna's relief, the adults agreed ahead of time that during the weekend at the *Marai* they would observe tradition and have an alcohol-free gathering. She had been nervous about Per being exposed to what, for her, is a dark side of her family. She was glad he was kept at least one step removed from her childhood reality.

❧

Now that her children are grown, Anna has been trying to visit New Zealand every few years. Like the first visit, these trips bring mixed feelings. Though in many ways they are wonderful, they also cause feelings of estrangement toward her history and family to rise closer to the surface. After all her years away, Anna cannot relate to her siblings the way she would like. Some of her sisters feel the same way. They have lived too long without her to expect a close bond: "I'm just there on holiday, so I don't know what their lives are about, and, you know, I'm just visiting them, and what I say and what I think, it doesn't mean anything to them. 'Oh she's just passing, passing through' . . . so I really don't know what it's like."

The first few times she returned to New Zealand, Anna spent all of her time with her siblings. Now when she visits, she wants to do more. New Zealand is an incredibly beautiful country with a rich culture, and Anna wants to experience it in a way she could not as a child: "In a way it's not a very good experience, I think, going home. I just go home to see how my family is . . . and I get to be together with them, but that's it. When I come there, I sit in their four walls until I want to move [to] the next house and sit in those four walls. Nobody ever says like, 'Oh, do you want to go to the park?' or 'Shall we go to the aquarium?' They just don't think like that. So I go to the next one and sit there, and it's really pretty boring."

One sister has expressed some resentment that Anna left and now comes back as a tourist. This hurts, but Anna feels justified: "They can think whatever they want, but I go and work and save money so I can go on holiday. And because things are so expensive in Norway, I wait and buy things when I get there. She only sees the one side of me. And it's a shame, but I don't think I would ever come on the same [wave]length with my younger sister, because she was only eight years old when I left." Her family does not understand why Anna wants to visit the sights around Auckland or rent a car and drive through the countryside. Anna's Norwegian side looks at them and wonders why they do not take the initiative to see more of their own country.

Anna has changed since she moved to Norway, and though she knows this, the occasional reminders still take her by surprise. A few years ago, a teenaged niece came from New Zealand to spend several months with Anna and Olav. Anna was delighted: she would finally be able to share the way she lives, her home, and her friends with one of her New Zealand relatives. But as when Anna visits New Zealand, her feelings afterward were mixed. Having her niece there reminded Anna of how Norwegian she has become: "Maori people, they're very loving people and considerate and friendly people. And I feel that many times. But then again, I'm not as loving, because I see my niece—you know, I've had her here for these three months, and, you know, she's my blood, she's very close to me—but, then, I can't really show her how I feel. And when I talk to her, I don't have this typical Maori loving way of being. I feel it myself." With her niece, Anna felt herself holding back emotionally, being more reserved than she would like to be but unable to bring what she calls her "Maori me" to the surface.

Anna's affections quickly became channeled into making sure her niece had everything she might need. She found herself worrying that her niece might feel uncomfortable if she did not have the right clothes for when they went out on a boat, walking in the woods, or out to dinner. She also wanted her niece to have the types of clothes young Norwegian women wear, she said, "because I wanted her to fit in, and I didn't want her to feel out of place. . . . I'm just thinking of her, how she would feel. And I just want to make it easier for her to be able to move in these different circles while she's here. . . . If I see that she needs this, then I'll go to town, and I'll buy it for her. I don't want her to not have what she should have. It's just that I've got this—I have this funny way of showing [my feelings]. . . . [I]t's like [I show them with] material things."

Anna had always been uncomfortable with how much effort and concern Norwegians put into outward appearances, but she also knew that this attitude had rubbed off on her. Now it was glaringly evident just how much she had been influenced by these values. Actions motivated by love and concern prompted a painful realization for Anna: some of what she most loved about her "Maori me" had been replaced by an almost involuntary Norwegian-ness.

❧

With her New Zealand family Anna feels self-consciously Norwegian; in Norway she is sometimes confronted with her Maori background. In New Zealand: "I feel funny. I feel funny going there, being there. You know, I feel that I don't really belong there. No, I feel—I like it there, and I like being with my family, and I have a lot of memories from there, but I don't—I don't feel that it's mine, my home; I really don't." Anna loves New Zealand and wants to continue going back to visit—but not unless Olav or one of her children is with her. No matter how much she enjoys seeing her siblings and being in her childhood home, she feels alone in New Zealand without them.

About Norway, Anna says, "I feel very Norwegian here, in that way that I've taken, I've learned so much; everybody learns through their life, but I've integrated, adapted, to the Norwegian society. I feel myself Norwegian. . . . Even Norwegian people say, 'You're so Norwegian.' . . . I've got a better life, and I feel that my life is more fulfilled here, and I know I'm more open to things." Anna is now a foreigner in both of her homes. She is not entirely Maori, but she is also not fully Norwegian. She does not feel she belongs completely in either place.

When Anna came to Norway, she really did not know what she wanted her life to look like. It had not occurred to her that her cultural identity might shift. Anna believes that as young adults "we're easier to form," and this is why she has been so influenced by Norwegian life. She began doing things the Norwegian way so she would fit in. After a time, not only Norwegian behavior but also the Norwegian way of thinking started to come naturally.

Though she cannot describe exactly how, Anna knows that if she had stayed in New Zealand, she would be a different person. If she had stayed, she wonders, would she be more relaxed and less ambitious than she is now? It is unlikely that she would have owned a home or had the financial resources she has in Norway. But, then again, if she had stayed in New Zealand, maybe these things would not have become important to her.

Norway is no longer Anna's home by default; it is her home because she has carved out a place for herself there. The more recent additions to Anna's life—her two granddaughters—only reinforce Anna's bond to Norway. After the first grandchild was born, Anna was thrilled: "So we have a grandchild, and we're very pleased with our lives. It's really nice, because everybody's talked about having a grandchild—'Oh, it's an experience'—and I know what they're talking about. . . . And, you know, I feel part of this child, this little baby. . . . I think it's lovely. The same with Granddad [Olav]. Yeah, he spoils her too." The grandchildren bring Anna incredible joy. When she speaks of them, her face changes—her smile broadens, and the light shines in her eyes.

That Anna is a foreigner is not something she dwells on now: "In the beginning, you compare. Even though I didn't say much, I compared. You know, I wouldn't do this and I wish my family were this." But now "it doesn't matter what I don't like about [Norway]." And she is quick to point out that there is little that she does not like.

Still, Anna regularly gets small reminders that she is from elsewhere. At those times she has to fight the feeling that she is an outsider or excluded somehow from the inner circle of Norwegian life. It happens on holidays when Norwegians wear *bunads*, when someone notices her accent, or when she is reminded of the things about Norway that she is not comfortable with. She feels awkward, for example, with the way she sees Norwegian families relating. "Family" gatherings in Norway are frequently limited to immediate families. In New Zealand, the Maori concept of family is more inclusive. There, "everybody is your auntie," and all are welcome, all the time. Olav's siblings and parents do not spend much time together, and this still seems strange to her. After all these years in Norway, however, Anna is uncertain whether this is because of personality differences or culture: "You know, we're just getting older, and maybe this is the way life's supposed to be. . . . [Olav] and his family, they don't have that much contact. . . . [E]verybody's so busy. Is that society, or is it culture, or is it just us getting older and searching for something else?"

Anna is no longer the only obvious foreigner in town—even Norway's rural areas and small towns have now become multicultural. However, with the increasing number of refugees and immigrants in Norway, the issue of foreigners has become increasingly politicized. When a crime is reported, it is almost always noted if the suspect is foreign: "Ninety percent of the time I don't feel foreign. . . . [I]t's only that, when different issues pop up on the news . . . when I hear it on the news, if it's something—I don't know, if it's criminal or politically, it kind of rings a bell. That little percent that I don't feel Norwegian, it rings, 'Oh you know they're talking about us.' And then again I feel a little bit unsure. So there is always this little percent that tells me that I'm not Norwegian."

To Norwegians, Anna will always be an immigrant, no matter how Norwegian she has become: "It doesn't matter how much I've changed. In my eyes I would see myself as Norwegian. But there's always this thing behind: How do I look in their eyes? You know? How do I look in their eyes?"

Anna and Olav are now middle-aged. They are at a point in their lives when they think about how they want to spend their retirement years. For a long time, Anna wondered if some day she might return to New Zealand after retirement. But thoughts of living in New Zealand no longer draw her: "What would happen if all of a sudden I said, 'No, I want to go home'? I don't know where to start; I don't know where to start thinking at all, because what am I going to do there? I just have my family. How am I going to live, and . . . what about my kids and their families? I can't imagine moving back to New Zealand and starting anew, because I don't want to start anew. I mean, why should I? This is my home."

The people Anna feels closest to are not in New Zealand; they are in Norway. They are her husband, her children, her grandchildren, and her friends. If there were an illness or emergency, for example, Anna would go to her friends for help before she would call any family from New Zealand: "I wouldn't call on [them] to help me with anything. . . . [N]o, I wouldn't do that, because my closest friends would be [here]. I mean, they know me better. . . . You know, they're family! Who said that blood is thicker than water?"

Anna had her fiftieth birthday party recently. Afterward she sent thank-you cards to the friends who celebrated with her, and on the cards was a photo of Anna taken at the party. She is standing on the front steps of her Norwegian house and holding with both hands a full-sized flag of New Zealand. This significant birthday was not spent in New Zealand but in Norway with the friends who have become her family. Knowing she could always choose to return to New Zealand gives Anna comfort: "'Cause I think maybe there's more about New Zealand in the back of my mind than I—than I think, than I feel or that I would let out, I guess."

Though Anna holds on to the flag of New Zealand, she chooses to stand on the soil of Norway, and this is where she will stay. "I wonder if the older I get, the more . . . I think I really belong." She feels clear that even if something happened to Olav, she would not leave Norway: after all, "this is where my kids are. My friends are here. My life is here."

Lisa

Lisa considers herself an American. She holds a U.S. passport and makes her home in Miami. Her nationality is simple, but her identity is not. In addition to being an American, Lisa is a Jew, an immigrant, an office manager, a wife, a mother, and a friend. She is also Christian-raised, a sister, a daughter, a South African, and a Canadian. Incorporating all of these labels has been a process. Lisa has had to learn how to retain them all, moving within and between them, without losing any one part of herself. She is adept at adding or removing layers of these varied identities like articles of clothing. The layers she wears on the outside are visible to everyone. Other layers are not noticeable immediately. They peek out at the hem of her sleeve or under her collar. The most intimate, personal layers lie hidden next to her skin—a secret part of her that she does not share with the world.

If asked about her religion, Lisa will respond that she is Jewish. She converted to Judaism more than twenty years ago, has raised her children as Jews, and attends a temple. Her relationship to Judaism is nevertheless questioned at times, both by herself and by others: "See, a lot of Christians don't see me as Jewish, because they know that I converted and they know that my family is not Jewish. So they think maybe I'm, like, partly Christian, which maybe I really am, because that's how I'm kind of raised. That's a whole complicated subject."

Internalizing one religious identity over another remains a challenge: "You know, those first few years we were married, I didn't really feel Jewish; I still don't feel Jewish really. Oh, I don't want my kids to hear that!" Regardless of these conflictive feelings, Lisa's loyalty and connection to Judaism and to her local Jewish community does not waver: "I'm committed to those people now, the people at the synagogue. I feel like, as part of the congregation we're committed."

And despite the discordant feelings Lisa has with regard to winter holidays, incorporating Judaism into her life has been positive: "The greatest thing about the religion is that you get to question everything; you don't just have to sit there and accept what the religious leader is telling you. . . . See, that's partly why I feel so good about where I am, where my family is, because now I've studied some, just a tiny little bit of Judaism, a tiny little bit. And I feel that I have a leg up, because I've got that tiny little bit of Christianity that I have, and the tiny bit of Judaism, and now I have more knowledge, so I have a greater understanding of people and the world, you know?"

Lisa's mother-in-law once asked Lisa how she would feel if one of her children decided to marry a non-Jew. Her reply, though initially about religion, prompted Lisa to also think about whether she would recommend that her children immigrate:

I told her I would try and steer them toward somebody of the same upbringing. And that means not just religious but community too. I told her what I did I would not recommend. I would not recommend [it] to anybody because it's so hard. It's so much harder because when you shift religions, you have to leave your family almost. That's how it feels; it feels like there's a wall now between me and my family, and that's very hard. And she understood that. We were speaking more about religion. But I think that also applies to immigrating. When you change countries, it is like another religion. . . . Just the physical distance alone is a big issue. So I thought that was kind of interesting that I really knew how I felt about that, because it was hard, it was very hard. . . . I'd like to be more—closer and connected to my family. . . . I don't think that feeling ever ends, and that's kind of sad, but that's just the fact of life, and it's not the worst thing that can happen, right?

Nevertheless, Lisa is committed to the United States:

What makes me feel like I'm an American? I feel responsible for what happens in America. You know, you start with your community—you feel responsible for what happens in your community—and then on a bigger scale, [you] feel a responsibility to the country after having become a citizen. . . . I think a lot of the international community likes to just forget, conveniently forget, all the good things America does in the world. Just the money that goes out there to help—I really believe it's happening—it does go out there in a variety of ways to help in places like Africa and India and all over the world. But people tend to forget that part. They only remember all the bad stuff.

But no matter how deep her commitment, Lisa's ambivalence remains: "Oh, it's so hard to face. . . . [I]t's hard coming to grips with being a citizen of a different country. . . . I love the United States. Canada still is a special place for me, [but] . . . I've lived in Miami longer than anywhere. . . . When you live somewhere for a long while, you get really accustomed to your place; you know the smell of it, the color of it, the look of it, the feel of it, everything. . . . I think that you're kind of torn, torn between wanting to be somewhere else but then the connections that you've made."

The differences between the United States and Canada are always on the surface of her consciousness, and they nag at her: "I feel them all the time. I do. I feel them all the time." In Miami, Lisa feels she has to be on guard, especially in the car:

Here, [driving is] a challenge. You have to be alert. Sometimes you have to be aggressive; sometimes you have to be submissive. You definitely have to be wide awake, paying attention all the time. People don't obey the rules here; why is that? Every single day I can give you an example of something that happens on the road, and it's not that way [in Canada]. People just kind of drive along; they make space. But remember, too, up there I didn't live in the city. . . . You know, it's the way that people drive, the way that they talk to each other. Even in the grocery store, up there, if I address someone in the grocery store, they look me in the face, and there's an exchange. . . . But [in Miami], very rarely do you get that kind of attention.

Some days, Lisa will tell you that she wants nothing more than to leave the burning sun and humidity of Miami for the chill of the Canadian winter. On those days the United States is full of violence and superficiality. Other days, she rambles on about the unique beauty of the Florida Everglades, the amazing opportunities the United States provides, the value of the friendships she has formed in Miami, and the depth and meaning that Judaism has brought into her life. Lisa is not fickle; she is complicated by virtue of her multiple identities and loyalties.

The immigrant status of Lisa, a blond, white woman, is not obvious in the United States. Her accent is so slight that it usually goes unnoticed. When someone recognizes that she is an immigrant, it pleases her:

You know, I was getting to the point where I was thinking I was so Americanized that I didn't even have an accent anymore, until I left the dance class two or three weeks ago. I go to pay my parking, and the man—he's always there—he says, "Are you from England?" And I said, "No, but can you hear my accent?" He says, "Yeah." I said, "Where do you think I'm from?" and he couldn't guess. But it turns out he's from Nigeria. So I told him I was born in South Africa and we lived in Zambia. So we had a nice little conversation. I thought, "Darn, I thought I lost that accent." You know, I wanted to, but on the other hand, I don't really want to lose it because I'm proud of my heritage, and I think to lose the accent I'd kind of lose part of the heritage.

⟡

Lisa's mixed feelings about Canada and the United States surface when she speaks about her siblings: "I think that my siblings have a little bit of a hard time relating to the new me—not the new me so much but my life. That was kind of evident when my brother did come [to Miami] recently. We're in a different economic bracket than they are, and I think that has a little bit of effect on how they perceive our life and what we do here. I think so."

Lisa's brother, James, lives in a rural farming community in British Columbia. His everyday life is very unlike Lisa's urban existence. When she drove him around Miami Beach to see the sights, he was uncomfortable with the ostentatious display of affluence and materialism: the mansions, yachts, sports cars, and billboards hawking designer clothing and new condominiums. The amount of violence on television and in video games in the United States contrasted dramatically to what he sees in Canada.

When James commented on this, Lisa was once again reminded how far apart she is from her family. They have their familial bond and earnest love for one another, but Lisa's siblings do not always understand what her life in Miami is like. She sees that her children, although not raised permissively by U.S. standards, are exposed to much more than their Canadian cousins.

The irony here is that Lisa and Jason are far from materialistic compared to many Americans. They live simply, are environmentally conscious, and restrict the types of video games and television their children have access to. Lisa is a pacifist and tries very hard to shield her children from exposure to violent media. But the fact is that the American media present more violent content than their Canadian counterpart. Lisa frequently worries about the effect television will have on her children. She worries, too, about consumer culture and what she refers to as the "weight of possessions" for both herself and her children. For Lisa this is as much about environmental responsibility as it is a response to her childhood experience of moving around the world with one trunk.

Given Lisa's limited contact with her siblings, the divergence between their lives is not surprising. But understanding this does not prevent the emotional ache it causes. During an intense interview, Lisa became tearful: "And like, this kind of conversation that we're having? I've never had a conversation like that with my sisters, ever. The youngest one is enough younger than me that it's almost a different generation. So that's understandable. My brother I can understand because he's a man, and it's a little bit different there. But my other sister—I mean, I feel very sisterly towards her. But I've lived away for so long, and I really hate that—I hate that we just have that one-week-a-year kind of relationship. We don't talk on the phone all that much; once in a blue moon I'll phone her or she'll call me. And, you know, it's different when you're face to face and you can see each other and really have a conversation. You can't replace that on the telephone." And yet Lisa feels a strong bond with her sister: "I feel extremely close to her, you know, more than a friend. It's hard to put into words, but I feel very close to her."

Like other pieces of her immigrant life, the one with her family in Canada is fraught with ambiguity. Reminders of this unhealable wound can come at any time. When their children were small and Lisa and Jason wanted a night out, they called a babysitter. But their friends had family to call: "In most families here that I know, when their kids are little, especially when they're teeny tiny babies, if they need a night out, they call their sister. They call their mother. You know, they call someone within their family unit to come and take care of that precious brand-new baby. I didn't have anybody to call."

Her children are not babies any more, but the issue remains. Once when the children went away to a summer camp, Lisa and Jason decided to take their own camping trip. Since they would not be accessible by phone, they needed to give the children's camp a relative's phone number in case of emergency. The only available relatives were Lisa's, but that would not do because they were not located within the U.S. borders. Facing this kind of problem, while not dramatic, is a consistent reminder of Lisa's foreignness and the geographical space between her family: "I have those feelings all the time. . . . [D]ay to day, it's a longing kind of feeling: I wish they were here, just so we could visit, really. And then when there's occasions, big events, I wish they were here, or I was there so we could share them, share those things, because even though we're luckier than most and we see each other quite often, maybe once or twice a year on average, I still feel that maybe we're not quite part of their lives. And that's sad; it's sad."

The logistics of travel mean that Lisa misses the landmark events in the lives of her nieces and nephews, just as they miss those of her children: "When they're away, you really lose so much. I see that when I see my nieces and nephews now; they're almost grown, and I wish I had been more of a part of their life, all these years. When I see them, I adore them, and the rest of the year I adore them from a distance. It's all you can do."

To fill the gap, Lisa substitutes family with friendships. Though it took many years for her to feel connected and close to anyone in Miami, these relationships are now what give Lisa a feeling of permanence and belonging in Florida:

I don't really think anything replaces [family]. . . . Your friends become like your family. They really do. I think that's why I have such good friends. . . . [T]hey do become like your family, when your family is far away, I think. You know, if I'm agonizing over something, I don't call my sister; I call my friends, because they are in the same community as me, [and] they have children the same age. They have the same kind of life that I do, with all the different responsibilities. . . . [T]hat's, I think, a very important point. When you live away from your siblings, you adopt sisters. . . . And now, I have; I'm overwhelmed with great people. I can't believe all these great people.

⁓

For the most part, Lisa's life reflects her individuality and how she wants to live in the world. But in some respects, her choices are bounded by the fact that she is a foreigner. There is a slight constraint in all of her decisions: a concern that how she behaves will identify her to others as a stranger or cause some sort of problem. Her mother, with her own experience of multiple immigrations, says that immigrants must "live carefully." Lisa follows this philosophy, too, though she does not always like it:

That's kind of how I am . . . and maybe that comes from being an immigrant; you live in control, all the time. I think that, even now, I'm very rule abiding. . . . And I often wonder if it's because I'm an immigrant . . . because I don't want to get into trouble, I don't want to cause a disruption, [and] I don't want to be noticed. . . . I don't know whether it's just my personality or being an immigrant. But my parents are that way too. . . . Even today, like picking up [William] at the school. There's a certain place where you're supposed to pick up. So I told him, you must go up to the first stop, because I'm not supposed to stop back here. Where everybody else, they just do whatever they want!

Every few years, Lisa becomes frustrated enough with "living carefully" that she reaches a boiling point. Disagreements about something simple become elevated and symbolic of Lisa's compromise. The disagreement with her parents over the millennium New Year was one example; another occurred when Lisa found out that her husband had allowed their oldest son, Michael, to see *Black Hawk Down*, an R-rated movie about the American military in Somalia. She was furious:

One of the things I've been very sure about with parenting is I think for children to have too much exposure to too much really graphic violence is possibly destructive to them, to their personal growth.

You know, following my parents' lead, we never saw violence growing up, either in real life or on TV, in movies. [Michael] mentioned
that they saw this movie. . . . And I had like a nervous breakdown. I
cried for two hours, could not drive the car . . . and I just cried and
cried and cried and cried. . . . And then I finally got control of myself
[and] drove the car home. I could not come in the house. I refused.
I sat in that car for like two more hours. . . . I was so upset I could
not come in this house. I wanted to stay in that car, and I wanted
to drive it in a diagonal line till I hit Vancouver. It's almost like, I
don't know, do I hold Jason to a higher standard because I'm an immigrant? And I think that a lot of my reaction, or my overreaction,
is years and years and years of holding in some of those feelings.
Resentment, anger, you know, from being an immigrant.

Lisa believes that the immigrant experience has helped her become a
stronger, more self-confident person. This took some years. She has seen
herself change over time:

That's actually a very positive thing about being an immigrant—
that you're able to perhaps perceive those changes in yourself a
little more readily than if you weren't an immigrant, right? I think
so, because there's such a division between before and after [immi-
gration]. . . . I wouldn't be who I am today if I hadn't had all these
things happen, but still there are some things I could have done
without. . . . I have thought about that. Who would I be if I still
lived in the same place? Who would I have married? And I can't
even imagine it. I just can't. I can't even imagine it. I can't.

The "new, post-forty Lisa," as she calls herself, is not a pushover but a
person who now knows which battles she is willing to fight and which ones
she can let go: "I had to learn. . . . I mean, people even told me, 'You're such
a marshmallow.' You know, and I still, to this day, I tread lightly on certain
subjects. You know, I don't always tell people exactly how I feel, because
I don't want to hurt their feelings or I don't want to criticize them. I don't
want to have a confrontation; that's a big one. But I learned."

Lisa supposes that because she spent so many years adjusting and
adapting to a new country, it took her longer to find confidence than it
otherwise might have: "I think it's—maybe that's why maturity took so
long, because I moved in the middle of growing up. I think it delayed me,
because it did take me a long time to become more self-possessed. I was
just kind of floundering. Floundering is not really the right word, but I was
looking for myself. I don't know whether the post-forty comfortable zone is
more a maturity thing or an acceptance of my new life, twenty years later."

This newly found confidence is the result of pride about how she has
raised her children, feeling comfortable in her surroundings, and having

success in her work: "The only way you can really be happy is if you make yourself happy. I've just learned that kind of recently, probably around the year 2000!" When asked if she is glad she moved to the United States so many years ago, Lisa replied, "Oh yeah. Can I say that out loud? *Yes!* I made a great decision to come here."

Shirine

Shirine was finished with Denver. The time had come to move on, to be done with the past. At forty-seven, she was starting over. Living in France, she would renew and heal her relationship with her mother, support herself by painting, and live in an environment that inspired and nurtured her. She would be back to Denver for the occasional visit, but her children would come to France more than she would go to them. This was Shirine's plan, but as often happens, the plan and reality did not precisely match.

The idea of leaving Denver had been occupying Shirine's thoughts for years. What started out as a vague fantasy slowly infused all of her thoughts about the future until she was finally ready to put her ideas into motion. For several months before she left, the minutiae of extricating herself from Denver had completely filled her days. When Shirine finally got off the plane in Nice, there were no more errands to run, people to call, or details to attend to. But rather than feeling excited or ready for adventure, Shirine felt strung out. After selling the big house where she had raised her children and saying good-bye to more than twenty-five years of her life, Shirine was exhausted.

Having reached her goal, Shirine was suddenly faced with an indistinct idea of her future. Focused intensely on leaving Denver, she had not put much energy into planning the next step. She was no longer looking forward to living in France: she was there. Now Shirine had to construct the new life she had embarked on: "A lot of times in my life I know what I want, the main plan. And then the small details I don't plan out; I just let it happen. . . . I just go for it. I think I've done this since I was really young . . . because otherwise I'll never make the leap. . . . I think the thing is just putting the power out there to manifest."

Every morning Shirine awoke feeling tired and stressed. Sunny Mediterranean weather could not ease her anxiety about the future. For several months, the happiness that came with the move was counteracted with worry that she may have left too soon. Shirine missed her children and worried that they might not have been ready for separation. She had no idea how much time would pass before she started earning an income. Shirine recognized the underlying feelings she was having. Though it had been many years, she remembered what it felt like to be uprooted, and she also knew that the uncertainty and worry would eventually dissipate. The best response was to allow herself time to adjust and not expect too much.

Shirine moved into a furnished apartment in the same building as her mother. The apartment was tiny but had the advantage of a balcony overlooking the city. It was close but separate from her mother. Learning to be together after the many years apart was sometimes difficult: "It was hard with my mom; there were some disappointments about her and the relationship with her." This was balanced by acts of nurturing: "It was fine because in some ways I was taken care of for the first time. I didn't have to clean the house; I didn't have to do laundry. It just was very nice, after so many years of doing all this by myself and for the kids, to just sit there and veg almost. But, you know, I knew that wasn't my life. . . . [I]t was just temporary."

Instead of jumping into work, Shirine spent slow days reading, taking long walks, and resting: "I got really lazy. I just kind of let go. I don't know. I think it's because I had worked so hard and done everything on my own." Her mind needed to shift focus from the details of the move to a freer space where her creativity could awaken again. Shirine was starting over, but she was not without resources; nor was she in a completely unknown place. She spoke French fluently, so she did not have to worry about language. Though she is a foreigner in France, the country does not feel foreign to Shirine, and she had no trouble adjusting to French culture.

The greater challenge was finding social outlets. Though she had long been visiting the area, Shirine had no friends of her own in Nice. Her mother included Shirine in social activities, but her mother's friends were other Persian exiles. For the first time in many years, Shirine was surrounded by Persian culture. She was speaking Farsi, eating Persian food, and listening to Persian music.

After about four months in Nice, Shirine saw an ad for an international women's club meeting. From experience she knew that the way to find friendships would be through other foreigners: "When I first went, first of all, I didn't want to be with the Persians; I'm friendly with them, but I knew from the beginning that I didn't want to get stuck in that social scene. So I said to myself, 'I've got to meet people; I want to meet people that are from all over the world.' I have never in my entire life joined anything, but I thought to myself, 'How else am I going to meet anyone?' The thing is that when people come together and they're in a foreign country, the bond is, I think, deeper."

Feeling more settled now, Shirine set up her small apartment as a studio and began to paint again. The canvases she worked on were larger and even more abstract than anything she had done before, with an intensity of color and shape. Shirine felt she was expanding, moving into the future with her work. Then suddenly the door to the future seemed to slam shut. In February, after Shirine had been in France for only five months, Jackson unexpectedly became involved in a new business that required him to be away from Denver for two months. Louis was still in his senior year of high school, and neither Shirine nor Jackson wanted him to be left alone. Shirine felt she must go back to Denver immediately.

Shirine returned to Denver in February. Soon it became clear that Jackson would need to be gone much longer than he originally thought. If Shirine did not want Louis to be alone, she would have to stay in Denver through May. Going back and forth to France was not feasible: the flights were too expensive and Shirine had no income. She was living off the sale of her house and had to make that money last. Reluctantly she agreed to live in Jackson's house with Louis until Jackson returned.

Just a few short months before, Shirine had deliberately said good-bye to Denver. The last thing she wanted now was to be back where she started. After five months in Nice near both green hills and ocean, the Denver winter was uninspiring. Though the city is beautiful after a snow, the streets are soon dirty and bordered by brown slush. The surrounding mountains trap polluted air and the city feels closed in. Shirine felt disoriented and confused. Denver was not where she lived anymore, and yet there she was. Throwing herself into work, Shirine focused on producing enough art for an exhibit at a local gallery. The distraction was good for her. Between organizing the event, designing and sending the invitations, and creating the art, Shirine had little time to dwell on her frustrations.

The one thing that felt right about Denver was being with her children. Francesca came home from college almost every weekend, and the three of them spent time together. All along, the urge to leave Denver had been tempered by concern about leaving her children, and Shirine was glad to be with them again.

While Shirine was away from France, she found a new sense of clarity about the decision to uproot herself from Denver: "I feel that it was good for me to come back and have such a hard time these five months . . . to really make that final move without looking back. . . . [W]hat's good is that I've really come to appreciate the fact that I live where I live now [in Nice]. I'm more excited now than I was then." When Shirine finally went back to Nice, the ambiguity she felt after the initial move was replaced by a renewal of energy and enthusiasm.

Cultivating connections in the European art world was now Shirine's first priority. She needed to create a network in the art world and consciously decided to draw on the social skills she had learned as the child of a diplomat. She takes some pride in overcoming her lifelong shyness to manage that: "I was out there trying really hard to promote myself. But only now do I feel really comfortable. . . . That's coming a long way. I'm not scared of anything. I'm not scared of anybody. I can go to any country. And that's because, you know, I pushed myself, because I just was not like that. I think it's a desire."

Going back and forth between Denver and France was not Shirine's intent when she packed up her house and moved. But family and finances restrained her choices. Instead of following a straight road, she had to accept a more circular route to her new life. For three years essentially the same schedule was followed: Jackson traveled during the winter and early spring, and while he was gone, Shirine came to Denver and stayed in his house. Though both of her children were now out of high school, Shirine felt it was important to be available to them. Eventually, however, Louis and Francesca began to move into their own adult lives. Francesca moved to London to finish college, and Louis went to both Mexico and France to study languages. Every year Shirine was able to spend less time in Denver until finally Nice became her primary residence.

◦

Shirine's commitment to her art and her belief in spiritual guidance for her choices have not wavered:

> One day I woke up and claimed myself as a painter. I've been very, very faithful to my own belief system about what's right for me, and I know that by the end of my life I will have been right about the choice I made. . . . It's a long-term process . . . and for some reason God has supported me through all of it. And I've learned not to panic, because I truly know this is what I should do. And I know I'll be supported to do it. . . . I will, by the end of my life, achieve something that I feel is significant. If your work is good, I think it will just flow. And if I've achieved at the end of my life something that speaks to people, like good music, like classical music that makes them happy, moves them, puts a smile on their face or what-ever, then I feel like I've achieved something. But, you know, that should be the goal.

Shirine's means of emotional healing was through her spiritual path and is integral to her painting. Art "comes hand in hand with my spirituality." She has long believed that through the process of painting, she can access a subconscious level of what she calls "archaic knowledge" and symbolism. When she was a child, Shirine wrote letters to God. Now she paints to connect with her spiritual side.

Reviewing her work one day, Shirine noticed some symbols she had not been aware she was painting. Amid the abstract swirls of color were Persian-looking shapes and calligraphy. Seeing anything reminiscent of Persian culture was surprising: Shirine has long been aware that her work represents much beyond her conscious thought, but this was the last thing she expected. Even more surprising was that she liked the way the paintings looked. The next time she sat down to paint, she deliberately included some Middle Eastern patterns.

After a lifetime of turning away from anything Persian, Shirine has be-gun to open herself, little by little, to her cultural history and recently went back to using her family surname: "I'm more connected with Persians now. I speak Farsi better than I ever did before and am, in general, more comfort-able with Persians than I was in the past. It's not that I'm more Persian but more accepting of the culture. Instead of shunning everything, I'm accepting and letting it support me. Maturity has taught me to accept help and support rather than always move away from it. And this includes my mother and sister, along with my culture. It's funny; things have come full circle."

Shirine's sense of identity remains complex: "In France I don't feel French; I will probably always feel American in France, but I feel very comfortable. Every time people ask me where I'm from, I have the hardest time. . . . I'm Persian-born American; lately I've been saying that. . . . What I would like to say is that I'm a citizen of the world, but it sounds so pretentious. But that's how I'd explain it, because I don't feel Iranian. Probably I feel more American. No, here's what I feel; I feel Western. I relate to Western people, and that means Europeans and Americans. That's what I relate to."

Home for her is not bound by nationality or place. Home "is not necessarily . . . tangible; it's not an earthly feeling. . . . I found out where my home is, and it has nothing to do with the external. One of my biggest things I've realized in my life is that home is inside of me with my children. That's why I have so much peace now, because I don't really care. I don't have that struggle to belong anymore. I've never belonged. I don't think I ever will, really."

When Shirine left her life in Denver, she felt like she was "emerging from a dungeon." Her unhappiness was, she said, "not because of America or Americans. It's just feeling so stuck in my life and so stuck [in Denver]." She became a citizen of the United States in the hope that citizenship would create belonging. But the belonging citizenship gave was an illusion, just as getting married gave her the illusion of permanence and security. Shirine no longer wants to live in the United States, but she has never been sorry she became a citizen: "When I took that pledge to be American, I'm proud of it, and I don't take it back. . . . I mean, I always thought everybody in the States has received me with more than honor and more than respect, you know? The States and the people in the States have been more than kind to me." Her time in the United States was important for her. "I know the reason why I was in the States all these years was to find my inner self and my inner freedom."

❧

Coming to Denver as a young woman, Shirine felt "lost." Starting over in France in midlife was different. "I'm not scared anymore; that's the biggest thing. . . . Hopefully if one learns anything in life, it's to become more secure and solid." Shirine would not say that her life has turned out well, because as far as she is concerned, it has not "really even turned out quite yet. . . . It's a process. . . . I feel like I've lived centuries within my life— centuries of differences within my lifetime." Shirine knew she had to leave Denver, but both she and her children had to ease into the idea of separation. It took hard work to "release myself from my kids so that I can invite my new life in. I mean, I have been so bound to them and so determined to get them to a point where they feel well that I haven't given myself any chance to be open to anything. And so I think that that's why I've worked so hard . . . to get them to a point where they can fly. So then I can maybe have the chance at a life."

The life Shirine leads has diverged dramatically from what she knew as a child. The daughter of a diplomat, she never took public transportation—the family's driver would transport her wherever she wanted to go. Now, living in a small apartment that doubles as a work studio, Shirine takes the bus and watches her expenses. Over time she has come to a better understanding of her mother's earlier choices. She appreciates their renewed relationship and is happy they live near each other. Making a living with her art is challenging, but Shirine is hopeful: "I've given up on trying to [market my art] a certain way. I'm just open for whatever way it comes. It doesn't matter. I mean, it's basically for the people, and you've got to let go of how it's going to be distributed." Since moving to France she has had showings in Milan, Nice, Denver, Dubai, and London. Her painting style, like her life, continues expanding in new directions: "Yes. I mean, it's definitely getting there. I think I'm not going to really be there until I'm in my sixties. . . . [F]inally, my life is starting! Oh, God, I can't wait!"

Barrett

Barrett holds within herself distinct but blended identities. She can seamlessly transition from an efficient American businesswoman to a demonstrative Venezuelan mother figure. These are oversimplified labels, of course, but the contrasts between her different selves are real. Barrett can be whom she needs to be whether at a professional conference in New York or an intimate party in Caracas. Though she knows well the ins and outs of North American social rules, the relaxed graciousness of Venezuelan culture suits her better, and this is the side of Barrett's personality that she chooses to emphasize.

Though Barrett has lived a bicultural life for many years, her family is used to seeing only her American side. When they are exposed to the Venezuelan version of Barrett, it always seems to startle them—and this never fails to surprise and sometimes annoy Barrett. She tells the story of when she was visiting her brother Greg and his family in Chicago. Greg had neighbors who were originally from Caracas, and he invited them over to meet Barrett. When the couple came to the door, Barrett did what she always does when meeting new people in Venezuela: she extended her hand and then leaned in and kissed the other person's cheek. Speaking in Spanish, they greeted each other with smiles and amicable touches.

Barrett turned to speak to Greg and saw an expression of surprise on both his and his wife's faces. His wife blurted out, "Do you know each other?" "No," responded Barrett; they were meeting for the first time.

"And so what was the kissing thing about?" Amused, Barrett replied, "That's just the way you do things in Venezuela; I didn't even think about it." For Greg and his wife, however, this was the way to greet old friends, not someone unfamiliar, even if there was a personal connection. Barrett's openness seemed inappropriate and foreign to them, even though the Venezuelan couple was clearly at ease with her and handled the situation just as she did.

This kind of cultural discomfort can also occur between her coworkers from the United States and Latin America. At corporate meetings, interactions between the Venezuelan cable station and their cohorts from New York are sometimes awkward: "We were up at the channel for meetings this week in New York. And all of the people who work in International are kissy-huggy, you know, the two-kiss thing. And the Americans shake your hand. It's like, 'C'mon. Give me a kiss.' I mean, I know that there are certain guys up there that are uncomfortable around me, but they would also see that among our males, the people who work with me, they hug each other. And the Argentinean men kiss each other. I mean, they really kiss each other. It's not a kiss in the air; it's a kiss on the cheek."

American greetings feel stiff and formal to Barrett now. She has always been affectionate, and even as a child she did not understand why the men in her family were so reserved with each other: "I remember my brothers flipped out when the man I was named after, my Uncle Barrett, he used to kiss my father, and my brothers would greet my father with a handshake. And I can't believe that; it's like, 'Oh, what is the problem here?' And it's something that I obviously needed in my life, this kind of warmth. . . . As I said, it's not that my family isn't warm, because my family is warm. It's just so different."

Barrett describes herself as a person who had been searching for the right kind of nutrition—not one that would just suffice but one that would support and encourage an emotionally healthy life. When she first came to Venezuela, she "was desperately in need of finding that right formula." Finding a formula for her emotional nutrition gave Barrett the latitude to feel comfortable with herself. When she lived in the United States and England, her openness and receptive nature felt out of place. In Venezuela, her way of being with other people is not only accepted; it is assumed. Fitting in is not something she has to work for; it just is. And that brought an incredible sense of freedom: "I don't know what it is, but definitely, the possibility [exists], in Venezuela, of just being so absolutely *me*." Before moving to Venezuela, Barrett felt that her life seemed like "an eternal rehearsal for something, but it was not the real thing." She explains, "I was not the real me . . . until I was able to get immersed into this culture that embraced me in a different way."

Since Barrett began working at the cable television station, her life has shifted from total immersion in Venezuelan culture to a balance between the two cultural dimensions of her life. Working for a multinational corporation requires a fair amount of international travel and regular exposure to North American business and social situations. Her past and her present are no longer entirely separate. But Barrett is comfortable spending time in the United States only because she knows she does not need to live there: "I don't feel a relief to come back. . . . [A]s long as I know that I'm going home, I can come [to the United States] and operate here." When she's away, Barrett looks forward to returning to Caracas: "I just can't wait to just speak Spanish and feel like I'm at home, where I can be me. . . . I love being there, you know, and I love the weather, and I get home, and I just can't wait to be at home."

Barrett usually sees her family when they are at her mother's winter condo in Florida. But her mother often expresses her wish that Barrett would visit the house she grew up in, in New England: "My mother says, 'You haven't been home in over two years.' And I'm going, 'I haven't been home in over two years; what are you talking about? . . . I live at home—I mean, at *my* home.'"

Barrett's mother and brothers still seem to think of her immigration to Venezuela as a finite chapter of her life. Barrett does not believe they have ever fully grasped how committed she is to living there. When she attends family gatherings in the United States, she is still treated as a wanderer coming home to relate her adventures. Inevitably frustrated, she will tell them, "You know, I don't have any exotic stories for any of you people anymore. I live in Venezuela now. . . . [T]his is just my normal life." She can't conjure up witty anecdotes about expatriate life or travel adventures. When she is in Caracas, she lives in her familiar routine. When she visits the United States, Barrett feels she is away from home.

Though Barrett knows her family loves her, they do not understand her well, and she suspects that her visits can be equally trying for them: "I have this whole totally different vision of life and all of the things that happen in life and then what happens after life, and in [New England] there's no relation to that side of me. . . . It's like I am the strange one who's gone away, and I'm fun to be with, and everybody's glad to see me, but I know that there's a side to me that they'd just rather not deal with, and so it's much easier to deal with me on a sporadic basis."

❧

Barrett's emotional connection with Venezuela has an intertwined, dual quality. Her character naturally fits well with the culture, but over time the culture has also acted to shape her way of thinking and being in the world. Barrett is quick to point out that this influence does not mean she has become Venezuelan but that the country has become internalized in her: "I know that . . . so many things have happened to make this me, who I am, so much of Venezuela and America. Well, there's so much Venezuela in me, which is not necessarily Venezuel*an*—it's *Venezuela*; it's the country; it's the earth; it's the smells and the sounds of the country that are so intrinsic in everything. And I know that there's a physical thing; there's a physical difference in how I dress and how I carry myself. I have been in situations where I will come into the States on my American passport and people look at me like, 'You're not American.'"

Leaving the United States did not cause Barrett any feelings of remorse or sorrow. Any pain associated with immigration took place long before she left. Barrett had been grieving the loss of her "home" since she was a child and first recognized the pain of feeling like an outsider. When she moved to Venezuela, this grieving was finally over, because she had finally found a place where she could be who she wanted, without the pretense she felt was required of her in her hometown: "I went to Venezuela, and when it was what I had hoped it would it be, I just let my roots go into that ground." Venezuela became as much a part of her as her American past: "If you haven't lived in another country, it's very hard for you to understand what happens when . . . you are no longer from just one place."

Feeling accepted in Venezuela gave Barrett the chance to heal. Being physically and emotionally separate from the past helped move along the process of therapy and self-introspection: "There [has] been other griev-ing, and it's taken me all of these years to come into a kind of plenitude of myself. But that's me, and . . . it's not Venezuela's fault. . . . [F]ortunately, I was able to find the roads to a cure in Venezuela, which I didn't find in the States . . . because [there] I was not able to be me except in my own, literally, inner space, for so long." In Venezuela, Barrett does not feel the need to live up to her family's expectations for how she should live her life: "There are other pressures on me, but there's certainly not the pressures of trying to have me be something I never was—what they were hoping I would have been. What I really am is what I have grown up to be in Venezuela." Trusting that emotional and spiritual healing was possible, Barrett listened to her heart and let herself be pulled in a new direction.

In her description of her immigration experience, Barrett frequently re-turned to the theme of searching for the right location, a place where being true to herself did not cause her to feel like an outsider: "There was always something inside that kept me looking for something that I could morph into and feel like I was totally me. It was like a spirit that was in a physical context of my body . . . that was . . . not where I was supposed to be. But there was also an absolute certainty that there was some place, some physi-cal place, where I would no longer be an 'extraterrestrial.'"

Barrett has always been willing to take risks. She traveled to England with her cello and exposed herself to public critiques, moved to Venezuela, and changed careers at forty-two: "Why am I so fearless? I don't know. Because I come from a situation where there was a lot of fear. I mean, it's not easy; there are things that are pretty daunting, but also this believing in fate—you know, I think the other formula that's really been important with all of this is being able to say and believe, completely, that God or life or whatever you want to call it never gives you more than you can handle. And so the idea is if we've come into a life to learn and to grow and to fulfill a mission, be [that] what it may, the worst thing you can do is deny that."

Having faith that she would be taken along the right path, Barrett has been able to face her demons head on. She has changed from what she describes as a "mousy, insecure" person to a dynamic, strong individual with an amazing personal presence: "I'm not a daredevil. . . . My fearlessness has another quality to it, which is the fearlessness of being in a situation where I feel like this is what life is dealing me. And so deal me in, sure. I'm not going to be stupid, but deal me in. Let me learn; let me go up the next step in my spiritual growth."

Barrett started looking for spiritual fulfillment when she was just a child, exploring ways of understanding the world that did not fit with her upbringing. Her yearning for a place where she could belong was not just about location; it was also about finding herself and trusting that she knew the best way to go about that, despite the skepticism of those around her.

That she found a home in Venezuela was not a surprise to her. She had known for a long time that there was a special place for her and that eventually she would be led there:

> Everything that's happened to me has confirmed something that I already knew. . . . [I]t was for my health, my spiritual health, I had to go somewhere else. . . . And time has not proven me wrong. . . . I don't know why I was born needing something else. But I know that this need for something else was from the beginning . . . and I'm grateful for whatever it was that I had in my makeup that allowed me to be able to go on that road. . . . [I]t's not an easy road; it's a road full of hardships and so on. But as you travel it, you know that you cannot do anything else. . . . [I]f I hadn't done it, I just can't imagine how horrible it would have been; I just can't imagine it. And thank goodness that I was able to listen and smell the road.

As the years have passed, Barrett has become more and more content: "I remember when I turned forty. I was [in Venezuela] with my friends, and I said, 'I'm so happy. I'm so much happier than I was when I was thirty.' And when I turned thirty, I was so much happier than when I was twenty. And turning fifty has been the best. So, evidently, my life is not the kind of life that faded out; my life has gotten better and better. 'Cause I've just let it."

⤴

Barrett loves Venezuela perhaps as much as any native-born person could. She steers away from politics, however, and keeps some emotional distance from what is happening in the country that is outside her realm. Still a U.S.

citizen, she maintains an aspect of closeness to as well as distance from the United States and her family there:

> I think everything about my life is—the best way to say it is in Spanish: *lejanía cercana* or *cercanía lejana* . . . close but far away and far away but close at the same time. . . . I'm as close as I can be, but no matter how close I am, I'm still far away. And that's always been the case . . . like a Chagall painting that you see outside of the glass. . . . All of this stuff is happening, but there's always something between me and everything else. And when I was growing up in the States, I was there, but I was so far away. And now that I live in Venezuela, it's different, because I'm very close to some things but there will also be a distance, or I will be very far away from other things but there are distances that never really exist.

Living closely distant to Venezuela means that while Barrett loves the country, she is well aware of its shortcomings and tries to avoid them. But as she points out, in any relationship the good must come with some bad. Venezuela is a beautiful country, with a rich culture and heritage, but it is also a country in political and economic turmoil. There is poverty and crime along with warmth and beauty. The health care system has serious flaws. Her livelihood is dependent on the Venezuelan economy, and so her financial future, like that of many people in the world, has a precarious side.

Unable to vote in national elections, she is reminded that she has no control of or input into the future of the country: "I don't share the philosophy of the government; I don't share the philosophy of the opposition. I find myself more and more distant from all of that. I surround myself with as much spiritual protection as I can, every time I go anywhere, so that I don't think about it."

Barrett feels disenfranchised in the United States as well. What happens in the United States feels remote and disconnected to her daily activities and associations. She has little desire to participate in the politics of the country and little faith that her absentee ballot would count for anything. Her relationships with both the United States and Venezuela are in some respects detached, and though she feels an intimacy with Venezuela, she remains one step removed from both countries.

Being "close and far away at the same time" also describes her relationships with family in the United States. When Barrett is with them, they engage easily, but when they are apart, she communicates regularly with only her mother. Barrett's brothers were young when she left home for college. As adults, the siblings have never lived near each other, so there has never been an opportunity to develop or maintain close relationships. Phone calls between them are uncommon; they send her jokes via e-mail but not personal letters. Other members of her family call her when she is visiting her mother but never call her in Venezuela. Barrett accepts their relationships the way they are: "I'm far away, but I'm as close as they want me to be."

꙳

In Venezuela it is always spring, and time passes without a visible change of seasons. Without the demarcation of the changing colors of leaves, cold winters, and hot summers, time has a different texture than it does up north. The passage of time is slower and its impact softer. Barrett once suggested that when living near the equator there is less emphasis on the future or past and more consciousness of the here and now: "Maybe the essential part of my love affair with Venezuela is that it has always allowed me to live in the present. Fully, completely, absolutely present. And all of the good things about living in the present." Learning to focus on the present has brought Barrett abundance—perhaps not in terms of the financial security her family wishes for her but in ways that, for her, are more important: the sense of being surrounded by devoted and loving friends and a culture that fits her personality and needs.

As a child, Barrett idealized the concept of living far away from home—someplace where instead of feeling awkward because she was different, she would feel that her differences were valued. Feeling foreign in New England hurt, but in Venezuela the hurt has been transformed into contentment: "Definitely the other country experience was much more satisfying, gratifying, and self-esteeming" than living in the United States. In Venezuela, Barrett fell in love with everything—good and bad—about her surroundings, and that made loving herself easier as well. She feels accepted and included by her communities of professional colleagues, friends, and the many children she has helped to raise—all relationships that have created attachment and a sense of home for her.

For Barrett, Venezuela is a place of emotional, intellectual, creative, and spiritual growth. It is a place of freedom and peace. Her family sees her as someone who ran away from home, and Barrett acknowledges that there is some truth to this perception. But Barrett's need to follow her own road was less about leaving than moving toward something better: "I knew that I had to leave the atmosphere that I was growing up in; I knew that. But . . . I was *going to* something. I had to go to something, to find something." That Barrett decided to stay in Venezuela on her own means everything to her: "Because my life in Venezuela is my life; it's *my* life. . . . [T]he fact that I've chosen that life is so important to me."

Staying in her adopted home and living out her choices is what Barrett needs: "I just want to be able to continue doing what I have to do. I want to be in a place where I can feel that I am able to meet life's challenges, that I'm able to embrace situations that are dealt to me. And, you know, I envision myself working in Venezuela . . . imagine myself in Venezuela. I don't want to flee."

Barrett wrote in a letter, "The essence of immigration . . . is the whole idea of hope. . . . [P]eople need to hope there is a better life somewhere else. You emigrate to wherever you imagine your dreams may actually come true, and then nothing else matters. You can leave family and everything familiar without even looking back. The promised land is a powerful magnet. . . . Hope spawns growth and is stronger than stagnant nostalgia." Hope and trust in her choices is what gives Barrett the strength to always be "closely far" emotionally, regardless of where she is physically, yet remain centered and calm through whatever storms approach.

LIVING "CLOSELY FAR"

Although their individual stories are different, the experiences of Anna, Lisa, Shirine, and Barrett suggest that immigrants' routes to attachment and belonging follow an indirect path. Their post-immigration lives share certain themes: all faced conflict involving separation and change in familial relationships, all reached a critical moment that compelled them to reevaluate their perceptions of home, and all came to new understandings of their composite identities. But these incidents and the shifts in perception they triggered were rarely linear.

Immigration has contoured all four women's lives in ways they could never have foreseen. Being an immigrant is not just about learning to live in another country; it is profoundly about the personal transformations that occur while a different kind of identity is being forged. Immigration is about drawing meaning and developing resilience from experiences, both good and bad (Ehrensaft and Tousignant 2006, 481).

The narrative lives of these four women must include stories of the pain and loss that accompanied them on their journeys. But positive outcomes are as significant to understanding how immigration affects individuals as are the negatives (Rudmin 2009, 117; Ehrensaft and Tousignant 2006). Discovering how immigrants find a sense of home reveals the constructive aspects of their characters and highlights immigrants' strength of purpose. How they approach the loss inherent in immigration correlates with the agency they have in shaping their own futures (Furman 2005, 111). Although Anna, Lisa, Shirine, and Barrett will continue to live with the tension and conflict of dueling identities and loyalties, beauty can nevertheless be found in the lives of these women, who, because of circumstance, have been given opportunities to find contentment, love, and wisdom in a new country.

Past Tense/Future Visions

The journey toward finding home includes not just the "where" but the "who." Included are the individual's outlook, choices, history, and internal emotional structure. All of the things that make us who we are will be affected by how we define home. For an immigrant, these questions of identity are magnified through the lens of difference. If they are to find a new sense of home, immigrants must to some degree reinvent themselves as individuals and create new understandings of themselves and their lives.

As strangers in a new country and culture, these four women were able to look at themselves as if in a photographic negative. In this reverse image, they could see themselves from the outside in. Observing their personal and cultural traits challenged their assumptions about themselves, from the ordinary to the unexpected. At times, there were parts of themselves and their personalities they felt the need to minimize or even suppress. This cultural shadow continually lurked beneath the surface of their outward identity. As they learned the rules of behavior, thinking, and language in their new world, keeping their shadow side contained became second nature. But when situations arose that triggered strong waves of memory and emotion, aspects of the shadow surfaced.

Shirine's European sensibilities, Lisa's feelings about holidays, and Anna and her "Maori me" were cultural shadows. Barrett had less trouble in Venezuela because there she actually felt less need to suppress herself than she had in Connecticut.

For years, Shirine tried to reject any traces of her Persian culture. Feeling trapped in Denver caused her to rebuff the American aspects of herself she had acquired by living for more than twenty years in that country. Now she has exposed what she once considered shadows and has circled back to a place of appreciation and acceptance of how both American and Persian cultures have shaped her. Barrett is able to function in both Venezuelan and American venues with comparative ease. When she is with Venezuelans, her Venezuelan identity is on the surface. When she is at a business meeting in New York, her direct, efficient American side can more easily appear.

These women are not being false or insincere when they shift between cultural traits. They have learned to loosen their grip on how they see themselves and to allow different facets of their personalities to emerge where and when they fit. The strength of one characteristic in one setting does not diminish the strength of another in a different setting. Additional culture learning can occur at a more leisurely pace, not in a rush or under the pressure they felt in the first years.

Fitting in is now a conscious decision, something that can be chosen or disregarded. Whether it is a result of having gained the confidence that comes with growing older or having attained comfort within their newer culture is not always clear. The "new, post-forty Lisa," strong, determined, and no longer a "marshmallow," came equally from Lisa's experience as a mother, an office manager, and an immigrant. These experiences were not mutually exclusive, and neither is the root of her self-confidence.

Adaptation to a new place and to our own changing rules and expectations is not an instantaneous trick. Age and time help the process along, especially for those who want to adjust with grace. By the time we are forty or fifty, many of us have augmented or shifted our identities multiple times and will do so as long as we continue to develop as individuals. Shedding old skins—allowing oneself to evolve in this way—requires seeing the apparent discontinuities in life as something to value and work with rather than to avoid. As Mary Catherine Bateson suggests, we compose our lives through improvisation (Bateson 1989) and in so doing face what life brings to us in the best way we can.

Anna, Lisa, Shirine, and Barrett were not always aware of how they were being transformed through immigration. The shifts in attitude and perspective were frequently so nuanced that until they started to describe their lives out loud to me, they did not realize exactly when change had occurred. At other times, the shifts crashed into their lives and could not be ignored: Shirine's divorce, Anna's first visit back to New Zealand, Lisa's and Barrett's moments of family crisis.

In different ways, all four women made use of challenging situations by taking what they learned and using it to reconcile the contradictions in their lives, to break old patterns and to discover a new frame of reference. Though not all of the issues in their lives are resolved, they now have a clearer vision of the trajectories of their lives than when they first emigrated.

As a cultural outsider, a person can find it easier to see his or her own identity with a measure of detachment and to evaluate which pieces are best let go to make room for new identities. The immigrant will always be an immigrant, never a native, never a complete insider. But as noted in Part II, the other side of this coin is the chance to explore new ways of being. Anna would agree with those who view "in-between" or liminal lives as an advantage. She observed that her relatives who had never left home seemed to be stuck in old ways of thinking and living, while she had been given the opportunity, through immigration, to expand her world and perspectives.

For all of these women, immigration engendered changes in identity that led to a sense of freedom. The Norwegian sense of order and practicality was a source of irritation for Anna until she visited New Zealand and realized how much of these traits she had absorbed herself. Unexpectedly, the positive aspects of both cultures became more apparent to her, and she realized the value of blending them. Shirine found freedom when she finally accepted that she would never belong in Denver. She had entered into American society as much as she was able, but it was not enough. Her acceptance gave her the strength not to fight to belong but to try something daring and new, something that represented freedom and belief in herself.

To a certain extent, adjusting has required each to release the struggle to maintain an identity based on only her first culture and former way of life. But as the women's turning points show, the surrender involved in letting go has not always been a negative experience; it has also been a route toward acceptance. Acknowledging the ongoing need to reconcile the disparities between the home they left and the home they have created helped their identities evolve and flow.

Nevertheless, living with your heart in more than one place can cause emotional fragmentation. As Katarzyna Marciniak remarks, "While it is fashionable nowadays to *theorize* in-betweenness, it is quite different to live it" (Marciniak 2006, 23; italics in original). None of these four women now want a complete return to their home of origin or their former identities. They are well aware that even if they made a physical return, the internal changes that have occurred in both themselves and those they left behind mean that home is no longer what it once was. In a globalized world, hybrid cultural identities may be advantageous in many respects, but there are also disadvantages and loss (Hall 1992, 311). Anna's ability to broaden herself also led to a painful alienation from those she left behind. The same was true for Barrett and Lisa; the more hybrid their identities have become, the less connected they feel to their homelands and families.

Acceptance of identity change does not mean forgetting. Lisa will always remember the Christmases of her youth with both fondness and sorrow. But while the yearly passing of the holidays will always cause heartache, she no longer stops short with pain every December. For Barrett, the struggle was less in accepting how Venezuelan she had become and more in recognizing that she still retained a measure of Americanness. Working for an U.S.-based corporation in Caracas, she could begin to value her American traits and cultural knowledge and stop wrestling with the dichotomy between her past and present.

For all four women, accepting that identity and belonging would be an ongoing challenge brought a new sense of ease about the idea of home. Acknowledging the conflict released some of the tension and perhaps an understanding that home is not necessarily where one is happiest but "where one best knows oneself" (Rapport and Dawson 1998b, 9). Self-knowledge provided the emotional room to reestablish their personal priorities. For Anna, Lisa, and Barrett, this understanding meant recommitting to their new home; for Shirine, understanding meant the need for yet another change.

⁓

Nostalgia is a concept that frequently appears in literature, both scholarly and otherwise, in conjunction with immigrant emotions.[1] Some writers consider nostalgia an emotional trap for immigrants, who are challenged to hold on to memories without letting an idealized past overwhelm the present (Akhtar 1999, 90, 94) or allowing the imagination to become the principal location of home (McLeod 2000, 211). In an oft-quoted passage, bell hooks differentiates nostalgia from remembering. While nostalgia is the "useless act" of "longing for something to be as once it was," remembering "serves to illuminate and transform the present" (1990, 147). Remembering, instead of causing a person to remain mired in the past, can be transformative, allowing one to move forward (Agnew 2005a, 9–10). Images of the past and future can then reflect and support one another.

Andreea Ritivoi, however, considers nostalgia a crucial factor in an immigrant's understanding of identity. Homesickness catalyzes individuals to take stock of their lives. In reviewing their personal history, identity, and options, immigrants are able to find a bridge between cultures (Ritivoi 2002, 3–5). Certainly, inhabiting familiar feelings of the past can console, but too much longing for something that cannot be recuperated can lead to sadness and dissatisfaction. Excessive nostalgia can cause an immigrant to constantly look over her shoulder and wonder whether she would be better off if she returned to her homeland. If yearning for the past prevents an immigrant from visualizing a potential future in a new place, feeling "at home" there would be incomprehensible.

For each of the four immigrants, the task of integrating their pasts and futures took different forms. All had feelings of grief and loss, and all still have occasional stretches of nostalgia during which they may romanticize how life "might have been." The counterweight to these feelings is the memories of why they left home in the first place, as well as the ongoing emotional investment in their new lives.

Of the four, only Lisa was under a spell of nostalgia that prevented her from separating from her past. Even as her children and day-to-day life absorbed her, she clung in her heart to the dream of living in Canada, which in turn kept her emotionally distanced from her life in Miami. But as she eventually recognized, her husband and children could never become a part of her past, and ultimately they were her priority. Once she could inhabit her life from a present perspective, she more easily embraced Miami and began to see her future differently. The change was not just in her vision of what might come next, but also in her perception of her own identity. She then moved from nostalgic melancholy into a more self-assured future.

Shirine was never able to see a future for herself in Denver. Visualizing a future there did not create bonds but feelings of constriction. Shirine did not idealize her past, but she did idealize her potential future, which she envisioned as unfolding in a different location. Shirine's idea of home is not easily defined, in part because after her many years of feeling dislocated, she has concluded that her search will continue. Being settled in France is only temporary. Like many immigrants, Shirine does not feel connected to any one nation and instead seeks to live with more ambiguously defined borders (Furman 2005, 112). In her words, she is "a citizen of the world." She deliberately gave up her grounded life in Denver for the uncertainty of a future she could ad-lib. Her future desires have not been formulated in terms of place but in terms of content. More than the other three, her search for a physical home continues, but her emotional rooting in her knowledge of herself is strong enough to carry her forward.

Barrett, like Shirine, spent many years hoping to find an unnamed but nurturing place to live. The moment she first stepped on Venezuelan soil, she knew that she would make that country her home. Still, it was not truly a home until she had attachments there. Her memories were formed by making *hallacas* in her friend's kitchen every Christmas and by watching her students as they progressed through school. Before Barrett made a home in Venezuela, she was primarily living in the future. Now, she feels comfortable in her environment and safe enough to let her roots grow.

Of the four women, Anna seems to have had the least conflicted relationship reconciling the past and present. Once she was in Norway, living in the present came easily, in part because she had little opportunity to dwell on the past. Her easygoing personality and ability to live in the moment benefited her as well. Anna does not recount experiencing nostalgia as such, but she did want to return to New Zealand and revisit her past. When she was finally able to return, unhappy reminders of childhood surfaced and at times overshadowed pleasant memories. She missed New Zealand but did not have a romanticized view of what her life there had been.

All four women carried both tension and ambivalence regarding their feelings about home. At different times and places, home has represented restriction and repression as well as comfort and security (see Gurney 1997). The aptitude for blending past, present, and future by incorporating, not erasing, their cultural and personal memories was a key factor in finding peace. They had to learn to reminisce without falling into either nostalgia or bitterness.

A sense of home, then, is like a sense of identity; it is active and fluid. Home entails "*creating* both pasts and futures through inhabiting the grounds of the present" (Ahmed et al. 2003, 9; italics in original). Because "being at home" is fundamentally about feelings and emotions, it is inherently full of contradictions and inconsistencies (Gurney 1997, 383). A home is built (not only in a physical sense but also in a spiritual and emotional sense) by finding a way to fit the past into a new life and the present into the former life—with the memories of family and friends who were left behind. The choice is not always about "where" home is; sometimes it is about how people approach the circumstances they find themselves in. Creating a sense of home comes with an acceptance of what there is to work with, including the interaction between individual personalities and the physical and social aspects of a location (see Moore 2000, 211). Home is the place from which the meaning of our lives is understood, but just as what and who we find meaning in can change, so can our definition of home.

Dual Realities

Living transnationally is frequently regarded as a positive alternative for immigrants (see Croucher 2009, 137). Seemingly, living dual lives might alleviate some of the emotional tension of separation. But for immigrants such as Anna, Lisa, Shirine, and Barrett, maintaining dual lives was not a practical reality, either personally or economically.[2] When they first emigrated, international travel and communication was far less manageable than it is today. As time passed, opportunities for connection with their homelands and families increased. But at the same time those opportunities began to appear, the prospect of sustaining concurrent relationships with their multiple homes became less possible.

Anna, Lisa, and Shirine had children. Attending to their children's needs and education, as well as those of their communities, required these three women to be physically present in one place. Motherhood altered their perspective of home and informed their decisions and desires regarding place and movement. They were for the most part bound to one location and too occupied with their everyday commitments to maintain ongoing continuity with their former lives. Economics similarly played a large part in limiting their choices. Working outside the home and contributing financially to their families' well-being was necessary at some juncture for all of them. Though Barrett did not have children, she too was limited by practicalities: the need to have a secure job and her own desires to create a sense of community in Venezuela.

Anna, Lisa, and Barrett all maintain significant ties to the homes they left behind. But for both emotional and practical reasons, all three women ultimately needed their sense of belonging and home to move toward a single location.[3] Belonging meant becoming a part of their adopted communities, learning, and internalizing a new culture and way of life.

Of the four women, only Shirine could be considered to have a somewhat transnational life. After many years stationary in Denver, Shirine now moves frequently between two countries. But this option presented itself only after her children were grown, she was divorced, and her economic situation allowed for it. For twenty years she appeared to be fully absorbed and assimilated into U.S. society. When she left, her aspiration was to settle in France, not create a peripatetic life. Eventually, going back and forth is something that she hopes will end.

The ability or desire to live in a transnational manner, then, cannot be assumed for all immigrants. Even when economic and political situations allow for ongoing, integral involvement with both sending and receiving societies, personal and familial circumstances affect the options immigrants have for maintaining transnational ties. Immigrants are not immune to the realities of life that affect all parents, particularly women, even when their lives are buffered by relatively privileged circumstances. Living dual lives is a luxury most people simply cannot manage.

The concept of emotional refueling mentioned in Part III took on a different meaning for these immigrants as time passed. During those first years as newcomers, visits "home" were looked forward to but usually became more of a reminder of conflict and longing than regeneration. Once acceptance and commitment to their new place or situation emerged, then refueling in fact became a possibility. After the millennium New Year "blowout," Lisa began to commit to the United States and release her hold on Canada. Now when she visits Canada, especially the Whistler condo, she does not feel pulled as strongly by difficult emotions, and she comes home to Florida feeling emotionally recharged instead of compressed.

Anna has also found a way to combine vacation time with her family visits in New Zealand, and this helps her feel less bound to her former identity. She can now be both a part of, and distinct from, her family and Maori roots when she is there. Shirine could not feel refueled by her visits to France while she was living in Denver. While giving her a taste of Europe, being in France also reminded her of her conflicted relationship with both her mother and her current life in Denver. Now that she lives in France, however, her visits to Denver recharge her connection to the American part of her identity. Barrett may never have the feeling of "refueling" in the United States, but this causes her less suffering than the others because she has never expected Connecticut to be a source of restoration.

The stories of these four immigrants illustrate that the transition to belonging in a new country is a long and many-layered process that continues to revisit immigrants as they go through the many phases of their lives. The circumstances they encountered steered them in the direction of assimilation and commitment to one home rather than dual homes. Still, the need to retain a significant part of their first cultural identities was never eclipsed. What led them to the eventual choices to stay, leave, or accept or reject the various aspects of their new homes was a product of their initial motivations as well as the situations they faced along the way.

The intermittent reappearance of turning points in the lives of these four women underscores that immigration is not an event and adaptation is not a phase: the interaction of belonging, identity, and home is an ongoing process. Being an immigrant becomes a way of life because acculturation and feelings of liminality are never completely resolved (see Bhatia and Ram 2009, 148; McLeod 2000, 210). The advice from Lisa's mother to "live carefully" is something most immigrants are likely to understand intrinsically, along with the awareness that there will always be an aspect of "foreigner" in their identities.

Destinations

Shirine and Barrett view their émigré lives as part of a conscious spiritual path. The meaning of their goals and experiences are found within the context of spiritual growth and a relationship with what is beyond the material world. Integrating the challenges and joys particular to both immigrant and ordinary aspects of life are part of a larger picture of how each woman interacts with the sacred. Though religious affiliation has been a primary focus in both Lisa's and Anna's lives, neither put great emphasis on their own spirituality. For both, religious expression holds value but belongs primarily in a tradition-bound context.

To find meaning in the world, Lisa focuses on nature. She sees the world more from a science-based perspective than from a spiritual one. Whether in the Everglades or the Canadian Rockies, Lisa finds peace in the outdoors. Though Lisa does not share Shirine's spiritual perspective, they both shared with me a similar insight: the possibility that their adult maturity was delayed, or at least altered, because of the experience of immigration. Lisa makes a direct connection between her own "growing up" and the development of her identity.

In both Canada and Miami, Lisa had to relearn how to fit in and shape her outward identity. Not until that became second nature could she consider who she had become underneath the surface. When she was finally able to consider this, issues of identity demanded her attention with intensity. Lisa may not include a spiritual element in her search for home, but she would agree that by living outside her comfort zone, she has reached a deeper level of understanding about her own personal life, her love and loyalties, and that this understanding has made a substantial difference in the happiness she finds in her daily life.

Anna refers to herself as a Mormon, but she has not been actively involved in the religion since she was a young child. Participation in Maori ceremonies brings her joy, but this is fulfillment based on cultural and personal history, not on the spiritual. The Lutheran church in Norway does not draw her, but she understands the importance of the ritual and rites of passage and willingly had her children christened and confirmed in the church. Her reasons for doing this were not based on religion but on ensuring that her children felt Norwegian and would not face the issues of belonging that she had. Anna did not set out to leave her home in New Zealand. But finding her new life was more than just luck. In her quiet way, Anna took risks, trusted her instincts, and allowed herself to follow a different path. The ability to follow her intuitive sense of what was best for her, even though it contradicted conventional wisdom, is a trait Anna shares with Lisa, Shirine, and Barrett. All four of these women were willing to take a chance and start their lives anew, not knowing what lay ahead.

When I first began to conceptualize this book, I resisted accentuating the theme of spirituality. Though I see developing self and identity as linked to spiritual understanding, I was not sure this would be an appropriate perspective from which to interpret these four women's lives, and I worried that I might risk imposing my own viewpoint. But as I concluded the work, it became increasingly apparent that I could not omit the dimension of spiritual exploration from their stories. Zygmunt Bauman suggests that to find meaning in the modern word, it is necessary to live life as a pilgrimage, always walking forward while continuing to reflect back. Meaning and identity can be acquired together along the way but will never be fully realized (Bauman 1996, 21–22). The window from which I observe the lives of these four women influences me to see them as unintentional pilgrims, on a perpetual search for meaning as they walk their individual journeys. While they move forward, they must remain committed to having trust in the journey itself rather than to anything more material or earthbound.

For these four immigrants, finding belonging and feeling "at home" has come to symbolize the search for an understanding of themselves. The "promised land" Barrett referred to was not a literal destination; it was a spiritual quest and a metaphor for inward discovery. The only way for these immigrants to reach their destination, then, was to leave behind the desire to look back to their first home, or forward to some future one, and instead to look inside themselves. Rather than a place, home became the acceptance of a creative, individual understanding of identity: who they are, who they will become, what they want, and where they belong.

Lives often include at least one story of adjustment. How to manage and integrate these adjustments is not always obvious. Every circumstance is somewhat different, and there are no prescribed instructions to follow. Even if immigrants have lived in an adopted country for years, in all probability aspects of their past are sometimes still difficult to incorporate into their present and future.

With each step on this journey, each of these immigrants was seeking somewhere solid to stand—a base that they could hold on to and make their own. What they found along the way has had as much to do with their ability to receive as what has been offered by the places they have sojourned. Belonging was not an automatic process. It required accepting a relationship with their new place that was not adversarial and letting go of resistance to identity change. Living in a place that was not their own did not make the search for self-understanding easier, but in the long run, it made it more profound.

Though an immigrant may seem completely adapted to a new country, he or she will undoubtedly have a compelling story to tell. That story is likely to begin with the focal events of leaving and arriving, yet the everyday moments that culminate into the transitions and turning points in their lives are the deeper narratives that need to be heard. Conveying that story to a listener who truly wants to comprehend their evolving stories provides validation for their experiences. Through the act of recounting, the storyteller is able to determine the meaning of the events and thus feel a sense of agency or influence over her own life (Jackson 2006, 14–18). Sharing the story relieves isolation and helps a person who feels like an outsider gain a sense of belonging (Bolen 1994, 110–112). Each retelling to an engaged listener, then, is a key part of the process of bringing an immigrant home.

Acting as a witness in turn affects the listener, who by receiving the story can benefit from it. Listening to the stories of immigrants provides insight into and inspiration for how we might move through our own worlds and remember how easily we can be transformed through our experiences, the people who surround us, and our physical locations. Truly listening to immigrant stories, however, requires going beyond the preliminary question of "Where are you from?" to questions about what it means to belong and be at home in a new country. Such meaningful conversation invites a deeper understanding about belonging and home over the course of time and place.

In our dynamic, multicultural world, asking immigrants to tell their stories about home provides an opportunity to enrich all of our lives.

John Berger writes that "home is no longer a dwelling but the untold story of a life being lived" (1991, 64). For each of the immigrants whose stories you, as reader, have witnessed, a unique sense of home has emerged. What was once a new and unfamiliar landscape is now comfortable and familiar, a place where it is gratifying to return. They have given up commitment to one location and replaced it with another, but each woman, in her own way, holds those pieces of her past home that give her strength. In their struggle to combine cultures and smoothly move through the grind of everyday life, they have managed to find their way toward both satisfaction and a strong sense of themselves.

The stories of Anna, Lisa, Shirine, and Barrett do not end here. They have many more years to sort out who they are and where and how they will belong. What the word "home" means to them today may not be what it means a few years from now. They will continue their journeys toward home and belonging as long as they move along their personal paths. We will leave them at midlife, all of them with more years lived in their adopted homes than their first ones.

Always "closely far" from both past and present homes, each woman has found her own way of accepting and valuing where her choices have led. Conflict and fragmentation steered each of them to internal transformation and slowly coalesced into new expressions of identity. At times, the differing aspects of these identities still feel incompatible, and belonging sometimes still fluctuates between locations. But as time has passed, each has found a measure of balance and constancy with her own sense of belonging. Each of their identities is richly blended and gently fills the space in their hearts that is devoted to home.

NOTES

INTRODUCTION

1. The number of *accidental immigrants* at any given time or in any specific locale is difficult to determine. The nature of this category is the unpredictability of individual intentions and decisions, over time, that are influenced by emotions and changing life circumstances. The evolution of these personal events cannot be recorded in visa applications, census data, or citizenship registers. For further discussion about the changing nature of immigrant decisions regarding permanency, see Redstone and Massey 2004 and Massey and Bartley 2005.

2. For an excellent discussion of migrants of privilege, see Croucher's (2009) *The Other Side of the Fence*. For research on women and socioeconomic class in the United States, see Ostrander's (1984) *Women of the Upper Class*.

3. Conversations with participants necessarily included information about the many people who helped create their life stories: parents, siblings, husbands, children, and friends. Because I interviewed only the four study participants, the depictions of events and personalities are theirs alone. To protect their own privacy and that of their families, all four participants requested anonymity and were therefore assigned pseudonyms. Identifying details such as the names of certain locations, employers, and family members were also changed.

4. For further reading about personal narrative analysis, see Clandinin and Connelly 2000; Maynes, Pierce, and Laslett 2008; and Behar 1993.

5. The findings of Walsh and Horenczyk (2001) indicate that the differences in men's and women's sense of self affect their response to immigration. They suggest that women tend to place a stronger emphasis on belonging, while men tend to focus on competence. Craig Gurney's research supports the idea of gendered responses to home and suggests that women tend to provide more complex emotional responses, both negative and positive, in response to questions about the meaning of home. For a more detailed discussion of the relationship between gender, home, and place, see Bilinda Straight's (2005) collection *Women on the Verge of Home* and the work of Doreen Massey, including "Double Articulation: A Place in the World" (1994a) and *Space, Place and Gender* (1994b).

6. Gurney's research indicates that emotional events such as falling in love, getting married, having children, and mourning are intimately connected to finding meaning in the concept of "home" (1997, 383).

7. The idea of a conversation, in this context, is derived from Clandinin and Connelly 2000, 136.

8. Because feelings around belonging, home, and identity are inherently personal, theories of identity formation, global cultures, and assimilation must not rely on abstract or external viewpoints but on research connected to the actual practices of migrants (Smith 2007, 1097).

PART I

1. A comprehensive analysis of globalization is beyond the scope of this book. Readers who are interested in globalization, movement, and culture should see Arjun Appadurai's (1996) *Modernity at Large*.

2. While the concept of place is implicated by and overlaps with issues of home, theories illuminating the meaning and significance of "place" are outside the focus of this book. For further reading on place, see Relph 1976; Feld and Basso 1996; Gupta and Ferguson 1997a, 1997b; Massey 1994a, 1994b; and Tuan 1980.

3. Feminist research has questioned conceptualizing home as a refuge for women (see Gurney 1997; Després 1991, 106; Straight 2005; and Martin and Mohanty 1986).

4. For additional discussion about the meaning of "home," see Case 1996 and Hollander 1991; for a discussion of how the physical environment of home affects identity, see Després 1991.

5. For a more in-depth discussion of the politics of identity, see Hall 1996a and Croucher 2004.

6. Psychologist Greg Madison (2010) has coined the term "existential migrant" to refer to voluntary migrants who are motivated by the desire for self-discovery and fulfillment.

PART II

1. Unfortunately many refugees and exiles know from the outset that they will never be able to return home. This book, however, does not focus on immigrants who feel torn from their homes but on those who have left home by choice.

2. Readers interested in immigration policy in Norway are referred to Wikan's (2002) book *Generous Betrayal* and Gullestad's 2002 article "Invisible Fences: Egalitarianism, Nationalism and Racism."

3. Readers interested in the recent history of Miami are referred to Portes and Stepick's (1993) *City on the Edge*.

4. Research and literature on the concept of transnationalism and its effects on nation building and migrant belongings is prolific. See, for example, Glick Schiller, Basch, and Szanton 1992; Glick Schiller and Fouron 2001; Portes and Rumbaut 2006; Ong 1999; Westwood and Phizacklea 2000. Transnationalism and its application to the four women profiled here is discussed further in Part IV.

5. Many scholars consider the juxtaposition and/or overlap of assimilation and transnationalism. See, for example, Croucher 2009, 201–203; O'Flaherty, Skrbis, and Tranter 2007; Smith 2007; Kivisto 2001; Faist 2000; Guarnizo, Portes, and Haller 2003; Portes, Guarnizo, and Haller 2002; Portes, Guarnizo, and Landolt 1999; Portes and Rumbaut 2006; Brubaker 2001; Waldinger and Fitzgerald 2004; and Brettell and Hollifield 2008, 18.

6. The topics of acculturation psychology and acculturative stress, which are complex, are more thoroughly explored in cross-cultural psychology literature. In-

terested readers are referred to Phinney et al. 2001; Berry 1997; Deaux 2006; and Akhtar 1999. Aspects of the acculturation framework have been criticized in recent years. For a critical analysis of Berry's research, see Chirkov 2009; Rudmin 2009; and Bhatia and Ram 2009.

7. A significant body of work by Homi Bhabha and Stuart Hall, among others, concerns postcolonial notions of identity. Interested readers are referred to McLeod's (2000) *Beginning Postcolonialism* for an insightful discussion of the sometimes overlapping genres of postcolonialism, migrancy, and diaspora studies. Those interested in Homi Bhabha's writings might begin with *The Location of Culture* (1994) and "Culture's In-Between" (1996); for Stuart Hall's work, see "The Question of Cultural Identity" (1992) and "New Ethnicities" (1996b).

8. These elements of pilgrimage are borrowed from the work of Dubisch and Winkelman (2005), although their discussion does not include a comparison of immigration to pilgrimage. The reference to liminality in the context of pilgrimage is applied here not as a literal representation of a rite of passage but rather as a metaphor for personal transformation. For more discussion on the idea of liminality and identity change through pilgrimage, as well as the meaning of pilgrimage, see Turner and Turner 1978.

9. For a discussion of the concept of liminality as applied to immigrants, see Gibb, Hamdon, and Jamal 2008, 6. See Borysenko and Dveirin 2006, 149, for the application of the concepts of spiritual transformation and liminal states to life-changing transitions generally.

10. See Case 1996, 8, for discussion of the passage of time and a sense of home.

PART III

1. The concept of a "paradigm shift" in scientific theory was developed by Thomas Kuhn (1962) and has been applied broadly in the social sciences as well as in popular culture.

2. The influence of states on belonging (for example, citizenship law, marriage law, and residency regulations) is discussed here only insofar as these issues were addressed by the participants. For further reading on the relationships between citizenship, transnationalism, and assimilation, see Croucher 2004; Portes and Rumbaut 2006; Brubaker 2001; Faist 2000; Waldinger and Fitzgerald 2004; and Smith 2007. For a discussion of nationalism and identity in the postcolonial, globalized world, see Gupta 1997.

3. See Mahoney and Yngvesson 1992 for an analysis of motivation and agency in feminist anthropology and psychology. For a discussion of agency and identity, see Gupta and Ferguson 1997b, 13, and Norindr 1994.

4. The same holds true for the assumption that "home" necessarily means "rooted." For more on the relationship between home and movement versus rootedness, see Malkki 1997 and Rapport and Dawson 1998b.

PART IV

1. The well-known writings of Eva Hoffman and Salman Rushdie, for example, carry a nostalgic tone about lost home. Readers interested in immigrants and nostalgia are referred to Ritivoi's (2002) *Yesterday's Self*.

2. For discussion of socioeconomics, class, and their relationships to transnationalism, see Portes, Guarnizo, and Haller 2002; Guarnizo, Portes, and Haller

2003; O'Flaherty, Skrbis, and Tranter 2007, 839; and Marciniak 2006, 24–25. The idealistic view of mobility and transnationality that has recently developed is ironic, given the largely disparaging view of itinerant people in Western cultures, such as the Romani. Homi Bhabha makes a similar point about diversity, economics, and social class (1994, xiv).

   3. I am not suggesting that the lives of these women illustrate optimum circumstances or that women, and in particular mothers, should not opt for a more transnational way of moving through the world if they are able. The emphasis here does not represent an antifeminist conception of home and family; it represents the practical reasons why transnational models of immigrant life and home are not always applicable (see Hart 2005, 136–137; Marciniak 2006, 25).

REFERENCES

Agnew, Vijay. 2005a. "Introduction." In *Diaspora, Memory, and Identity: A Search for Home*, edited by Vijay Agnew, 3–17. Toronto: University of Toronto Press.
———. 2005b. "Language Matters." In *Diaspora, Memory, and Identity: A Search for Home*, edited by Vijay Agnew, 23–47. Toronto: University of Toronto Press.
Ahmed, Sara, Claudia Castañeda, Anne-Marie Fortier, and Mimi Sheller. 2003. "Introduction." In *Uprootings/Regroundings: Questions of Home and Migration*, edited by Sara Ahmed, Claudia Castañeda, Anne-Marie Fortier, and Mimi Sheller, 1–19. Oxford: Berg.
Akhtar, Salman, 1999. *Immigration and Identity: Turmoil, Treatment, and Transformation*. Northvale, NJ: Aronson.
Appadurai, Arjun. 1996. *Modernity at Large: Cultural Dimensions of Globalization*. Minneapolis: University of Minnesota Press.
Bammer, Angelika. 1994. "Introduction." In *Displacements: Cultural Identities in Question*, edited by Angelika Bammer, xi–xx. Bloomington: Indiana University Press.
Basso, Keith H. 1996. "Wisdom Sits in Places: Notes on a Western Apache Landscape." In *Senses of Place*, edited by Steven Feld and Keith Basso, 53–90. Santa Fe, NM: School of American Research Press.
Bateson, Mary Catherine. 1989. *Composing a Life*. New York: Grove Press.
———. 1994. *Peripheral Visions: Learning along the Way*. New York: HarperCollins.
Bauman, Zygmunt. 1996. "From Pilgrim to Tourist." In *Questions of Cultural Identity*, edited by Stuart Hall and Paul du Gay, 18–36. London: Sage.
Behar, Ruth. 1993. *Translated Woman*. Boston: Beacon Press.
Bell, Jill Sinclair. 2002. "Narrative Inquiry: More Than Just Telling Stories." *TESOL Quarterly* 36 (2): 207–213.
Benmayor, Rina, and Andor Skotnes. 1994. "Some Reflections on Migration and Identity." In *Migration and Identity*, edited by Rita Benmayor and Andor Skotnes, 1–18. Oxford: Oxford University Press.
Berger, John. 1991. *And Our Faces, My Heart, Brief as Photos*. New York: Vintage International.
Berry, John W. 1997. "Immigration, Acculturation and Adaptation." *Applied Psychology: An International Review* 46 (1): 5–67.
———. 2006. "Contexts of Acculturation." In *The Cambridge Handbook of Acculturation Psychology*, edited by David L. Sam and John W. Berry, 43–57. Cambridge: Cambridge University Press.
———. 2008. "Globalization and Acculturation." *International Journal of Intercultural Relations* 32:328–336.

Bhabha, Homi K. 1994. *The Location of Culture*. London: Routledge.

――――. 1996. "Culture's In-Between." In *Questions of Cultural Identity*, edited by Stuart Hall and Paul du Gay, 53–60. London: Sage.

Bhatia, Sunil, and Anjali Ram. 2009. "Theorizing Identity in Transnational and Diaspora Cultures: A Critical Approach to Acculturation." *International Journal of Intercultural Relations* 33:140–149.

Bolen, Jean Shinoda. 1994. *Crossing to Avalon*. New York: HarperCollins.

Boneva, Bonka S., and Irene Hanson Frieze. 2001. "Toward a Concept of Migrant Personality." *Journal of Social Issues* 57 (3): 477–491.

Borysenko, Joan Z., and Gordon F. Dveirin. 2006. *Saying Yes to Change: Essential Wisdom for Your Journey*. Carlsbad, CA: Hay House.

Brettell, Caroline. 2008. "Theorizing Migration in Anthropology." In *Migration Theory: Talking across Disciplines*, edited by Caroline Brettell and James F. Hollifield, 113–159. 2nd ed. New York: Routledge.

Brettell, Caroline, and James F. Hollifield. 2008. "Introduction—Migration Theory: Talking across Disciplines." In *Migration Theory: Talking across Disciplines*, edited by Caroline Brettell and James F. Hollifield, 1–29. 2nd ed. New York: Routledge.

Brubaker, Rogers. 2001. "The Return of Assimilation? Changing Perspectives on Immigration and Its Sequels in France, Germany, and the United States." *Ethnic and Racial Studies* 24 (4): 531–548.

Case, Duncan. 1996. "Contributions of Journeys Away to the Definitions of Home: An Empirical Study of a Dialectical Process." *Journal of Environmental Psychology* 16:1–15.

Casey, Edward S. 1996. "How to Get from Space to Place in a Fairly Short Stretch of Time: Phenomenological Prolegomena." In *Senses of Place*, edited by Steven Feld and Keith Basso, 13–52. Santa Fe, NM: School of American Research Press.

Chirkov, Valery. 2009. "Introduction to the Special Issue on Critical Acculturation Psychology." *International Journal of Intercultural Relations* 33:87–93.

Clandinin, D. Jean, and F. Michael Connelly. 2000. *Narrative Inquiry, Experience and Story in Qualitative Research*. San Francisco: Jossey-Bass.

Croucher, Sheila L. 2004. *Globalization and Belonging: The Politics of Identity in a Changing World*. Lanham, MD: Rowman and Littlefield.

――――. 2009. *The Other Side of the Fence: American Migrants in Mexico*. Austin: University of Texas Press.

Deaux, Kay. 2006. *To Be an Immigrant*. New York: Russell Sage Foundation.

Després, Carole. 1991. "The Meaning of Home: Literature Review and Directions for Future Research and Theoretical Development." *Journal of Architectural and Planning Research* 8 (2): 96–115.

Dovey, Kim. 1978. "Home: An Ordering Principle in Space." *Landscape* 22 (2): 27–30.

Dubisch, Jill, and Michael Winkelman. 2005. "Introduction: The Anthropology of Pilgrimage." In *Pilgrimage and Healing*, edited by Jill Dubisch and Michael Winkelman, ix–xxxvi. Tucson: University of Arizona Press.

Ehrensaft, Esther, and Michel Tousignant. 2006. "Immigration and Resilience." In *The Cambridge Handbook of Acculturation Psychology*, edited by David L. Sam and John W. Berry, 469–483. Cambridge: Cambridge University Press.

Eyles, John. *Senses of Place*. 1985. Cheshire, UK: Silverbrook Press.

Faist, Thomas. 2000. "Transnationalization in International Migration: Implications for the Study of Citizenship and Culture." *Ethnic and Racial Studies* 23 (2): 189–222.

Feld, Steven, and Keith Basso, eds. 1996. *Senses of Place*. Santa Fe, NM: School of American Research Press.

Fielding, Tony. 1993. "Migration and Culture." In *Migration Processes and Patterns: Research Progress and Prospects*, edited by Tony Champion and Tony Fielding, 201–212. London: Belhaven Press.

Fortier, Anne-Marie. 2000. *Migrant Belongings: Memory, Space, Identity*. Oxford: Berg.

Frank, Gelya. 1979. "Finding the Common Denominator: A Phenomenological Critique of Life History Method." *Ethos* 7 (1): 68–94.

Furman, Frida Kerner. 2005. "The Long Road Home: Migratory Experience and the Construction of the Self." In *Psychological, Political, and Cultural Meanings of Home*, edited by Mechthild Hart and Miriam Ben-Yoseph, 91–125. New York: Haworth Press.

Geertz, Clifford. 1996. "Afterword." In *Senses of Place*, edited by Steven Feld and Keith Basso, 259–262. Santa Fe, NM: School of American Research Press.

Gibb, Tara, Evelyn Hamdon, and Zenobia Jamal. 2008. "Re/Claiming Agency: Learning, Liminality and Immigrant Service Organizations." *Journal of Contemporary Issues in Education* 3 (1): 4–16.

Gilroy, Paul. 1993. *The Black Atlantic: Modernity and Double Consciousness*. Cambridge, MA: Harvard University Press.

Glick Schiller, Nina, Linda Basch, and Christina Blanc Szanton, eds. 1992. *Towards a Transnational Perspective on Migration: Race, Class, Ethnicity, and Nationalism Reconsidered*. New York: New York Academy of Sciences.

Glick Schiller, Nina, and Georges Eugene Fouron. 2001. *Georges Woke Up Laughing: Long Distance Nationalism and the Search for Home*. Durham, NC: Duke University Press.

Gmelch, George. 1992. *Double Passage: The Lives of Caribbean Migrants Abroad and Back Home*. Ann Arbor: University of Michigan Press.

Guarnizo, Luis Eduardo, Alejandro Portes, and William Haller. 2003. "Assimilation and Transnationalism: Determinants of Transnational Political Action among Contemporary Migrants." *American Journal of Sociology* 108 (6): 1211–1248.

Gullestad, Marianne. 2002. "Invisible Fences: Egalitarianism, Nationalism and Racism." *Journal of the Royal Anthropological Institute* 8:45–63.

Gupta, Akhil. 1997. "The Song of the Nonaligned World: Transnational Identities and the Reinscription of Space in Late Capitalism." In *Culture, Power, Place: Explorations in Critical Anthropology*, edited by Akhil Gupta and James Ferguson, 179–199. Durham, NC: Duke University Press.

Gupta, Akhil, and James Ferguson. 1997a. "Beyond 'Culture': Space, Identity, and the Politics of Difference." In *Culture, Power, Place: Explorations in Critical Anthropology*, edited by Akhil Gupta and James Ferguson, 33–51. Durham, NC: Duke University Press.

———. 1997b. "Culture, Power, Place: Ethnography at the End of an Era." In *Culture, Power, Place: Explorations in Critical Anthropology*, edited by Akhil Gupta and James Ferguson, 1–29. Durham, NC: Duke University Press.

Gurney, Craig. 1997. "'. . . Half of Me Was Satisfied': Making Sense of Home through Episodic Ethnographies." *Women's Studies International Forum* 20 (3): 373–386.

Hall, Stuart. 1992. "The Question of Cultural Identity." In *Modernity and Its Futures*, edited by Stuart Hall, David Held, and Tony McGrew, 273–316. Cambridge, UK: Polity Press.

———. 1996a. "Introduction: Who Needs Identity?" In *Questions of Cultural Identity*, edited by Stuart Hall and Paul du Gay, 1–17. London: Sage.

———. 1996b. "New Ethnicities." In *Stuart Hall: Critical Dialogues in Cultural Studies*, edited by David Morely and Kuan-Hsing Chen, 441–449. London: Routledge.

Hart, Mechthild. 2005. "The Nomad at Home." In *Psychological, Political, and Cultural Meanings of Home*, edited by Mechthild Hart and Miriam Ben-Yoseph, 127–141. New York: Haworth Press.

Hoersting, Raquel C., and Sharon Rae Jenkins. 2011. "No Place to Call Home: Cultural Homelessness, Self-Esteem and Cross-cultural Identities." *International Journal of Intercultural Relations* 35:17–30.

Hoffman, Eva. 1989. *Lost in Translation: A Life in a New Language*. New York: Penguin Books.

Hollander, John. 1991. "It All Depends." *Social Research* 58 (1): 31–49.

hooks, bell. 1990. *Yearning: Race, Gender, and Cultural Politics*. Boston: South End Press.

Jackson, Michael. 1995. *At Home in the World*. Durham, NC: Duke University Press.

———. 2006. *The Politics of Storytelling: Violence, Transgression and Intersubjectivity*. Copenhagen: Museum Tusculanum Press.

Kaplan, Caren. 1987. "Deterritorializations: The Rewriting of Home and Exile in Western Feminist Discourse." *Cultural Critique* 5:187–198.

Kivisto, Peter. 2001. "Theorizing Transnational Immigration: A Critical Review of Current Efforts." *Ethnic and Racial Studies* 24 (4): 549–577.

Kosic, Ankica. 2006. "Personality and Individual Factors in Acculturation." In *The Cambridge Handbook of Acculturation Psychology*, edited by David L. Sam and John W. Berry, 113–128. Cambridge: Cambridge University Press.

Kübler-Ross, Elisabeth. 1997. *On Death and Dying*. New York: Scribner.

Kuhn, Thomas. 1962. *The Structure of Scientific Revolutions*. Chicago: University of Chicago Press.

Lechuga, Julia, and Norma P. Fernandez. 2011. "Assimilation and Individual Differences in Emotion: The Dynamics of Anger and Approach Motivation." *International Journal of Intercultural Relations* 35:196–204.

Lueck, Kerstin, and Machelle Wilson. 2011. "Acculturative Stress in Latino Immigrants: The Impact of Socio-psychological and Migration-Related Factors." *International Journal of Intercultural Relations* 35:186–195.

Madison, Greg A. 2010. *The End of Belonging: Untold Stories of Leaving Home and the Psychology of Global Relocation*. Rev. ed. London: CreateSpace.

Magat, Ilan N. 1999. "Israeli and Japanese Immigrants to Canada: Home, Belonging, and Territorialization of Identity." *Ethos* 27 (2): 119–144.

Mahoney, Maureen A., and Barbara Yngvesson. 1992. "The Construction of Subjectivity and the Paradox of Resistance: Reintegrating Feminist Anthropology and Psychology." *Signs* 18 (1): 44–73.

Mak, Anita S., and Drew Nesdale. 2001. "Migrant Distress: The Role of Perceived Racial Discrimination and Coping Resources." *Journal of Applied Social Psychology* 31 (12): 2632–2647.

Malkki, Liisa H. 1997. "National Geographic: The Rooting of Peoples and the Territorialization of National Identity among Scholars and Refugees." In *Culture, Power, Place: Explorations in Critical Anthropology*, edited by Akhil Gupta and James Ferguson, 52–74. Durham, NC: Duke University Press.

Mallett, Shelly. 2004. "Understanding Home: A Critical Review of the Literature." *Sociological Review* 52 (1): 62–89.

Marciniak, Katarzyna. 2006. *Alienhood: Citizenship, Exile, and the Logic of Difference*. Minneapolis: University of Minnesota Press.

Martin, Biddy, and Chandra Talpade Mohanty. 1986. "Feminist Politics: What's Home Got to Do with It?" In *Feminist Studies, Critical Studies*, edited by Teresa de Lauretis, 191–212. Bloomington: Indiana University Press.

Masgoret, Anne-Marie, and Colleen Ward. 2006. "Culture Learning Approach to Acculturation." In *The Cambridge Handbook of Acculturation Psychology*, edited by David L. Sam and John W. Berry, 58–77. Cambridge: Cambridge University Press.

Massey, Doreen. 1994a. "Double Articulation: A Place in the World." In *Displacements: Cultural Identities in Question*, edited by Angelika Bammer, 110–121. Bloomington: Indiana University Press.

———. 1994b. *Space, Place, Gender*. Minneapolis: University of Minnesota Press.

Massey, Douglas S., and Katherine Bartley. 2005. "The Changing Legal Status Distribution of Immigrants: A Caution." *International Migration Review* 39 (2): 469–484.

Maynes, Mary Jo, Jennifer L. Pierce, and Barbara Laslett. 2008. *Telling Stories: The Use of Personal Narratives in the Social Sciences and History*. Ithaca, NY: Cornell University Press.

McAdams, Dan P. 2006. *The Redemptive Self: Stories Americans Live By*. Oxford: Oxford University Press.

McLeod, John. 2000. *Beginning Postcolonialism*. Manchester, UK: Manchester University Press.

Moore, Jeanne. 2000. "Placing *Home* in Context." *Journal of Environmental Psychology* 20 (3): 207–217.

Norindr, Panivong. 1994. "Coming Home on the Fourth of July: Constructing Identities." In *Displacements: Cultural Identities in Question*, edited by Angelika Bammer, 233–250. Bloomington: Indiana University Press.

O'Flaherty, Martin, Zlatko Skrbis, and Bruce Tranter. 2007. "Home Visits: Transnationalism among Australian Migrants." *Ethnic and Racial Studies* 30 (5): 817–944.

Ong, Aihwa. 1995. "Women out of China: Traveling Tales and Traveling Theories in Postcolonial Feminism." In *Women Writing Culture*, edited by Ruth Behar and Deborah A. Gordon, 350–372. Berkeley: University of California Press.

———. 1999. *Flexible Citizenship: The Cultural Logics of Transnationality*. Durham, NC: Duke University Press.

Ostrander, Susan A. 1984. *Women of the Upper Class*. Philadelphia: Temple University Press.

Phinney, Jean S., Gabriel Horenczyk, Karmela Liebkind, and Paul Vedder. 2001. "Ethnic Identity, Immigration, and Well-being: An Interactional Perspective." *Journal of Social Issues* 57 (3): 493–510.

Portes, Alejandro, Luis Eduardo Guarnizo, and William J. Haller. 2002. "Transnational Entrepreneurs: An Alternative Form of Immigrant Economic Adaptation." *American Sociological Review* 67 (2): 278–298.

Portes, Alejandro, Luis E. Guarnizo, and Patricia Landolt. 1999. "The Study of Transnationalism: Pitfalls and Promise of an Emergent Field." *Ethnic and Racial Studies* 22 (2): 217–237.

Portes, Alejandro, and Rubén G. Rumbaut. 2006. *Immigrant America: A Portrait*. 3rd ed. Berkeley: University of California Press.

Portes, Alejandro, and Alex Stepick. 1993. *City on the Edge: The Transformation of Miami*. Berkeley: University of California Press.

Rapport, Nigel, and Andrew Dawson. 1998a. "Home and Movement: A Polemic." In *Migrants of Identity: Perceptions of Home in a World of Movement*, edited by Nigel Rapport and Andrew Dawson, 19–38. Oxford: Berg.

———. 1998b. "The Topic and the Book." In *Migrants of Identity: Perceptions of Home in a World of Movement*, edited by Nigel Rapport and Andrew Dawson, 3–18. Oxford: Berg.

Redstone, Ilana, and Douglas S. Massey. 2004. "Coming to Stay: An Analysis of the U.S. Census Question on Immigrants' Year of Arrival." *Demography* 41 (4): 721–738.

Relph, E. 1976. *Place and Placelessness*. London: Pion.

Ritivoi, Andreea Diciu. 2002. *Yesterday's Self: Nostalgia and the Immigrant Identity*. Lanham, MD: Rowman and Littlefield.

Rudmin, Floyd. 2009. "Constructs, Measurements and Models of Acculturation and Acculturative Stress." *International Journal of Intercultural Relations* 33:106–123.

Rushdie, Salman. 1992. *Imaginary Homelands: Essays and Criticism 1981–1991*. London: Penguin Books.

Sam, David L. 2006a. "Acculturation: Conceptual Background and Core Components." In *The Cambridge Handbook of Acculturation Psychology*, edited by David L. Sam and John W. Berry, 11–26. Cambridge: Cambridge University Press.

———. 2006b. "Acculturation of Immigrant Women and Children." In *The Cambridge Handbook of Acculturation Psychology*, edited by David L. Sam and John W. Berry, 403–418. Cambridge: Cambridge University Press.

Sixsmith, Judith. 1986. "The Meaning of Home: An Exploratory Study of Environmental Experience." *Journal of Environmental Psychology* 6:281–298.

Smith, Michael Peter. 2007. "The Two Faces of Transnational Citizenship." *Ethnic and Racial Studies* 30 (6): 1096–1116.

Straight, Bilinda, ed. 2005. *Women on the Verge of Home*. Albany: State University of New York Press.

Tsuda, Takeyuki (Gaku). 2003. "Homeland-less Abroad: Transnational Liminality, Social Alienation, and Personal Malaise." In *Searching for Home Abroad*, edited by Jeffrey Lesser, 121–161. Durham, NC: Duke University Press.

Tuan, Yi-Fu. 1980. "Rootedness versus Sense of Place." *Landscape* 24 (1): 3–8.

Tucker, Aviezer. 1994. "In Search of Home." *Journal of Applied Philosophy* 11 (2): 181–187.

Turner, Victor, and Edith L. B. Turner. 1978. *Image and Pilgrimage in Christian Culture*. New York: Columbia University Press.

United Nations Development Programme (UNDP) Human Development Report. 2009. *Overcoming Barriers: Human Mobility and Development*. Available at http://hdr.undp.org/en/reports/global/hdr2009.

Waldinger, Roger, and David Fitzgerald. 2004. "Transnationalism in Question." *American Journal of Sociology* 109 (5): 1177–1195.

Walsh, Sophie D., and Gabriel Horenczyk. 2001. "Gendered Patterns of Experience in Social and Cultural Transition: The Case of English-Speaking Immigrants in Israel." *Sex Roles* 45 (7/8): 501–528.

Watson, Lawrence C., and Maria-Barbara Watson-Franke. 1985. *Interpreting Life Histories: An Anthropological Inquiry*. New Brunswick, NJ: Rutgers University Press.

Westwood, Sallie, and Annie Phizacklea. 2000. *Trans-nationalism and the Politics of Belonging*. London: Routledge.

Wikan, Unni. 2002. *Generous Betrayal: Politics of Culture in the New Europe.* Chicago: University of Chicago Press.

Wolf, Eric R. 1982. *Europe and the People without History.* Berkeley: University of California Press.

Zandy, Janet. 1990. "Introduction." In *Calling Home: Working-Class Women's Writings*, edited by Janet Zandy, 1–13. New Brunswick, NJ: Rutgers University Press.

INDEX

Language learning, 2, 16, 52, 81, 148; compared to religious conversion, 66, 83; through television and comics, 46, 74. *See also* Anna: and childhood; Anna: and transitions; Barrett: and transitions; Shirine: and childhood

Learning: about different cultures, 12, 84, 87, 148, 153, 155; and language (*see* Language learning). *See also* Anna: and childhood; Anna: and resolutions; Anna: and transitions; Barrett: and transitions; Lisa: and resolutions; Lisa: and transitions; Shirine: and childhood; Shirine: and resolutions; Shirine: and transitions

Leaving home, 39–40, 86, 114, 120, 155

Legal status, 45, 50, 76, 115, 116

Lejanía cercana, 145. *See also* "Closely far"

Life history, 4–6. *See also* Life stories; Narratives; Stories

Life stories, 4–8, 11–12, 84. *See also* Narratives; Stories

Limimality, 86–88, 149, 154, 161n8, 161n9

Lisa: and childhood, 18–24; and resolutions, 128–135; and transitions, 52–62; and turning points, 95–101

"Living carefully," 133, 154

Lutheran church, 47

Madison, Greg, 160n6 (pt. I)

Maoris: and adoption, 14; ceremonies and traditions of, 14, 92–93, 123–124, 155; culture of, 125, 127; language of, 16. *See also* Anna

Marai, 13, 14, 52, 123–124

Marciniak, Katarzyna, 150

Marriage, 5, 11, 12, 39, 42, 86, 110, 114; and accidental immigration, 2, 3; as analogy to immigrant commitment, 109; and immigration, 1, 41, 79, 84, 96, 110, 116, 121. *See also* Anna; Barrett; Lisa; Shirine

Martin, Biddy, 7

Maturity, 134, 139, 155

Media, 1, 3, 10, 131; American, 133–134. *See also* News

Memories, 5, 7, 89, 111, 114, 120, 151; of childhood, 89; and nostalgia, 111, 150; and sense of home, 87, 89; and visits home, 111–112, 152

Methodology, 6

Meyer, Barrett. *See* Barrett

Miami, 53, 95; ethnic and racial issues in, 56, 96; Jewish population of, 55; and Mariel boatlift, 56. *See also* Barrett: and resolutions; Lisa

Micvah, 55–56

Mohanty, Chandra, 7

Mormonism, 13, 15, 16, 40, 155. *See also* Anna: and childhood

Mother: death of, 110, 120 (*see also* Anna: and transitions; Anna: and turning points); relationship with, after immigration, 154 (*see also* Barrett: and resolutions; Barrett: and turning points; Lisa: and resolutions; Lisa: and turning points; Shirine: and resolutions; Shirine: and transitions; Shirine: and turning points)

Motherhood, 83–84, 148; and transnationality, 153, 162n3. *See also* Anna: and transitions; Lisa: and transitions; Shirine: and transitions; Shirine: and turning points

Movement, 1, 3, 8, 9, 10, 87, 90, 153, 161n4; illegal, 3

Moving out, 39

Moving to a foreign country. *See* Immigration

Multicultural, 56, 127, 157

Narrative inquiry, 6

Narratives, 4–6, 8, 147, 156

Nationalism, 115, 139

New England, 40. *See also* Barrett

News, 1, 106, 109, 127. *See also* Media

New Year's Eve, 97–98, 101, 115, 133, 153

New Zealand: British influence in, 15–16; Maori culture in (*see* Maoris); and Mormonism, 13–14; race issues in, 15–16. *See also* Anna

Nichols, Lisa Dwyre. *See* Lisa

Nielsen, Anna. *See* Anna

Northern Rhodesia, 19

Norway, 49, 149; and Constitution Day, 121–122; immigration and foreigners in, 49, 127, 160n2 (pt. II); religion in, 47, 155. *See also* Anna

Nostalgia, 100, 111, 147, 150–152, 161n1 (pt. IV). *See also* Memories

Outsider, feeling like an, 83, 85, 89, 113, 120, 121, 149, 156. *See also* Anna: and resolutions; Barrett: and childhood; Barrett: and resolutions; Lisa: and childhood; Shirine: and childhood; Shirine: and transitions

Paradigm shift, 110, 161n1 (pt. III)

Passport, 21, 53, 116, 122, 128, 143

Persian culture, 24. *See also* Shirine

Carol E. Kelley is an anthropologist and former lawyer who has worked as a research consultant for universities and nonprofit organizations.